浙江省高职院校"十四五"重点立项建设教材

跨文化交际

（第二版）

主　编　李晓红

副主编　唐黎卿　吴　倩

编　者　陈　玥　佘雄飞　全俊宏

INTERCULTURAL COMMUNICATION

(2nd Edition)

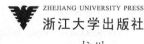

ZHEJIANG UNIVERSITY PRESS

浙江大学出版社

·杭州·

图书在版编目（CIP）数据

跨文化交际：英文 / 李晓红主编. -- 2版. -- 杭州：浙江大学出版社，2024.6（2025.6重印）

ISBN 978-7-308-24304-9

Ⅰ．①跨… Ⅱ．①李… Ⅲ．①文化交流－英语－高等职业教育－教材 Ⅳ．①G115

中国国家版本馆CIP数据核字（2023）第196479号

跨文化交际（第二版）

KUAWENHUA JIAOJI（DI-ER BAN）

李晓红　主　编

唐黎卿　吴　倩　副主编

责任编辑	郑成业
责任校对	李　晨
封面设计	春天书装
出版发行	浙江大学出版社
	（杭州市天目山路148号　邮政编码　310007）
	（网址：http://www.zjupress.com）
排　版	杭州林智广告有限公司
印　刷	杭州宏雅印刷有限公司
开　本	787mm×1092mm　1/16
印　张	19.25
字　数	496千
版 印 次	2024年6月第2版　2025年6月第2次印刷
书　号	ISBN 978-7-308-24304-9
定　价	59.00元

FOREWORD

前　言

随着世界经济全球化、信息技术飞速发展、国际文化交流日益频繁，中国与世界接轨的步伐不断加快，不同文化背景的个体和群体之间的交流在深度和广度上实现着前所未有的突破，跨文化交际已经成为"地球村"的普遍现实。然而，文化之间的差异往往会导致交际的困惑、误解、矛盾和冲突，因此，培养对文化差异的敏感度和宽容度、发展跨文化意识是"地球村"公民的共识，跨越交际障碍、构建人类命运共同体是当今世界的迫切诉求。

党的二十大报告指出：构建人类命运共同体是世界各国人民前途所在，促进各国人民相知相亲，尊重世界文明多样性，以文明交流超越文明隔阂、文明互鉴超越文明冲突、文明共存超越文明优越、共同应对各种全球性挑战。跨文化交际人才培养是二十一世纪人才培养至关重要的任务。

在此背景下，我们对《跨文化交际》教材进行了修订，具体修订内容如下：

1. 增加单元导读，明确各章的知识目标、能力目标和育人目标；

2. 增加第十三章，主题为Acculturation and Cultural Identity；

3. 优化各章Section A和Section B，并增加主题相关的图片，使教材图文并茂；

4. 优化二维码内容，增加可视化资源，提高阅读体验和学习效度；

5. 优化各章课后练习，并增加具有时代价值和育人元素的案例分析题。

《跨文化交际（第二版）》以提升高职学生知识、能力和素质为设计宗旨，充分考虑知识性、趣味性和实用性的结合，富有多模态资源。全书以模块串联内容，共分六个模块：第一模块介绍了文化、交际和跨文化交际的基本概念；第二模块分析了两个最具影响力的文化价值理论；第三和第四模块阐释了跨文化语言交际和非语言交际的内涵；第五模块讨论了跨文化交际中的障碍和如何搭建跨越障碍的桥梁；第六模块讲述了三大跨文化交际情境——商务情境、旅游情境和教育情境。

教材各模块相互独立，又层层递进，每个模块增加具有时代特色的育人案例，培养学生的价值判断能力、价值选择能力和价值塑造能力。每个模块下设单元，共十六单元，每个单元包含影视片段、阅读材料和案例听力三部分。同时，教材适应"互联网＋"教学和碎片化学习的时代需求，设有二维码，二维码中的内容与各单元

FOREWORD

主题相关，便于学生实现时时学和处处学，拓展知识和能力。影视片段和教学视频能够帮助学生构建跨文化交际的真实情境，形成对跨文化交际的具象认知；阅读材料是对跨文化交际的理论介绍，深入浅出，简洁精练；案例听力是理论联系实际和解决问题的过程。每一单元的练习都设有主观题和客观题，便于学生理解和思考。

教材可以与跨文化交际在线课程配套使用，网址如下：智慧职教MOOC（icve.com.cn）。此外，本教材提供配套课件，可扫描右方二维码，以供学习使用。每个单元的教学大约需要4课时，完成整本教材大约需要64课时。

扫一扫
下载配套课件

《跨文化交际（第二版）》是集体智慧和劳动的结晶。主编是浙江旅游职业学院的李晓红教授，她编写了第三、六、七、八、十一、十二、十三、十四、十五和十六单元，浙江同济科技职业学院的吴倩副教授编写了第一单元和第二单元，浙江旅游职业学院的唐黎卿老师编写了第四单元和第五单元，浙江旅游职业学院的陈玥老师和佘雄飞老师编写了第九单元和第十单元，中国国旅（浙江）国际旅行社有限公司高级英文导游全俊宏对教材的部分内容进行了材料整理和练习设计。二维码中的教学视频由浙江旅游职业学院的外教和中国教师共同完成。在编写教材的过程中，参考了大量的国内外专著、教材和论文，得到了有关专家的倾心指导，也得到了浙江大学出版社郑成业编辑的大力协助，敬请接受本人的深深谢意。

本教材可以作为高职院校英语专业学生的用书，也可以作为大学生人文素养通识课程的参考用书，还可以供对跨文化交际感兴趣的社会人士阅读。

由于编者的水平和能力有限，书中疏漏和谬误仍在所难免，敬请使用者批评指正，便于今后完善。谢谢！

编者
2024年3月

目 录
CONTENTS

CONTENTS

Module 1
Basic Concepts

Unit 1　Culture

- **Knowledge Objective:**

  Guide students to master the definitions, metaphors, and features of culture.

- **知识目标：**

  指导学生掌握文化的定义、关于文化的比喻和文化的特点。

- **Ability Objective:**

  Guide students to evaluate Chinese and foreign value concepts through case studies, and learn to introduce fine traditional Chinese culture, such as silk, porcelain, tea and the like in approximately 200 English words.

- **能力目标：**

  指导学生通过案例分析评价中外价值观，能用 200 词左右的英文介绍中华优秀传统文化，如丝绸、瓷器、茶叶等。

- **Educative Objective:**

  Guide students to think about the tremendous changes China has undergone in the eyes of foreigners by analyzing the five-episode documentary series *From Chung Kuo to China*. Guide students to understand that "all the extensive Chinese civilization was created by the Chinese people".

- **素质目标：**

  通过分析五集系列纪录片《从〈中国〉到中国》，引导学生思考外国人眼中中国文化的变迁，引领学生了解"所有博大精深的中华文明都是中国人民创造的"。

Section A　Video Clip Appreciation

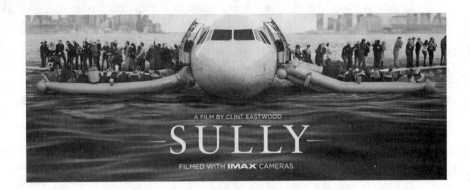

I. Introduction to the Movie *Sully*

Based on a real event, the movie follows Sullenberger's emergency landing of the US Airways Flight 1549 on the Hudson River, in which all passengers and crew survived with only minor injuries, and the subsequent publicity and investigation. On January 15, 2009, pilot "Sully" (the affectionate nickname of Sullenberger) and the first officer Jeff Skiles took off for Charlotte Douglas. Barely three minutes before the flight, the plane hit a group of geese, which crippled both engines of the plane. Without engine power and any airport within range, Sully glided his disabled plane onto the frigid waters of the Hudson River, saving the lives of all 155 aboard. However, even as Sully was dubbed a hero by the press for his actions, an unfolding investigation threatened to destroy his reputation and career.

II. Introduction to the Video Clip

Although Sully was being heralded by the public and the media for his unprecedented feat of aviation skill, the National Transportation Safety Board believes that the accident may have been pilot error. Because preliminary data from ACARS suggest that the port engine was still running at idle power. Theoretically, this would have left him with enough power to return to LaGuardia or land at Teterboro. Furthermore, the Board claims that several confidential computerized simulations show that the plane could have landed safely at either airport without engines. Sully has to defend himself to the commission. Will he succeed?

III. Script of the Video Clip

Video Clip

Investigator 1: Multiple airports, runways, two successful landings. We are simply mimicking what the computer already told us.

Investigator 2: A lot of toes were stepped on in order to set this up for today. And frankly, I really don't know what you gentlemen plan to gain by it.

Sully: Can we get serious now?

Investigator 2: Captain?

Sully: We've all heard about the computer simulations and now we are watching actual sims. But I can't quite believe you still have not taken into account the human factor.

Investigator 2: Human piloted simulations showed that you could make it back to the airport.

Sully: No, they don't. These pilots were not behaving like human beings, like people who are experiencing this for the first time.

Investigator 2: Well, they may not be reacting like you did.

Sully: Immediately after the bird strike, they are turning back for the airport. Just as in the computer sims, correct?

Investigator 2: That is correct.

Sully: They obviously knew the turn and exactly what heading to fly. They did not run a check. They did not switch on the APU.

Investigator 2: They had all the same parameters that you faced.

Sully: No one warned us. No one said, "You are going to lose both engines at a lower altitude than any jet in history. But be cool. Just make a left turn for LaGuardia like you're going back to pick up the milk." This was dual engine loss at 2,800 feet followed by an immediate water landing with 155 souls on board. No one has ever trained for an incident like that. No one. The Teterboro landing, with its unrealistic bank angle, we were not the Thunderbirds up there. I'd like to know how many times the pilot practiced that maneuver before he actually pulled it off. I'm not questioning the pilots. They're good pilots. But they've clearly been instructed to head for the airport immediately after the bird strike. You're allowed no time for analysis or decision-making. In these simulations, you've taken all of the humanity out of the cockpit. How much time did the pilots spend planning for this event? For these simulations? You're looking for human error. Then make it human.

Skiles: This wasn't a video game. It was life and death. Sully's right. That's worth a few
    seconds.

Sully: Please ask how many practice runs they had.

Elizabeth: Seventeen.

Sully: Seventeen?

Elizabeth: The pilot who landed at Teterboro had seventeen practice attempts before the
    simulation we just witnessed.

Investigator 2: Your reaction decision time will be set at 35 seconds.

Skiles: Thirty-five seconds. That's not enough time.

Sully: We only had 208 seconds total, so I'll take it.

Investigator 1: Upload the link. Return to LaGuandia. Now with an added 35-second delay in
    response time.

Pilot 1: Birds.

Pilot 2: Okay, I saw them. Give me 35 seconds.

Pilot 1: Thirty-five seconds. Time's up.

Pilot 2: Here we go. Flight path vector. Going for 1-3.

Pilot 1: Okay.

Pilot 2: Activate confirm.

Pilot 1: All right—You are confirmed.

Pilot 2: We are heading right for the airport.

Broadcast: Caution, obstacle. Caution, obstacle.

Pilot 1: We're about seven miles from the runway.

Broadcast: Caution, obstacle. Terrain, terrain. Pull up. Pull up. Pull up. Pull up. Too low,
    terrain. Too low, terrain.

Pilot 1: We got a little extra speed. You want some flaps? (Too low, terrain. Too low, terrain.)

Pilot 2: No, leave the flaps up. Too low, terrain. (Too low, terrain. Too low, terrain. Too low,
    terrain.)

Investigator 2: Let's try Teterboro.

Investigator 1: Upload the link, please.

Pilot 3: Birds.

Pilot 4: Auto pilot off. Flight Director off. Hack the time.

Pilot 3 & 4: Thirty-five seconds.

Pilot 3: Engine one and two fail. Turn.

Pilot 4: Okay. Let's see if we can make it.

Pilot 3: Heading sub 2-9-8. You seeing Teterboro out there?

Pilot 4: I do. Way too low.

Broadcast: Obstacle. Obstacle. Pull up. Pull up. Pull up. Pull up. Pull up. Pull up.

Pilot 4: Not gonna work, not gonna work. (Pull up. Pull up. Pull up. Pull up.)

Sully: Does anyone need to see more simulations?

Skiles: Now that we've seen what could have happened, can we, uh, listen to what actually we did?

Investigator 2: We will look at all the results at a later date. Elizabeth.

Elizabeth: For the record, this is the CVR of US Airways Flight 1549, January 15th, 2009. Gentlemen, headsets.

Sully: Birds.

Skiles: Shit.

Sully: Oh, yeah. We got one rolling back. We have both of them rolling back. Ignition start. I'm starting the APU. My aircraft.

Skiles: Your aircraft.

Sully: Get out the QRH.

Skiles: Priority left.

Sully: Loss of thrust on both engines. Mayday, mayday, mayday. This is Cactus 1549. Hit birds. We've lost thrust on both engines. We are turning back towards LaGuardia.

Patrick: Okay, you need to return to LaGuardia? Turn left heading 2-2-0.

Sully: 2-2-0.

Patrick: Which engine did you lose?

Sully: Both. Both engines.

Skiles: If fuel remaining, engine mode, select your ignition. Ignition.

Sully: Ignition.

Skiles: Thrust levers, confirm idle.

Sully: Idle.

Skiles: Airspeed. Optimum relight, 300 knots. We don't have that.

Sully: No, we don't.

Patrick: Cactus 1549, if we can get it for you, do you wanna try to land runway 1-3?

Sully: We are unable. We may end up in the Hudson.

Skiles: Emergency electrical power, emergency generator not online.

Sully: Online.

Skiles: ATC notified. Squawk 7700. Distress message transmit. We did that.

Patrick: Cactus 1549, it's gonna be left traffic, runway 3-1.

Sully: Unable.

Patrick: Okay, where do you need to land?

Broadcast: Wind shear.

Skiles: FAC 1 off, then on.

Patrick: Been 10 seconds. Captain. Come on. Talk to me. Cactus 1549, runway 4's available if you wanna make left traffic to runway 4.

Sully: I don't think we can make any runway. Uh, what about over to our right? Anything in New Jersey? Maybe Teterboro?

Patrick: Okay, yeah. Off your right side is Teterbor Airport. LaGuardia Departure, got an emergency inbound.

Airport Traffic Controller: This is Teterboro tower. Go ahead.

Patrick: Cactus 1549 over the GW Bridge needs to go to the airport right now.

Airport Traffic Controller: Check. Does he need assistance?

Patrick: Yes. Bird strike. Can I get him in for runway 1? Cactus 1549, you wanna try and go to Teterboro? Obstacle.

Broadcast: Obstacle. Obstacle. Obstacle. Pull up. Clear of conflict.

Skiles: No relight after 30 seconds, engine master one and two, confirm off.

Sully: Off.

Skiles: Wait 30 seconds.

Broadcast: Too low, terrain. Too low, terrain. Too low, terrain. Too low, terrain.

Sully: This is the captain. Brace for impact.

Patrick: Cactus 1549, turn right 2-8-0. You can land runway 1 Teterboro.

Sully: We can't make it.

Patrick: Okay. Which runway would you like at Teterboro?

Sully: Go ahead. Try number one.

Skiles: Number one. No relight.

Sully: We're gonna end up in the Hudson. (Too low, terrain.)

Patrick: I'm sorry. Say again. Cactus? (Too low, terrain. Too low, terrain.)

Sully: All right, let's put the flaps out. Put the flaps out.

Skiles: Flaps out.

Patrick: Cactus 1549, radar contact lost. You also got Newark off your two o'clock in about seven miles.

Skiles: Got flaps out. Two hundred fifty feet in the air. 170 knots. Got no power on either one. Try the other one.

Sully: Try the other one.

Patrick: 1549? Still up?

Skiles: One hundred and fifty knots. Got flaps two. You want more?

Sully: No, let's stay at two.

Patrick: You got runway 2-9 available at Newark. It'll be two o'clock in seven miles.

Sully: You got any ideas?

Skiles: Actually not.

Broadcast: Terrain. Terrain. Pull up. Pull up. Pull up. Pull up. Pull up. Pull up. Pull up. Pull up.

Sully: We're gonna brace. (Pull up.) Thirty. (Pull up.) Twenty. (Pull up.)

Sully: I need to take a quick break. What did you think? Hearing the CVR just now? Let me tell you what I think. I'm just so damn proud. And you, you were right there, through all that distraction. With so much at stake. We did it together. We were a team.

Skiles: Thanks, Sully.

Sully: We did our job.

Skiles: We did our job.

Larry: Hey, you did good.

Investigator 2: I'd like to call this hearing back to order. If we could settle, please? Take your seats. That is honestly the first time that I have listened to a crash recording while actually sitting with the captain and the first officer. It's extraordinary.

Skiles: That was no simulation.

Investigator 2: No, it wasn't.

Elizabeth: Gentlemen, I want to inform you that the left engine has been recovered. We just received a comprehensive report. There was extensive damage to both the guide vanes and fan blades of the engine. Five compressor blades were fractured and eight variable gudie vanes missing.

Sully: So, no thrust?

Elizabeth: As you testified, it was completely destroyed. The ACARS data was wrong. I'd like to add something on a personal note. I can say with absolute confidence that after speaking with the rest of the flight crew, with bird experts, aviation engineers, after running through every scenario, after interviewing each player, there is still an "X" in this result and it's you, Captain Sullenberger. Remove you from the equation, and the math just fails.

Sully: I disagree. It wasn't just me. It was all of us. It was Jeff and Donna and Sheila and Doreen and all of the passengers, the rescue workers, air traffic control, ferry boat crews and the scuba cops. We all did it. We survived.

Elizabeth: First Officer Skiles, is there anything you'd like to add? Anything you would have done differently if you had to do it again?

Skiles: Yes, I would have done it in July.

New Words

simulation 模拟，模仿

parameter 参量，参数

maneuver 精巧动作

humanity （统称）人，人类

activate 开动，激活

caution 谨慎，小心，慎重

obstacle 障碍，阻碍，妨碍

upload 上传（程序或信息）

ignition 点火器

Mayday （船只、飞机发出的）无线电求救信号

knot 节，飞机或轮船的航速以及流速单位（1 节约等于 1 海里 / 小时）

distress 受苦，遇难，遇险

testify 作证，证明

Phrases and Expressions

pull off 驶向路边短暂停靠

at stake 有风险，处于危急关头

Notes

gonna 将要（等于 going to）

APU 辅助动力装置

CVR 驾驶舱话音记录器，即"黑匣子"

QRH 快速检查单

ATC 空中交通管制

GW Bridge 乔治·华盛顿大桥，位于哈德逊河之上，为纽约的一条交通要道

ACARS 飞机通信寻址与报告系统

IV. Exercises for Understanding

1. Decide whether the following statements are true or false according to the video clip you have just watched. Write "T" for true or "F" for false.

_____ (1) In the beginning, the men of the National Transportation Safety Board thought it was not necessary to settle on the Hudson River.

_____ (2) The computer simulations indicated that the plane could have landed at LaGuardia or Teterboro safely.

_____ (3) Elizabeth claimed that the left engine was idle and still functioning.

_____ (4) Sully argued that what the Board did not take into account was the "human factor".

_____ (5) Sully failed to defend his reputation and career.

2. Put the following sentences in the right order according to the video clip you have just watched.

_____ (1) The only announcement Sully made to the passengers was "Brace for impact".

_____ (2) The plane hit a flock of Canada geese, which crippled both engines.

_____ (3) With its nose raised, Flight 1549 completed an unpowered ditching on the Hudson River.

_____ (4) With no thrust and little altitude, Sully decided that gliding back to LaGurardia was not possible.

_____ (5) Sully decided that landing at Teterboro was not viable.

3. Explore interculturally.

(1) Do you think Sully is a hero? Why or why not?

(2) Watch the movie _The Captain_ (《中国机长》). What are the similarities and differences between Chinese and American heroes? What are the cultural factors underlying them?

Section B   Reading

微课

What Is Culture?

"What is culture?" is a question that is impossible to answer crisply. It may seem obvious but culture is what makes the Japanese Japanese, the Germans German and the Brazilians Brazilian. Culture is a complex, abstract and pervasive matrix of social elements that functions as an all-encompassing form or pattern for living by laying out a predictable world in which an individual is firmly oriented. Culture enables us to make sense of our surroundings, aiding the transition from the womb to new life.

Definitions of Culture

E. B. Tylor, the forefather of culture study, conceived culture as "the complex whole which includes knowledge, belief, art, morals, law, custom, and any other capabilities and habits acquired by man as a member of society". According to R. Benedict, what really binds men together is their culture—the ideas and the standards they have in common. In the eyes of Clyde Kluckhohn, an anthropologist, culture means the total life way of a people, the social legacy the individual acquires from his group. Or culture can be regarded as a part of the environment that is the creation of man. D. Brown regarded culture as a collection of beliefs, habits, living patterns, and behaviors which are held more or less in common by people who occupy particular geographic areas. In 1981, I. Robertson thought the culture of every society is unique, containing combinations of norms and values that are found nowhere else. The definition by G. Hofstede is as follows: the collective programming of the mind that distinguishes the members of one group or category of people from another. The "mind" stands for the head, heart, and hands—that is, for thinking, feeling, and acting, with consequences for beliefs, attitudes, and skills. Edward Hall defined culture very simply. He proposed that culture is communication and communication is culture.

Metaphors of Culture

Culture is like an iceberg. The iceberg metaphor for culture shows a cruise ship sailing close to the iceberg. Part of the iceberg is immediately visible, part of it emerges and submerges with the tides, and its foundations go deep beneath the surface.

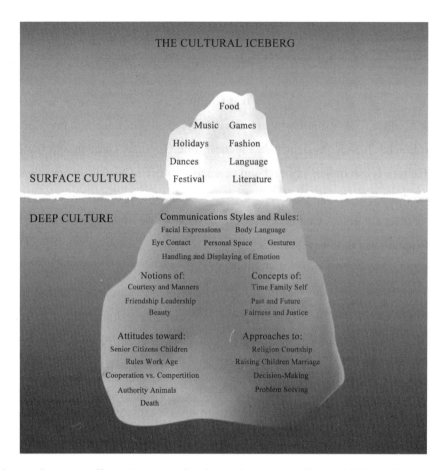

Above the water line: Aspects of culture that are explicit, visible, and taught. These include written explanations as well as those thousands of skills and information conveyed through formal lessons, such as manners or computing long division or baking bread. Also above the water line are the tangible aspects: from the "cultural markers" tourists seek out such as French bread or Guatemalan weaving, to the conformity in how people dress, the way they pronounce the letter "R", how they season their food, and the way they expect an office to be furnished.

Below the water line: "Hidden" culture—the habits, assumptions, understandings, values, judgments... that we know but do not or cannot articulate. Usually these aspects are not taught directly. Think about mealtime, for example, and the order you eat foods at dinner: Do you end with dessert? With a pickle? With tea? Nuts and cheese? Just have one course with no concluding dish? Or, in these modern times, do you dispense with a sit-down meal altogether? Or consider how you know if someone is treating you in a friendly manner: Do they shake hands? Keep a respectful distance with downcast eyes? Leap up and hug you? Address you by your full name? These sorts of daily rules are learned by osmosis—you may know what tastes "right" or when you're treated "right", but because these judgments are under-the-waterline, it usually doesn't occur to you to question or explain those feelings.

Culture is our software. Culture is the basic operating system that makes us human around the world physically pretty much the same. There are variations in body size, shape and color, but the basic equipment is universal. We can think of our physical selves as the hardware, but we cannot be said to be human until we are programmed and each of us is programmed by our home culture.

Humans are unique among all the animals on earth in that the infant is weak and incapable of survival for an exceptionally long period of time. At birth the infant is only a potential human. It must learn how to be human and it learns that in a culturally specific way. It is the culture that provides the software. As with any good software, we are only vaguely aware of it as we use it. It fades into the background and we just know that we can be, that the computer works, or perhaps sometimes does not work because it is incompatible with someone else's software.

Culture is like the water a fish swims in. Like any creature, a fish scans its environment to find food, reproduce and protect itself from danger. It notices everything except the water it is swimming in. The fish takes the water for granted because it so totally surrounds the fish that it really cannot imagine another environment. The same is true for us. Our culture is so much a part of who we are and what the world is like for us that we do not notice it—we take it for granted. For most people for most of their lives, everything they see and do takes place in the same culture. Everyone is swimming in the same water. They couldn't describe the water even if they wanted to.

Culture is the story we tell ourselves about ourselves. Every cultural group has a story that provides a way for members of the group to understand who they are and what the world is like. People tell themselves their story in their folklore, arts, in politics and in intimate conversations among friends and family members. The stories may be very old and include legends of how the group was created, but stories also change to adapt to changing circumstances.

For instance, Americans often say they are an immigrant nation. If you ask an American about his culture, he will probably tell you something about his ethnic or religious background. He may tell you where his ancestors came from and how they happened to go to America. He will tell you how his life and his family's life are unique. This story emphasizes the diversity within American culture. In fact, it is not important whether the story is true or not. What is significant is that people tell the story to show themselves and others who they are.

Culture is the grammar of our behavior. Culture is what people need to know in order to behave appropriately in a society. It includes all the rules that make actions meaningful to those acting and to the people around them. In learning to speak, everyone learns to use the grammar of their native language, but they use it automatically with little or no awareness of the rules of grammar. Similarly, people learn their cultural grammar unconsciously and apply its rules automatically. Just as native speakers of a language are usually unable to describe the grammatical rules of that language unless they have specifically studied grammar, most people find it difficult to describe the meaning system of their own culture. Like the grammar of a language, cultural grammars are repetitive. They are made up of basic patterns that occur again and again. For instance, an important pattern in Chinese culture is the distinction between inside and outside. This pattern shows up in the language, traditional architecture and in social relationship.

Culture is a toolbox. Every situation and every person is different. For culture to endure, it must be flexible enough to accommodate many different circumstances. One useful metaphor for culture is the toolbox—one that comes with a stack of reference manuals. Instead of saying "in this culture we make tables THAT way, we raise children or cook a meal THIS way", we acknowledge that culture gives us a set of tools for the task, along with a guide book that suggests how we might use those tools and what the results should look like. Cultural "tools" for making dinner would include heat source and cooking vessels, knowledge of food stuffs, recipes, knives, and rules for what items are served at which time of day to which kinds of guests.

Culture is a set of options. More broadly, one can think of culture in mathematical terms as a set (albeit with fuzzy boundaries) that contains accepted options, tools, and reference books. If you have a friend over to dinner, you have a number of culturally appropriate choices—you can order out for pizza, cook them a gourmet meal, take them to a restaurant, or have a barbeque.

Other options are possible but less likely these days, such as killing and plucking a chicken in their honor; these exist at the margin of the cultural set—on their way in or out. The stars represent yet other potential responses which lie "beyond the pale" and would not even be considered, such as roast dog, or sending the guest to the neighbors to beg food because you don't have enough.

This way of conceptualizing culture helps account for the many differences within a culture. Context, personality, and subcultures will affect which options people perceive and carry out, while still maintaining group boundaries about what is normal and acceptable. This metaphor also helps explain why culture endures, because options that prove satisfactory will continue to be selected and reinforced by a variety of people in many contexts over time. "Sets of options" also gives intercultural trainers a way of talking about cultural patterns that avoids the simplistic "THE Japanese do it THIS way" stereotype while still giving foreigners guidance about typical or workable options.

Features of Culture

Culture is learned. Culture is not born innate. The process begins immediately after birth. We begin to consciously or unconsciously acquire and learn our culture in our early life through senses and from experience, habits, skills, and knowledge. Interaction with family members and friends is the most common way for us to learn about our culture. Other sources for culture learning are schools, churches, media, folk tales, art and the like. Culture propagates through generations, which adopt their old customs and traditions as a part of their culture. Culture values are imparted from one generation to another, thus resulting in a continuum of traditions that are part of culture. Moreover, nobody has to remain for a life-time locked inside only one time, but accurately get inside them and act according to what is expected in them. Many people have learned more than one culture and move comfortably within them. When circumstances dictate, they make the transition from one culture to another easily.

Culture is subject to constant changes. Culture loses some of its traits and gains new ones. The aspects of culture that change vary across societies. Cultures change in the process of transmission from generation to generation, group to group, and place to place. With the passage of time, new technologies emerge, new modes of work come up, social thinking undergoes transitions and so does culture. Technological inventions, disasters, cultural contact and environmental factors account for the changes of culture.

Culture also furnishes attitudes. Attitudes are feelings about things, based on values. People from different cultures have different attitudes towards the same things. In Mexican culture, a death of an aunt is an event that business associates are expected to view as significant to family members. A boss is expected to have an understanding attitude toward an employee who is not able to get a report done by a deadline because of the funeral and family needs. In Britain, however, the attitude toward a business associate's loss of an aunt is that this is a private affair, regrettable and perhaps very sad, but something that should not affect work to a great extent. Reports should come in on time if possible.

Exercises for Understanding

1. Answer the following questions according to the passage you have just read.

(1) Which of the metaphors of culture given in the passage do you prefer? Why?

(2) Brainstorm examples of culture. Then classify them into the visible and invisible parts of the iceberg.

(3) According to the passage, what constitute the changes of culture?

(4) What are the functions of conceptualizing culture when culture is regarded as a set of options?

(5) Create your own metaphors. Culture is like a _____.

2. Choose the most appropriate answers to the following questions.

(1) How many definitions of culture are mentioned in this passage?

    A. 6   B. 7   C. 8   D. 9

(2) Which of the following is NOT above the water line?

    A. Assumptions

    B. Dressing style

    C. Pronunciation of "R"

    D. Office furnishing

(3) That culture is our software implies the following EXCEPT that _____.

    A. the physical body is like the hardware of the computer

    B. it is programmed by our own culture

    C. an infant learns how to be human in a culturally specific way

D. we are strongly aware of the "software" as we use it

(4) Culture is compared to the grammar of our behavior in that _____.

    A. cultural grammars are learned consciously

    B. cultural grammars occur infrequently in daily life

    C. cultural grammars can be illustrated easily

    D. culture grammars determine appropriate behaviors

(5) Which of the statements of culture is NOT true?

    A. Culture is transmissible.

    B. Culture is adaptive.

    C. Culture is dynamic.

    D. Culture is static.

3. Decide whether the following statements are true or false according to the passage you have just read. Write "T" for true or "F" for false.

_____ (1) Culture is innate as soon as a person is born.

_____ (2) Culture is acquired through socialization.

_____ (3) Man is the producer of culture and the product of culture.

_____ (4) People from different cultures are likely to have overlapping opinions.

_____ (5) One's actions and attitudes are independent of his or her culture.

4. Case study.

Watch the 5-episode documentary series *From Chung Kuo to China* and discuss about the tremendous changes that China has undergone in the eyes of foreigners.

FROM CHUNG KUO TO CHINA

Section C   Case

The Scenario

Scan and Listen

Dinner with Friends

Janice is a young American engineer working for a manufacturing joint venture near Nanjing. She and her husband George, who is teaching English at a university, are learning Chinese and enjoying their new life. They have been eager to get to know Chinese people better so were pleased when Liu Lingling, Janice's young co-worker invited them to her home for dinner.

When Janice and George arrived, Lingling introduced them to her husband Yang Feng, asked them to sit down at a table containing 8 plates of various cold dishes, served them tea and then disappeared with her husband into the kitchen. After a few minutes, Lingling came back and added water to their tea. Janice offered to help in the kitchen but Lingling said she didn't need help. She invited the couple to look at their new CD player and their color TV and then disappeared again.

A half hour later she came back and sat down and the three began to eat. Yang Feng came in from time to time to put dish after dish on the table. Most of the food was wonderful but neither George nor Janice could eat the fatty pork in pepper sauce or the sea cucumbers, and there was much more than they could eat. They kept wishing Yang Feng would sit down so they could talk to him. Finally, he did sit down to eat a bit, but quickly turned on the TV to show them all its high-tech features. Soon it was time to go home.

George and Janice felt slightly depressed by this experience, but returned the invitation two weeks later. They decided to make a nice American meal and felt lucky to find olives, tomato juice, crackers and even some cheese in the hotel shops. They put these out as appetizers. For the main course they prepared spaghetti and a salad with dressing made from oil, vinegar, and some spices they found in the market.

When Liu Lingling and Yang Feng arrived, they were impressed by the apartment and asked the price of the TV, video player, vacuum cleaner and other things. Janice politely refused to answer their questions. They took small tastes of the appetizers and seemed surprised when both George and Janice sat down with them. They ate only a little spaghetti and did not finish the salad on their plates. George urged them to eat more but they refused and looked around expectantly. Janice and George talked about their families and jobs and asked the Chinese couple about theirs. After a while, George cleared the table and served coffee and pastries. Yang Feng and Lingling each put four spoons of sugar into their coffee but did not drink much of it and ate only a bite or two of pastry.

After they left, George said that at least they had a chance to talk, but Janice was upset. "We left their place so full that we couldn't walk and they're going to have to eat again when they get home."

📝 Exercise

Listen to the case above and answer the following questions.

(1) What are Janice and Liu Lingling?

(2) How did Janice and her husband feel when Liu Lingling invited them to have dinner at home?

(3) What were Liu Lingling and her husband busy with most of the time? How did Janice and her husband feel?

(4) How did the American couple treat Liu Lingling and her husband when they returned the invitation?

(5) What are the differences between Chinese and American ways of hospitality?

Unit 2 Communication

● **Knowledge Objective:**

Guide students to master the definition, models, and constituent elements of communication.

● **知识目标：**

指导学生掌握交际的定义、模型和构成要素。

● **Ability Objective:**

Guide students to reduce "noises" and use communication elements for effective communication, and to distinguish and analyze the different communication modes and values embedded in Chinese and foreign cultures.

● **能力目标：**

指导学生减少"噪声"并综合运用交际要素进行有效沟通，同时辨析中外文化不同的交际模式和其中蕴藏的不同价值观。

● **Educative Objective:**

Guide students to analyze Li Ziqi's short video *The Life of Rice* and think about how Li Ziqi uses YouTube for effective international dissemination of fine traditional Chinese culture, inspiring students to have a sense of responsibility to promote fine traditional Chinese culture. Guide students to understand that "we need to uphold the beauty of each civilization and the diversity of civilizations in the world. Each civilization is the crystallization of human creation, and each is beautiful in its own way. The aspiration for all that is beautiful is a common pursuit of humanity that nothing can hold back. There would be no clash of civilizations as long as people are able to appreciate the beauty of them all".

素质目标：

通过分析李子柒的短视频《水稻的一生》，引导学生了解如何运用 YouTube 助力中华优秀传统文化的国际传播，激发学生弘扬中华优秀传统文化的责任感和使命感。引导学生了解"坚持美人之美、美美与共。每一种文明都是美的结晶，都彰显着创造之美。一切美好的事物都是相通的。人们对美好事物的向往，是任何力量都无法阻挡的。各种文明本没有冲突，只是要有欣赏所有文明之美的眼睛"。

Section A　Video Clip Appreciation

I. Introduction to the Movie *La La Land*

La La Land tells the story of Mia, an aspiring actress, and Sebastian, a dedicated jazz musician, who meet and fall in love in Los Angeles while pursuing their dreams. Set in modern day, Los Angeles, this original musical about everyday life explores the joy and pain of pursuing dreams.

II. Introduction to the Video Clips

Sebastian, a pianist who holds on to an ideal version of jazz, wants to open his own club. Mia, an incurable romantic, is fascinated by the allure of the old Hollywood. These two proper L. A. dreamers are simply meant for each other despite getting off to a bad start. Soon they are blissfully in love and move in together. In Clip 1, Sebastian is playing the piano at home. Mia comes home, and Sebastian begins singing *City of Stars* as he plays. Mia joins him on the piano bench and joins in, making the song a duet. Later, Mia is on the phone with her mother. She is being asked about Sebastian and defensively tells her mom that he's going to open a jazz club but admits he doesn't have the money yet. The truth of the comment hits home for Sebastian and he takes the job offered by Keith, his old friend, to play in a newer-style jazz band that he doesn't really believe in. After that, Sebastian is always on tour. In Clip 2, when Mia gets home, Sebastian is back making a meal as a surprise for her. They talk with each other happily at first but end up with a quarrel. On the following night, Sebastian misses Mia's performance because of a photoshoot of the band. After that, Mia breaks off the relationship, saying she's going to move back to her hometown and give up acting. A casting agent contacts Sebastian, looking for Mia for a film audition. Sebastian tracks her down to her hometown and drives her to the meeting. In Clip 3, Sebastian and Mia are discussing their future after the audition. In Clip 4, both are successful with their careers. Sebastian opens his own jazz club and Mia has her desired career as a famous actress and married someone else. The two former lovers encounter each other five years later when Mia's husband takes her to Sebastian's jazz club.

III. Script of the Video Clips

Clip 1

Video Clip 1

[*Lyrics of the song*]

City of stars

Are you shining just for me?

City of stars

There's so much that I can't see

Who knows?

I felt it from the first embrace I shared with you

That now our dreams

They've finally come true

City of stars

Just one thing everybody wants

There in the bars

And through the smokescreen of the crowded restaurants

It's love

Yes, all we're looking for is love from someone else

A rush

A glance

A touch

A dance

To look in somebody's eyes

To light up the skies

To open the world and send them reeling

A voice that says

I'll be here and you'll be alright

I don't care if I know

Just where I will go

'Cause all that I need's this crazy feeling

A rat-tat-tat on my heart

I think I want it to stay

Clip 2

Sebastian: I thought... Surprise! I gotta leave first thing in the morning, but I just—I had to see you. It's so nice to be home.

Video Clip 2

Mia: I'm so glad you're home.

Sebastian: How's the play going?

Mia: I'm nervous.

Sebastian: You are? Why?

Mia: Because... what if people show up?

Sebastian: Pishi Kaka. You're nervous about what they think?

Mia: I'm nervous to do it. I'm nervous to get up on that stage and perform for people. I mean, I don't need to say that to you.

Sebastian: It's gonna be incredible.

Mia: You don't get it but I'm terrified.

Sebastian: They should be lucky to see it. I can't wait.

Mia: I can. When do you leave? In the morning?

Sebastian: 6:45. Boise.

Mia: Boise?

Sebastian: Boise.

Mia: To Boise.

Sebastian: You should come.

Mia: To Boise?

Sebastian: Yeah. You can knock it off your bucket list.

Mia: Oh. That would be really exciting. I wish I could. What are you doing after the tour?

Sebastian: Why can't you?

Mia: Come to Boise?

Sebastian: Yeah.

Mia: 'cause I have to rehearse.

Sebastian: Yeah, but can't you rehearse anywhere?

Mia: Anywhere you are?

Sebastian: I mean—I guess.

Mia: Well, all my stuff is here and it's in two weeks. So I don't think really think that would be...

Sebastian: Okay.

Mia: The best idea right now, but... I wish I could.

Sebastian: We're just gonna have to try and see each other, you know, so that we can see each other.

Mia: I know, but when are you done?

Sebastian: What do you mean? I mean...

Mia: When you finish with the whole tour?

Sebastian: After we finish, we're gonna go to recording and then we'll go back on tour. You know, we tour so we can make the records so we can go back to tour the record.

Mia: So it's like the long haul?

Sebastian: What do you mean the "long haul"?

Mia: I mean the long haul that you're gonna stay in this band for a long time. On tour.

Sebastian: I mean, what did you think I was going to do?

Mia: I don't... I hadn't really thought it through. I didn't know the band...

Sebastian: You didn't think we would be successful?

Mia: No, that's not really what I mean. I just mean that y-you... I mean... you'll be on tour for what? Months now? Years?

Sebastian: Yeah, I don't mean—this is it... I mean, this is—it could feasibly be—yeah for... I could be on tour with this... for a couple of years, at least, just this record.

Mia: Do you like the music you're playing?

Sebastian: I don't. I don't know... What—what it matters?

Mia: Well, it matters because if you're going to give up your dream. I think it matters that you like what you're playing on the road for years.

Sebastian: Do you like the music that I play?

Mia: Yeah, I do. I just didn't think that you did.

Sebastian: Yeah well, you know...

Mia: You said Keith is the worst and now you're gonna be on tour with him for years. So I just didn't...

Sebastian: I don't know what—what are you doing right now?

Mia: Know if you were happy?

Sebastian: Why are you doing this?

Mia: I don't...

Sebastian: What do you mean "Why are you doing this?" And it just sounds like now you don't want me to do it.

Mia: What do you mean I wanted you to do this?

Sebastian: This is what you wanted for me.

Mia: To be in this band?

Sebastian: To be in a band to have a steady job. You know, t—to be... you know.

Mia: Of course, I wanted you to have a steady job so that you can take care of yourself and your life and you could start your club.

Sebastian: Yes, so I'm doing that so I don't understand why aren't we celebrating?

Mia: Why aren't you starting your club?

Sebastian: You said yourself no one wants to go to the club. No one wants to go to a club called "Chicken on a Stick".

Mia: So change the name!

Sebastian: Well, no one likes jazz! Not even you!

Mia: I do like jazz just because of you!

Sebastian: And this is what I thought you wanted me to do! What am I supposed to do? Go back to play *Jingle Bells*?

Mia: I'm not saying that! I'm saying why don't you take what you've made and start the club! People will wanna go to it because you're passionate about it and people love what other people are passionate about. You remind people of what they've forgotten.

Sebastian: Not in my experience. Well, whatever alright. It's... it's time to grow up, you know. I have a steady job, this is what I'm doing. And now all of a sudden if you had these problems, I wish you would've said them earlier before I signed on the goddamn dotted line.

Mia: I'm pointing out that you had a dream that you followed, that you were sticking...

Sebastian: This is the dream! This is the dream!

Mia: This is not your dream.

Sebastian: Guys like me work their whole lives to be in something that's successful, that people like. You know? I mean, I'm finally in something th-th-th-th-that people enjoy.

Mia: Since when do you care about being liked? Why do you care so much about being liked?

Sebastian: You are an actress! What are you talking about? Maybe you just liked me when I was on my ass because it made you feel better about yourself.

Mia: Are you kidding?

Sebastian: No. I don't know...

Clip 3

Sebastian: When do you find out?

Mia: They said the next couple of days. But I'm not expecting to find anything out.

Video Clip 3

Sebastian: You're gonna get it.

Mia: I really might not.

Sebastian: Yes, you are.

Mia: I don't want to be disappointed.

Sebastian: I know. I know these things.

Mia: Where are we?

Sebastian: Griffith Park.

Mia: Where are we?

Sebastian: I know. I don't know.

Mia: What do we do?

Sebastian: I don't think we could do anything. Because when you get this…

Mia: If I get this.

Sebastian: When you get this, you gotta give it everything you got. Everything. It's your dream.

Mia: What are you gonna do?

Sebastian: I gotta follow my own plan. Stay here and get my own thing doing. You'll be in Paris. Good jazz there. And you love jazz now. Right?

Mia: Yes.

Sebastian: I guess we're just gonna have to wait and see.

Mia: I'm always gonna love you.

Sebastian: I'm always gonna love you too. Look at this view.

Mia: I've seen better.

Sebastian: It's the worst.

Mia: Yeah. I've never been here during the day.

Clip 4

Mia's Husband: Do you wanna check it out?

Mia: Okay.

Mia's Husband: This place is pretty cool.

Video Clip 4

[*Applauce*]

Sebastian: Cal Bennett on the sax! Javier Gonzalez on trumpet. The lovely Nedra Wheeler on bass. The one and only Cliffon "Fou Fou" Eddie on drums. And a little too good on the piano. So good that he's gonna own this place if I'm not careful. Khirye Tyler, everybody. Welcome to Seb's.

[*Sebastian playing the piano*]

Mia's Husband: You want to stay through another?

Mia: No, we should go.

Mia's Husband: Okay.

Sebastian: One, two, one, two, three, four.

New Words

incredible 难以置信的，不可思议的
haul 拖，拉
feasibly 可行地

Phrases and Expressions

knock off 除去
on my ass 处境恶劣

Notes

Boise 博伊西，美国爱达荷州首府
wanna 想要

IV. Exercises for Understanding

1. Decide whether the following statements are true or false according to the video clips you have just watched. Write "T" for true or "F" for false.

_____ (1) Sebastian fell in love with Mia because she was a famous actress.

_____ (2) Mia quarreled with Sebastian because he couldn't make big money.

_____ (3) Mia and Sebastian fought and reconciled and they didn't end up being together.

_____ (4) When Mia returned to L. A., she came across Sebastian's jazz club.

_____ (5) In the end, Sebastian conveyed all his hopes, wishes and longings about the life he and Mia had had through the notes he played.

2. Put the following sentences in the right order according to the video clips you have just watched.

_____ (1) Mia and Sebastian met in the Griffith park talking about their future plans.

_____ (2) Mia argued with Sebastian about whether Sebastian should get involved in the tour to Boise and make records.

_____ (3) Sebastian established a Jazz club called Seb's.

_____ (4) Mia and Sebastian played music of *City of Stars* together.

_____ (5) Mia dropped in at Seb's and recalled the happy time she had had with Sebastian.

3. Explore interculturally.

(1) Why do Mia and Sebastian fight? What goes wrong in their process of communication?

(2) What's conveyed in the last look Mia and Sebastian share in the video clip?

Section B Reading

微课

Ask any employee what they'd like to change about their company, and you're likely to hear "we need better communication around here".

Everyone around them nods in active agreement. But what are they agreeing about? What do they mean by this? It could be any number of things. Probing people's complaints about "poor communication" can lead to the core issues that need attention.

■ No one really understands my needs and ideas. (Issues of respect and listening skills)

■ Some of us are left out of information loops or decision-making. (Organizational structure issues)

■ The organization has levels and divisions that speak different languages (Language barrier issues, class/education boundary issues)

- People work alone or can't converse during work hours. (Work organization issues)
- Everything is put in writing; no one talks to me as a person. (Organization climate issues)
- We have such different worldviews that no one understands where I am coming from. (Diversity issues)
- We employees don't dare tell managers what's really going on. (Management style issues)
- We managers don't dare tell employees what's really going on. (Survival issues)

Definition of Communication

What is communication? Communication generally refers to the process in which participants create and share information with one another as they move toward reaching mutual understanding. Whether you live in a city of Canada, a village in India, a commune in Israel, or the Amazon jungles of Brazil, you participate in the same activity when you communicate. The results and the methods might be different, but the process is the same.

A Model of Communication

As to the elements of communication, there are 10 of them. They are: context, sender, encoding, message, channel, receiver, decoding, response, feedback, and noise.

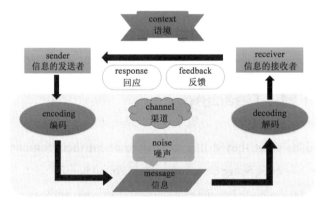

Elements of Communication

To understand the elements of communication, we have to mention our field of experience, or context. We each carry our own field of experience with us wherever we go. It is culture-specific. Although all aspects of a culture are part of the context, one of the most important aspects of culture is the establishment of the communication norms within the culture. Norms are the guidelines that we establish for conducting transactions. Norms exist at the beginning of a communication encounter and grow, change, or solidify as people get to know one another better. Norms tell us what kinds of message and behaviors are proper in a given context or with a particular person or group of people. Sometimes we don't know the norms. We have to learn them from experience.

Another important element in communication is message. It is the content of a communicative act. Communication takes place through the sending and receiving of messages. Everything a sender says or does has potential message value. The message is usually conveyed by a certain channel. A channel is both the route traveled by the message and the means of transportation. Messages are transmitted through a variety of sensory channels. We may use touch, smell, sound, sight, taste and so on to carry a message. Some channels are more effective at communicating certain messages than others, and the nature of the channels selected affects the way a message will be processed. Experiences show that most of us have channel preferences. We prefer to rely on one or more channel while disregarding others. But in general, the more channels used to carry a message, the more likely the communication will succeed. Most human communication is a mutual process rather than a one-way message flow. The participants frequently exchange roles as message originators and message receivers in the ongoing process of communication.

But communication is never perfectly effective. The receiver does not always decode a message into exactly the same meaning that the source had in mind when encoding the message. This is because of the noise. Noise is any stimulus, external or internal to the participants, that interferes with the sharing of meaning. Noise can be physical, psychological, perceptual, emotional, linguistic, and cultural. Much of our success as communicators depends on how we cope with these noises. The important point to remember is that noise can function as a communication barrier. As noise increases, the chances for effective communication usually decrease, and as noise decreases, the chances for effective communication usually rise. We must be fully aware of them. Finally, after receiving the message, the receiver usually gives certain feedback to the sender. Feedback returns information to the sender of a message, thereby enabling the sender to determine whether the message has been received or correctly understood. In any situation, paying attention to both verbal and nonverbal feedback allows us to behave in ways that increase understanding of our message. Feedback serves useful functions for both senders and receivers. It provides senders with the opportunity to measure how they are coming across, and it provides receivers with the opportunity to exert some influence over the communication process.

📝 Exercises for Understanding

1. Answer the following questions according to the passage you have just read.

(1) Why are norms important in conducting smooth communication?

(2) What channels do you usually prefer to use in communication? Why?

(3) What examples can you find to show that one channel is more effective than others in transmitting certain messages?

(4) What are the things that create noises in the process of communication?

(5) Why is feedback a very important element of communication?

2. Choose the most appropriate answers to the following questions.

(1) In communication, the following elements are changeable EXCEPT _____.

    A. methods

    B. results

    C. noise

    D. process

(2) The process of communication includes _____ elements.

    A. 9

    B. 10

    C. 11

    D. 12

(3) _____ is the process of putting an idea into a symbol.

    A. Decoding

    B. Channel

    C. Encoding

    D. Response

(4) _____ refers to the response of a receiver to a sender's message.

    A. Noise

    B. Channel

    C. Context

    D. Feedback

(5) Communication is never perfectly effective because of the following types of noise EXCEPT _____.

    A. psychological

    B. sentimental

C. cultural

D. emotional

3. Decide whether the following statements are true or false according to the passage you have just read. Write "T" for true or "F" for false.

_____ (1) People acquire communication norms from their life experiences.

_____ (2) There are rules for speakers to follow as to how messages are constructed and interpreted.

_____ (3) Communication is a one-way flow instead of a mutual one.

_____ (4) In most cases, intercultural communication is conducted without cultural "noises".

_____ (5) The sender plays a more important role than the receiver in communication.

4. Case study.

Watch the short video of *The Life of Rice* and discuss how Li Ziqi uses YouTube in the international dissemination of fine traditional Chinese culture. Then make and release an English short video about one representative cuisine in your hometown.

5. Small group task: A contest of English expressions of Chinese culture.

Step 1: Divide the class into 2 groups.

Step 2: In five minutes, each group prepares 5 words or expressions in the Chinese language that represent Chinese culture.

Step 3: Each group hands in the 5 words or expressions to the teacher.

Step 4: Start the contest. Group A expresses in English the words and expressions written by Group B. Group B expresses in English the words and expressions written by Group A. The group wins one point when its members express one word correctly. Take turns.

Step 5: The group that gets more points wins the game.

Section C Case

The Scenario

Scan and Listen

Where Is the Bus?

It was National Day and everyone had a long weekend, so the Foreign Affairs Office of a large university in Shanghai arranged a trip for its foreign teachers to the city of Hangzhou. Almost all the foreign teachers decided to go. They were accompanied by a number of mostly monolingual Chinese guides from the Foreign Affairs Office as well as some young teachers from the English, German, French and Russian faculties who accompanied their colleagues to act as interpreters. Altogether about 50 teachers, guides, interpreters and Foreign Affairs Office staff traveled to Hangzhou on a university bus.

When they got to Hangzhou, they were unloaded at a hotel on the outskirts of the city, given a nice dinner, and told to meet in the lobby at 8 the next morning. In the morning, when they were ready to set off sightseeing, the teachers were told that they would be taking the city bus. They didn't understand why they should take the crowded city bus when they had a comfortable touring bus, with a driver, in which they had driven to Hangzhou.

In fact, the Foreign Affairs Office had found out only after they got there that the city of Hangzhou had passed the Emergency Traffic Control Regulation prohibiting buses without Hangzhou registrations from entering the city for the few days before, after, and including the holiday. The interpreters were told NOT to pass this information on to the foreigners, since non-Chinese "wouldn't be able to understand the reasons" for it. The interpreters were instructed simply to insist to the teachers that they had to take the city bus, or if necessary to make up a reason.

The foreign teachers demanded explanations from their interpreters, who tried to explain that they hadn't made the decision and didn't know the reason. When they could get no real answer, the foreigners resigned themselves to taking the city bus. The interpreters, who were also friends and colleagues, could see that not knowing what was going on was affecting their foreign friends' enjoyment of the trip, so one by one they revealed the reason to the foreign teachers. The teachers were then annoyed with the Foreign Affairs Office staff for trying to deceive them. "Why couldn't they just have told us the truth in the first place?" they asked.

The Foreign Affairs Office was annoyed with the interpreters for not following directions. They blamed the interpreters for the fact that the foreigners were annoyed. By evening, everyone was annoyed with someone, and the holiday was turning out to be no fun at all.

📝 Exercise

Listen to the case above and answer the following questions.

(1) Who accompanied the foreign teachers during the trip to Hangzhou?

(2) How did they get to Hangzhou? Where did they stay?

(3) Why did they have to take the city bus to go sightseeing the next morning?

(4) Were the foreign teachers told the truth about the traffic control? Why or why not?

(5) What are the differences between Chinese and Americans in interpersonal communication?

Unit 3 Intercultural Communication

⏵ INTRODUCTION

● **Knowledge Objective:**

Guide students to master the definition, causes and variables of intercultural communication.

● **知识目标：**

指导学生掌握跨文化交际的定义、兴起的原因和变量。

● **Ability Objective:**

Guide students to differentiate and analyze different cultural values, customs and protocols between China and foreign countries through case study and to understand and solve conflicts and contradictions in intercultural communication.

● **能力目标：**

指导学生通过案例分析辨析中外不同的价值观、文化习俗和交际规约，学会理解和解决跨文化交际中的冲突和矛盾。

● **Educative Objective:**

Guide students to learn from Chinese German designer Liu Yang's *East Meets West* collection about how to seek common ground while reserving differences, how to deepen exchanges and mutual learning with other civilizations, how to cultivate sense of patriotism and international perspective, and understand the Chinese philosophy "similarities and differences coexist just as mixed colors complement each other".

● **素质目标：**

通过分析华裔女设计师刘扬《东西相遇》图集，引导学生在中外跨文化交际中学会求同存异、文明互鉴，培养家国情怀和国际视野，理解中国文化"同无妨异，异不害同，五色杂陈，相得益彰"的哲学思想。

Section A Video Clip Appreciation

I. Introduction to the Movie *The Second Best Exotic Marigold Hotel*

As the contented residents of the hotel begin settling into their new lives, Sonny Kapoor strives to balance the demands of planning his wedding with the responsibilities of purchasing a new property. Meanwhile, new guests Guy Chambers and Lavinia Beech find themselves in a predicament after arriving at the hotel to find there is only one vacancy. Perhaps with a  little innovation, new co-manager Muriel Donnelly can find a means of accommodating the hotel's latest occupants, but she'll have her work cut out for her as Douglas Ainslie and Evelyn Greenslade begin their new careers in Jaipur while flirting with the idea of a serious romance, like Norman Cousins and Carol Parr. With romance in the air, it's no wonder that Madge Hardcastle has her pick of handsome suitors, and as stalwart Muriel safeguards the many secrets of the vivacious residents, Sonny and Sunaina learn that planning a traditional Indian wedding can be a true test of commitment.

II. Introduction to the Video Clips

Clip 1

As the *Best Exotic Marigold Hotel* has only a single remaining vacancy, posing a rooming predicament for two fresh arrivals, Sonny Kapoor pursues his expansionist dream of opening a second hotel. He and his business partner Muriel flew to America to look for an investor, believing that being a franchise of Evergreen, an American based conglomerate, is the best way to proceed. Evergreen's response is that they will send someone to Jaipur to investigate on their behalf.

Clip 2

The world is seemingly Sonny Kapoor's oyster. He is financially secure enough that he and Sunaina can now get married. The British retirees who hoped to stretch their pensions by relocating to Marigold Hotel in Jaipur, India, begin to pair off romantically. Muriel Donnelly who safeguards many secrets of the vivacious residents, reflects on her old days in the hotel and her thinking about life and death.

III. Script of the Video Clips

Clip 1

Video Clip 1

Sonny Kapoor: Breathe the air, Mrs. Donnelly!

Muriel Donnelly: I'm eating dust.

Sonny Kapoor: The wind in your hair!

Muriel Donnelly: Put the bloody top back on, Sonny!

Sonny Kapoor: I will not hear your negativity. Madam, this is Route 66 and we are most assuredly getting our kicks!

Chet (Bellman): Hi. I'm Chet and I'll be happy to valet your car.

Sonny Kapoor: Not as happy as we are that you are happy to do so, my friend.

Muriel Donnelly: Just tell me... Just tell me there's a cup of tea and a biscuit waiting inside.

Doorman: That's a great accent. Are you from Australia?

Sonny Kapoor: The sound of destiny, Madam... calling us with her siren song. And go to her we must! For this is our moment. If not now, when? And if not us, who?

Muriel Donnelly: Later? Somebody else?

Sonny Kapoor: My hand is powdered, so the shake is firm and dry. My clothes precisely walk the tightrope between casual and relaxed formality.

Muriel Donnelly: Sonny, Sonny. Let me do the talking. Alright?

Sonny Kapoor: Okay.

Sonny Kapoor: Mr. Burley. While I am aware that... convention dictates that I should wait for your assessment of our proposal... please take my interruption less as rudeness than proof... of our profound excitement at the opportunity to meet yourself... and your fine company. And let me say right here and now...

Muriel Donnelly: Alright, that's enough, that's enough.

Sonny Kapoor: We agreed that my colleague would do the speaking and rightly so for... while her language may be... salty, it has great economy and pith.

Mr. Burley: I don't care about any of that.

Muriel Donnelly: No, listen and learn, son. Tea is an herb that's been dried out. So to bring it back to life, you have to infuse it... in boiling water. That is boiling water. Everywhere I've been in this country... they slap down a cup of tepid nonsense... you know with the teabag lying beside it... which means I've got to go through the ridiculous business of dunking it... in the lukewarm piss... waiting for the slightest change of color to occur. And at my age... I haven't got the time.

Sonny Kapoor: This is what I'm talking about.

Mr. Burley: Get her some boiling water. Now, Mrs. Donnelly. Tell me more about your establishment.

Muriel Donnelly: We've been going properly for about eight months now. But phase two of the development is more or less complete. Like life and a tortoise. It's not exactly fast-moving...

Sonny Kapoor: Mrs. Evelyn Greenslade.

Mrs. Evelyn Greenslade: Here.

Muriel Donnelly: ...but you only make progress when you stick your neck out.

Sonny Kapoor: Mr. Douglas Ainslie.

Mr. Douglas Ainslie: Here.

Muriel Donnelly: We have guests that come and go.

Sonny Kapoor: Mrs. Muriel Donnelly.

Mrs. Muriel Donnelly: Here.

Muriel Donnelly: But there's been a hard core of regulars from the beginning.

Sonny Kapoor: Mrs. Madge Hardcastle.

Mrs. Madge Hardcastle: Here.

Sonny Kapoor: Mr. Norman Cousins and Miss Carol Parr.

Mr. Norman Cousins and Miss Carol Parr: Both here.

Muriel Donnelly: We have monthly check-ups at the local clinic... and Sonny takes a rollcall every morning.

Sonny Kapoor: A most valuable precaution to ensure that nobody has died in the night.

Muriel Donnelly: Most of our guests don't just live in India, they now work there.

Evelyn Greenslade: These are lovely.

Dealer Hari: That is why they cost 10,000 rupees each.

Evelyn Greenslade: Every day? We have to do this every day?

Dealer Hari: Process, madam. We must respect the process.

Evelyn Greenslade: Very well. You and I both know that since a fine, genuine pashmina... requires the annual growth of at least three Changra goats... you and everyone in this market blend the yarn to give it more body. The reason I come to this stall is that whereas Bharat over there uses wool... and Mohan goes with the rabbit fur... you at least use a reasonable quality of silk. I'll give you 5,000 for four.

Dealer Hari: Done.

Evelyn Greenslade: Thank you. I'll see you tomorrow, Hari.

Dealer Hari: Tomorrow, Miss Evelyn. And thank you for your respect.

Muriel Donnelly: Two of the guests have made themselves useful at the local expats club, which is, shall we say, a little down on its uppers.

Customer: Norman...

Norman Cousins: Mmm?

Customer: I know the membership's dropping, times are tight, but... do you really have to water down the wine?

Norman Cousins: What?! I uncorked it myself. They're on to us. Let's try the red.

Muriel Donnelly: And others are doing jobs they never thought they could do.

Douglas Ainslie: One Queen was so close to her elephant... that when she passed away, the elephant stood beside her tomb for three days... before dying of grief. We should all know such love, just not necessarily from an elephant.

Muriel Donnelly: And sometimes they're right, they can't.

Tourist: Uh, when were these built?

Douglas Ainslie: I'm sorry?

Tourist: What period are we talking about?

Douglas Ainslie: What, um... period? Ah, uh... yeah. Um...

Boy: 17th... 17th century.

Douglas Ainslie: 17th century.

Tourist: Sure?

Douglas Ainslie: Absolutely positive.

Boy: Wait, wait, wait. Maybe 18th.

Douglas Ainslie: Oh, oh, oh...

Boy: Please admire the beautifully carved...

Douglas Ainslie: Now please admire these beautifully carved pillars...

Boy: that are engraved with typical Rajasthani...

Douglas Ainslie: which are engraved with typical Rajasthani carvings, typical carvings which... And, um, you, you, you can see...

Muriel Donnelly: Look, I could talk and talk... but all that counts in the end is this one had an idea. I know, I know, but it works. The proof of our success is we are victims of it. The Marigold Hotel is full up.

Sonny Kapoor: With nobody checking out. Until the ultimate check-out.

Muriel Donnelly: So we have to expand. There's a local place we've got our eye on.

Sonny Kapoor: The Supreme Quality Hotel.

Muriel Donnelly: You put up the notes, we buy it. And we become the furthest outpost of the Sonny Evergreen franchise.

Sonny Kapoor: Leading to a chain of hotels stretching across India and beyond... for those such as... this great lady... whose face is a map of the world... and whose mind, though failing, still contains many of the secrets of the universe, who had the chance to say, when she left her home for the Best Exotic Marigold Hotel... as others will do... "Why die here... when I can die there?"

Mr. Burley: If you'll indulge me. Evergreen is a different concept. We believe that the... well that the leaves don't need to fall. That these years, the mature years... are an opportunity for travel, for further education... for different work situations. Well, in a word, an opportunity for life. And for passing on the value of that life to others, I take it you would agree with me, Mrs. Donnelly?

Muriel Donnelly: I'm here, aren't I?

Mr. Burley: Are you talking to other companies about this?

Muriel Donnelly: We came to you first.

Mr. Burley: We do have competitors.

Muriel Donnelly: Not in our eyes.

Clip 2

Muriel Donnelly: I never understood why anyone would want to get married. I barely found a bugger I could spend a week with... let alone

Video Clip 2

a life. But I've been looking forward to this. And it turns out some things really are worth the wait. I'm not good with special occasions... or the gifts that go with them. So you'll have to make do with this letter instead. Written from the heart to the children I never had. I said at your party, I don't do advice. I do opinions. And my opinion of the groom is this: he gets plenty wrong... but never when it counts. And when he's right... (My friends...) it is something to behold.

Sonny Kapoor: I must tell you, the reception cannot take place at the Best Exotic Marigold Hotel. A bride as radiant as this one... deserves a more splendid setting for her wedding party... and I have just the place. Please, step into Vikram's beautiful minibus. And for those who are less close to it, or just move slower... you may use either of his cousin's and together... We shall ride to my new hotel! Don't look at me. —No, no, no. Don't look at him. Although, as the future unfolds, perhaps we will also take the Supreme Quality Hotel under our wing... and my old friend Kushal shall find himself working but a short distance beneath me... such is the level of my victorious magnanimity. But for now, to your chariots! And let us travel to the new jewel in my crown! The apple of my eye! Let us travel to the pearl in my oyster! No longer the Viceroy Club... but my gift on her wedding day... to the girl of my dreams, where I will welcome you. Ladies and gentle gentlemen... Oh, yes... to the Second Best Exotic Marigold Hotel! That is for you! Come! You see?

Douglas Ainslie: Ladies and Germs... I wonder if I could have your attention just for a moment. I have a few words I'd like to say. I cannot rest from travel: I will drink Life to the lees. All times have I enjoyed greatly... for always roaming with a hungry heart. Much have I seen and known; I am a part of all that I have met; Life piled on life Were all too little, and of one to me. Little remains; But every hour is saved. From that eternal silence, something more. A bringer of new things. A few words of Alfred, Lord Tennyson... speaking to something which we all know, and should never forget that every hour brings new things. And Sonny and Sunaina have today announced... that they want to face those hours... those things, this life together. And it's a privilege to be able... to send them on their way in

Douglas Ainslie: such remarkable style. Actually, talking of style... I had a fairytale wedding myself. Although mine was Grimm.

Boy: Pause for laugh.

Douglas Ainslie: Moving on... The two things we can give our children, it seems to me... it seems to me, are roots and wings. And Sonny and Sunaina's wonderful families have given them roots... And now... they can take flight.

Evelyn Greenslade: Read this.

Douglas Ainslie: ...together... and as they embark on this...

Boy: Vegetarian, non-vegetarian...

Douglas Ainslie: journey, um, yeah, uh... journey on which we send them with all our love... and, and, and tremendous... you know... um, not obviously...

Boy: This is what the... the young... This is what the young make us remember...

Douglas Ainslie: For this is what the young make us remember...

Boy: that in the end...

Douglas Ainslie: ...that in the end, it's all very simple... that all it takes is to look into someone's eyes... and say... "Yes..." This is what I want. "And for them to reply..." It's what I want, too... And there's nothing to be afraid of. Evelyn and I would like to wish the two of you... all the love and luck in the world. And so say all of us. Sonny and Sunaina!

Carol Parr: If you really want to try monogamy, even though I think it's for the young and very naive... I suppose we could give it a go. Norman?

Chandrima: You lied to me.

Guy Chambers: Well... well, I'm not a hotel inspector anymore and I am gonna write that book. So, actually, everything I said was true... just a few days early, that's all.

Chandrima: What about your wife?

Guy Chambers: Well that, that was true already.

Chandrima: You were my first since my husband died.

Guy Chambers: You weren't the first. But I think you could be the last. Please... come dance with me... Chandrima. Sonny told me.

Chandrima: I'm gonna kill that boy.

Madge Hardcastle: Thank you for coming.

Driver Babul: You called. Left or right, my lady?

Madge Hardcastle: Sorry?

Driver Babul: When we reach the turning, do you want to go left or right?

Madge Hardcastle: What do you do when you're faced with a difficult decision?

Driver Babul: I don't believe there is such a thing. Throw a coin in the air and we always know which side we want it to land. Left or right, my lady?

Sonny Kapoor: Mrs. Donnelly? Mrs. Donnelly? Are you in there, Madam?

Muriel Donnelly: Piss off back to your wedding. I'm having a rest.

Sonny Kapoor: Yes. Of course. Sorry to disturb.

Muriel Donnelly: Did you forget your dancing shoes?

Sonny Kapoor: No, Madam.

Muriel Donnelly: Then go and knock them dead.

Sonny Kapoor: Yes, Madam.

Muriel Donnelly: Sonny...

Sonny Kapoor: I'm going. I'm going.

****

Mr. Burley: Is there no one on reception? I thought this was a hotel?

Muriel Donnelly: What are you doing here?

Mr. Burley: Checking on my investment.

Muriel Donnelly: You've come to the wrong place.

Mr. Burley: I don't think so. I couldn't find you at the party. How are you, Mrs. Donnelly?

Muriel Donnelly: Why did you come here, really?

Mr. Burley: To pay my respects to you. There's nothing I admire more than someone planting trees... under whose shade they may never get to sit.

Muriel Donnelly: Others will. That's what counts. How long are you staying?

Mr. Burley: I fly tomorrow morning. It's a punishing itinerary, I'm afraid. In which of your hotels do you think I should spend the night? Second or the first?

Muriel Donnelly: I don't think you'll get a lot of sleep over there. I... I have to deliver this... then I'll check you in.

Mr. Burley: Thank you, Mrs. Donnelly.

Muriel Donnelly: I know you'll understand me missing the reception... and I hope you'll forgive me for not coming to say goodbye. Go and have the honeymoon you deserve. I'm sure there'll be somebody there to see you off. Thank you. There is no such thing as an ending. Just a place where you leave the story. And it's your story now. I spent 40 years scrubbing floors... and the last months of my life as co-manager of a hotel... halfway across the world. You have no idea now what you will become. Don't try and control it. Let go. That's when the fun starts. Because as I once heard someone say... "There's no present like the time."

New Words

valet 伺候客人停车

tightrope 危险的处境

dictate 导致，影响

assessment 评价，评定

pith 精髓，要旨

infuse 倾注

tepid 微温的

dunk 浸泡

rollcall 点名

genuine 真的

pashmina 羊绒（一种面料）

yam 山药

expat 移居国外者，侨民

grief 悲痛，悲伤

franchise 获得特许经销权的机构

victorious 胜利的

magnanimity 雅量，高尚

oyster 牡蛎

privilege 特权

itinerary 行程表

Phrases and Expressions

embark on 从事，着手

piss off 滚开，走开

knock sb dead 使……倾倒

Bharat （梵文）婆罗多，即印度

IV. Exercises for understanding

1. Decide whether the following statements are true or false according to the video clips you have just watched. Write "T" for true or "F" for false.

_____ (1) Sonny Kapoor was driving so fast that Muriel Donnelly felt uncomfortable.

_____ (2) Sonny Kapoor and Muriel Donnelly cooperated well with each other so that they finished the construction of the second Marigold hotel in time.

_____ (3) Douglas Ainslie pretended to be a knowledgeable tour guide with the help of a local Indian boy.

_____ (4) Guy Chambers didn't fall in love with Chandrima because Chandrima wasn't the first woman in his life.

_____ (5) Muriel Donnelly showed great affection towards Sonny Kapoor.

2. Put the following sentences in the right order according to the video clips you have just watched.

_____ (1) Sonny Kapoor conducted everyday morning roll call to ensure all the clients in Marigold Hotel were alive.

_____ (2) Sonny Kapoor and Muriel Donnelly went to America to invite investment for the establishment of the second Marigold hotel.

_____ (3) Norman Cousins watered down red wine.

_____ (4) Sonny Kapoor went from his wedding ceremony to check whether Muriel Donnelly was still alive.

_____ (5) Evelyn Greenslade went to local Indian market to buy some pashminas.

3. Explore interculturally.

(1) Why does Muriel Donnelly insist that teabag should go together with boiling water?

(2) How does Muriel Donnelly judge Sonny Kapoor? Why?

 **Section B Reading**

微课

Definition of Intercultural Communication

Intercultural communication is the communication between people whose cultural perceptions and symbol systems are distinct enough to alter the communication event. The need for intercultural communication is as old as humankind. From wandering tribes to traveling traders and religious missionaries, people have encountered others different from themselves.

These earlier meetings, like those of today, were often confusing and hostile. The recognition of alien differences and the human propensity to respond unkindly to them were expressed more than 2,000 years ago by the Greek playwright Aeschylus, who wrote "everyone's quick to blame the alien". This sentiment is still a powerful element in today's social and political rhetoric.

Reasons for the Popularity of Intercultural Communication

Although intercultural contact has a long history, today's intercultural encounters are far more numerous and of greater importance than in any previous time in the past. There are mainly three reasons, namely, the rise of new technology and information systems like communication networks, communication satellite, worldwide transportation, worldwide web, television, and so on; the changes in the world's population; and a shift in the world's economic, political and cultural arena.

First of all, McLuhan characterized today's world as a "global village" because of the rapid expansion of worldwide transportation and communication networks. The popularity of various communication networks, the exploration of communication satellites, the rapid development of worldwide transportation, the expansion of the Internet and all kinds of digital devices all contribute to the possibility and necessity of intercultural communication.

Besides, the swelling and migrating of world's population and changes in immigration patterns have also made it pressing for people to conduct intercultural communication. Within the boundaries of the United States, people are now redefining and rethinking the meaning of the word America. Neither the word nor the reality can any longer be used to describe a somewhat homogeneous group of people sharing a European heritage.

Last but not the least, the shift in the world's economic, political and cultural arena after the Second World War calls for the study of intercultural communication. Globalization of economy especially has further brought people together. This expansion in globalization has resulted in multinational corporations participating in various international business arrangements such as joint ventures and licensing agreements, which mean that it would not be unusual for someone to work for an organization that conducts business in many countries.

With or without your desire or consent, you are now thrust into contact with countless people who often appear alien, exotic, and perhaps even wondrous. Whether negotiating a major contract with the Chinese, discussing a joint venture with a German company, being supervised by someone from Mexico, counseling a young student from Cambodia, or working alongside someone who speaks no English, you encounter people with cultural backgrounds that are often strikingly different from your own.

Yet there is a fact that when people of different nationalities and ethnic origins who frequently speak different languages and hold different convictions attempt to work and live together, conflicts can easily arise.

The ineffectiveness of many international development projects, the failure to conduct American government programs designed to offer economic and scientific expertise to aid the developing countries in the 1950s were mainly due to the ignorance about the vital role culture plays in the process of communication. Intercultural communication study thus became important to address the problem of cultural illiteracy.

Elements of Intercultural Communication

As intercultural communication study is of great significance nowadays, then how to study intercultural communication well? We should be fully aware of the four variables in intercultural communication study: perception, verbal process, nonverbal process, and contextual elements.

The variable of perception, for example, includes beliefs, attitudes, values, and world views. These cultural value systems serve as message filters that determine, to a certain extent, the meaning each person assigns to the messages he/she encounters and thus, how to perceive the events these messages describe.

In living our lives and communicating with each other, our perception of reality is less important than reality itself. Some would argue that there is no ultimate reality, only the illusion of our perceptions.

Our perceptions are influenced by:

Physical elements—what information your eyes or ears can actually take in, how your brain processes it;

Environmental elements—what information is out there to receive, its context;

Learned elements—culture, personality and habit: what filters we use to select what we take in and how we react to it.

For example, colorblind people will not perceive "red" the way as other people do. Those with normal vision may physically see "red" similarly, but will interpret it culturally:

■ Red meaning "stop" or "anger" or "excitement" or "in debt" (US);

■ Red meaning "good fortune" or "revolution"(China).

Take verbal processes or language for example. Language is a major means of communication, heavily influenced by the culture in which it is developed. It can be a great stumbling block in intercultural communication. A great language problem is the tenacity with which some people will cling to one meaning of a word or a phrase in the new language, regardless of connotation or context. The variations in possible meaning, especially when inflection and tone are varied, are so difficult to cope with that they are often waved aside. This complacency will stop a search for understanding.

For example, in American English, to be "embarrassed" is to feel mildly uncomfortable, but to Spanish speakers, to be "embarrassed" connotes "to be pregnant". That's why the Spanish translation of the English advertisement of the bottled ink produced by Parker Pen Company "To avoid embarrassment, use Parker SuperQuink" was decoded into "To avoid pregnancy, use Parker SuperQuink".

Another variable in intercultural communication study is nonverbal process. Learning the language, which most visitors to foreign countries consider their only barrier to understanding, is actually the beginning. To enter into a culture is to be able to hear its special "hum and buzz of implication". People from different cultures inhabit different sensory realities. They see, hear, feel, and smell only that which has some meaning or importance for them. They abstract whatever fits into their personal world of reorganization and then interpret it through the frame of reference of their own culture. The misinterpretation of observable nonverbal signs and symbols—such as gestures, postures, and other body movements—is a definite communication barrier. But it is possible to learn the meanings of these observable messages usually in informal rather than formal ways.

Culture strongly influences our subjective reality and there are direct links among culture, perception, and behavior.

📝 Exercises for Understanding

1. Answer the following questions according to the passage you have just read.

(1) What are the reasons that bring about the popularity of intercultural communication study?

(2) What are the 4 variables in intercultural communication?

(3) How do Spanish people understand the meaning of being "embarrassed"?

(4) How do you understand a culture's hum and buzz of implication?

(5) Why is our subjective reality affected by culture?

2. Choose the most appropriate answers to the following questions.

(1) According to the passage, which of the following is NOT the reason for the popularity of intercultural communication study?

A. The rise of new technology and information systems

B. The changes of the world's geographical patterns

C. The changes in the world's population

D. The shift in the world's economic, political and cultural arena

(2) Which of the following is NOT a scenario of intercultural communication?

A. A Chinese company discusses with a German company about the establishment of a joint venture.

B. A Japanese seeks supervision from a Mexican in terms of agricultural planting.

C. An American counsels a young student from Cambodia who speaks no English.

D. The local municipal government advocates the rich to donate for the poor in Australia.

(3) Perceptions are affected by the following elements EXCEPT _____.

A. physical elements

B. cultural elements

C. habitual elements

D. genetic elements

(4) From the perspective of an American, RED does NOT mean _____.

A. stop

B. in debt

C. good fortune

D. anger

(5) Which of the following does NOT have a direct link with intercultural communication?

A. Perception

B. Language

C. Subjective reality

D. Body movement

3. Decide whether the following statements are true or false according to the passage you have just read. Write "T" for true or "F" for false.

(1) The study of intercultural communication appeared after the Second World War.

(2) The emergence of global village is mainly due to the globalization of world economy.

(3) The study of intercultural communication is an effective way to overcome cultural illiteracy.

(4) The variables of perceptions include contexts, beliefs, attitudes, values and world views.

(5) The correct understanding of a word or phrase must take cultural context into consideration.

4. Case study.

Learn some works from Chinese German designer Liu Yang's *East Meets West* collection and discuss how to seek common ground while reserving differences and how to deepen exchanges and mutual learning with other civilizations.

5. Small group task.

In *Teaching Culture: Strategies for Intercultural Communication*, Ned Seelye told the following story: Some years ago some scholars conducted a research study to see how well American students studying abroad in Colombia (Latin America) could communicate with their Colombian hosts. The result of the study was that American students who already spoke better Spanish when they arrived in Colombia were more likely to have miscommunication problems with their hosts. Surprisingly, there were fewer communication problems between the hosts and American students who didn't speak Spanish very well.

In groups, please discuss why the students who could speak better Spanish miscommunicate with their hosts.

Section C Case

Scan and Listen

The Scenario

Are You Mad at Me?

Jeff was pleased to have been assigned an international student as his roommate in his second year at a small liberal arts college in the US. Ji Bing was an easy-going guy, a good listener, warm-hearted, and always ready for a new experience. He apprenticed Jeff's explanations of American life and unfamiliar language. Jeff didn't think Ji Bing was any more difficult to get along with than the American roommate he had the year before, except that he seemed to want to study more than Jeff was used to and he sometimes borrowed Jeff's things without asking first.

One night, Jeff was working on a project that required some artwork. Ji Bing was at his desk studying for a test. Jeff's scissors were just too dull to do the job, so he asked Ji Bing, "Sorry to bother you while you're studying, but could I use your scissors for a while?"

Ji Bing said, "Sure," opened his desk drawer and handed Jeff the scissors. "Thanks, thanks a lot," Jeff said. A few minutes later, Jeff decided that his crayons were not going to do the trick. He addressed his roommate again, "Sorry to bug you again, but these crayons make this look like kindergarten. You know those colored pencils you have? Would it be OK if I used them for my project?"

Ji Bing got up and got them off the shelf and said, "Help yourself," and went back to reading as Jeff thanked him.

After another few minutes, Jeff said, "I must be driving you crazy, but have you got any glue or tape? Promise I will buy you another roll."

Ji Bing handed Jeff a roll of tape that was on his desk saying, "Use as much as you want. I don't need it". "Appreciate it," mumbled Jeff as he went back to his project.

Ji Bing went back to reading. As Jeff was finishing his project, he noticed that Ji Bing was watching him. He looked up and was surprised to hear his Chinese roommate ask him in a plaintive tone, "Are you mad at me?"

"Of course not," Jeff replied, "What makes you think like that?"

📝 Exercise

Listen to the case above and answer the following questions.

(1) What was Jeff's first impression of Ji Bing when they became roommates?

(2) What did Ji Bing learn from Jeff as roommates?

(3) What did Jeff borrow from Ji Bing on that night?

(4) Why did Ji Bing suspect that Jeff was mad?

(5) What do American and Chinese young people expect from friendship?

Module 2
Cultural Value Orientations

Unit 4 Hall's Culture Context Model

⊙ INTRODUCTION

● **Knowledge Objective:**

Guide students to master the content of Edward Hall's high- and low-context theory, its contributing factors and manifestations in intercultural communication.

● **知识目标：**

指导学生掌握霍尔高低语境文化理论的含义、形成原因及其在跨文化交际中的体现。

● **Ability Objective:**

Guide students to distinguish the differences of communicative responsibilities between high- and low-context cultures, to identify representative countries with high and low ratings and to apply the theory for effective intercultural communication.

● **能力目标：**

指导学生区分高低语境文化中交际责任归属的差异，识别高低语境文化的代表性国家，并运用高低语境文化理论有效地进行跨文化交际。

● **Educative Objective:**

Guide students to think about the popularity of the documentary *China* which starts from audience's acceptance of heterogeneous cultures to create a comprehensive, three-dimensional, and authentic image of China in an intercultural context with appropriate use of discourse methods based on respect, equality and mutual benefit between the subject and the object.

● **素质目标：**

通过分析纪录片《中国》，引导学生学习在跨文化语境下，从受众对异质文化的接受度出发，采用适当的话语方式，在主客体相互尊重和平等互利的基础上有效地传播好中国声音，讲好中国故事。

Section A   Video Clip Appreciation

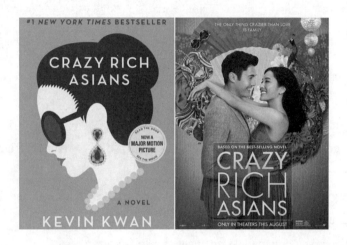

I. Introduction to the Movie *Crazy Rich Asians*

Crazy Rich Asians is a 2018 US romantic comedy based on the 2013 novel of the same name by Singaporean American novelist Kevin Kwan. It was directed by Chinese American filmmaker Jon M. Chu and praised in the United States since its release for its all-Asian cast. In the movie, Rachel Chu, an American-born Chinese economics professor who lives in New York, has been dating her boyfriend Nick Young for over a year when he invites her on a trip to his home country of Singapore to attend his friend Colin's wedding and meet his family. She's surprised to learn that Nick's family is extremely wealthy and he's considered one of the country's most eligible bachelors. Thrusted into the spotlight, Rachel must now contend with jealous socialites, quirky relatives and something far, far worse—Nick's disapproving mother.

II. Introduction to the Video Clips

Clip 1

Nick Young brings his girlfriend Rachel to meet his mother for the first time. They are having a brief talk in the kitchen.

Clip 2

Nick brings Rachel to his family gathering where people are wrapping dumplings. Later Rachel is kind of lost in the big building and Eleanor finds her.

III. Script of the Movie Clips

Clip 1

Video Clip 1

Nick: Mum.

Eleanor: You need a haircut. So unkempt. And you look tired from your trip. I'm gonna ask the cook to make you some herbal soup. I'll send it to the hotel later.

Nick: Mum, this is Rachel Chu.

Rachel: Oh, my gosh! I'm so happy to meet you, Mrs. Young. Or Auntie. Right? I'm learning the lingo.

Eleanor: I'm very glad to finally meet you, too. And I'm sorry Nick's father couldn't be here. He was called to business in Shanghai.

Nick: I told Rachel when duty calls, Dad answers.

Eleanor: As it should be. Nick tells me you're a professor, too. What do you teach?

Rachel: Um, I teach economics.

Nick: And she's brilliant. NYU's youngest faculty member.

Eleanor: So, economics... Sounds challenging. Are your parents academics as well?

Rachel: No. Well, my dad actually died before I was born, and my mom didn't even go to college. She actually hardly spoke any English when she immigrated to the United States. But she worked really hard, and she studied, and she earned her real estate license while she was waiting tables to support us. Now, she likes to say that she's Flushing's top real estate broker.

Eleanor: Self-made woman. She must be so proud of you.

Rachel: Well, she knows that I'm passionate about what I do, and she's always wanted that for me.

Eleanor: Pursuing one's passion. How American. Well, your mother's very open-minded, not like here, where parents are obsessed with shaping the life of their children.

Nick: That's dinner.

Eleanor: Go ahead. I'll be out in a minute. Rachel, it was lovely meeting you.

Rachel: Thank you. You, too. Okay, she hates me.

Nick: She takes a little minute to warm up, but we'll get there.

Rachel: A minute?

Clip 2

Aunt Alix: This is too much. We're hosting a rehearsal dinner, not feeding an army.

Eleanor: Better too many than have people say we're stingy.

Video Clip 2

Nick: So, right. You put the baby in bed. You tuck, tuck, tuck. Same on the other side. You give him a kiss good night.

Rachel: That's so cute.

Nick: How's that?

Rachel: And then you eat the baby.

Nick: Then you eat the baby after he's cooked.

Rachel: No, you gotta make sure he's cooked. Did your Ah Ma teach you that?

Nick: She did.

Oliver: I, on the other hand, was taught by Grand-Auntie Mabel. You put the Botox in the face, and then you pinch, pinch, pinch. Then, voila!

Rachel: Did you guys all learn when you were kids?

Astrid: We didn't have a choice.

Aunt Felicity: We taught you so you'd know the blood, sweat, and tears it took to raise and feed you monkeys.

Aunt Alix: Not like the ang-mohs microwaving macaroni and cheese for their own children. No wonder they put their parents in the old folks' home when they all grow up.

Aunt Felicity: I know!

Eleanor: Ah Ma says if we don't pass traditions down like this, they'll disappear.

Astrid: God forbid, we lose the ancient Chinese tradition of guilting your children.

Nick: It's totally worth it. Mother used to wait for me after school with a nice basket of these.

Astrid: Hey, I never got after-school dumplings.

Oliver: Well, that's because Auntie Felicity was doing after-school micro dermabrasion. Auntie, this is Dolce.

Aunt Alix: You speak Cantonese?

Rachel: No, I don't. It's just great seeing you guys all like this. When I was growing up, it was just me and my mom, which I loved. But we didn't really have a big family like this. It's really nice.

Oliver: Oh, that's so lovely of you to say, Rachel. We are all very lucky to have each other.

Rachel: That's a beautiful ring, Auntie Eleanor. I've never seen anything like it.

Eleanor: Nick's father had it made when he proposed to me.

Rachel: That's very romantic. How did you guys meet?

Nick: Actually, they met at Cambridge. They were both studying law together.

Rachel: Oh, I didn't know you were a lawyer.

Eleanor: I wasn't. I withdrew from university when we got married. I chose to help my husband run a business and to raise a family. For me, it was a privilege. But for you, you may think it's old-fashioned. It's nice you appreciate this house and us being here together wrapping dumplings. But all this doesn't just happen. It's because we know to put family first, instead of chasing one's passion.

Ah Ma: Ah, everyone's here!

Nick: Ah Ma... Thank you.

Ah Ma: Oh, Nick.

Nick: Come and sit.

Ah Ma: Oh, Nicki. You brought Rachel. Good. I can see you more clearly in the day. The shape of your nose is auspicious. Let me have a look, come closer... very nice looking. Sit. Sit.

Ah Ma: You made those dumplings? They don't look very good. You lost your touch.

****

Rachel: Oh, hi. I think I'm a little lost. This house is pretty big.

Eleanor: I'm glad I found you. I am afraid that I've been unfair.

Rachel: Oh, no, you know what? I'm sorry I made an assumption. I didn't mean to offend you.

Eleanor: Not at all. You asked about my ring. The truth is Nick's father had it made when he wanted to propose to me because Ah Ma wouldn't give him the family ring. I wasn't her first choice. Honestly, I wasn't her second.

Rachel: Gosh, I'm so sorry. I had no idea.

Eleanor: I didn't come from the right family, have the right connections. And Ah Ma thought I would not make an adequate wife to her son.

Rachel: But she came around, obviously.

Eleanor: It took many years, and she had good reason to be concerned. Because I had no idea the work and the sacrifice it would take. There were many days when I wondered if I would ever measure up. But having been through it all, I know this much. You will never be enough. We should head back. I wouldn't want Nick to worry.

New Words

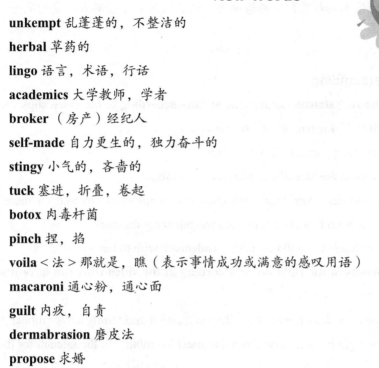

unkempt 乱蓬蓬的，不整洁的

herbal 草药的

lingo 语言，术语，行话

academics 大学教师，学者

broker（房产）经纪人

self-made 自力更生的，独力奋斗的

stingy 小气的，吝啬的

tuck 塞进，折叠，卷起

botox 肉毒杆菌

pinch 捏，掐

voila ＜法＞那就是，瞧（表示事情成功或满意的感叹用语）

macaroni 通心粉，通心面

guilt 内疚，自责

dermabrasion 磨皮法

propose 求婚

withdraw 退出（活动、组织等）

privilege 荣幸，光荣

auspicious 吉利的，幸运的

assumption 假定，臆测

adequate 适当的，能胜任的

Phrases and Expressions

real estate 地产，不动产

lose your touch 不如以往，变得不擅长

come around 转而接受

measure up 合格，符合标准

Notes

NYU 纽约大学，一所位于美国纽约州的世界顶尖私立研究型大学，为"常春藤"名校之一

Dolce & Gabbana 杜嘉班纳，总部位于意大利米兰，为奢侈品领域中最主要的国际集团之一

> **University of Cambridge** 牛津大学，一所位于英国牛津的世界顶尖公立研究型大学，在多个领域拥有崇高的学术地位及广泛的影响力，被公认为当今世界最顶尖的高等教育机构之一

IV. Exercises for understanding

1. Decide whether the following statements are true or false according to the video clips you have just watched. Write "T" for true or "F" for false.

_____ (1) Rachel was very happy to see Nick's mother.

_____ (2) Nick's mother liked the idea of pursuing one's passion.

_____ (3) Both Nick and his cousin Astrid had after-school dumplings when they were children.

_____ (4) Rachel didn't grow up in a big family, and she felt sorry for that.

_____ (5) Eleanor thought Rachel would not make an adequate wife to her son.

2. Put the following sentences in the right order according to the video clips you have just watched.

_____ (1) Rachel and Nick's mother talked about Rachel's career and family before dinner.

_____ (2) Nick Young brought his girlfriend Rachel to meet his mother in the kitchen for the first time.

_____ (3) Nick's Ah Ma came to meet Rachel.

_____ (4) Nick brought Rachel to his family gathering where people were wrapping dumplings.

_____ (5) Rachel was kind of lost in the big building and Eleanor found her.

3. Explore interculturally.

(1) What did Ah Ma say about the dumplings made by Nick's mother? Did Ah Ma like her daughter-in-law? Why do you think so?

(2) Why did Eleanor tell Rachel about the story behind the ring? What did she imply? What does this tell us about the way people communicate?

Section B Reading

微课

    Context is important in all kinds of communication, but it is relatively more important in some situations than in others. There are significant differences across cultures in the ways and the extent to which people communicate through context.

    In 1976, the well-known US anthropologist Edward Hall, the father of intercultural communication, originated the concepts of high-context culture and low-context culture. Hall based his concepts on the degree to which meaning comes from the context or from the words being exchanged.

In high-context cultures, much information is implied in the context. Context includes the situation or surrounding circumstances, relationships of the communicators, their family background, title, age, sex, education, status, and social networks. Relatively, little is provided in the verbal message itself. In low-context cultures, however, the majority of the information is contained in the verbal code, and the message is stated clearly and explicitly without depending on the context of the communication.

In high-context cultures, most of the meaning exchanged during an encounter is often not communicated through words. Information is provided through inference, gestures, and even silence. One reason that meanings frequently do not have to be stated verbally in high-context cultures is that there is normally a strong level of similarity among the people. Everyone, no matter what their culture is, communicates in this way in some situations. The most common example is communication between close friends and family members. Husbands and wives, and parents and children in all cultures typically communicate in this way. They are so familiar with one another that a glance, a turn of the head, or a slight change in facial expression carries more meanings than many words possibly could. In the intimacy of these relationships, people even discount what the other person is saying if what is said is not consistent with the context.

In low-context cultures, lack of a large pool of common experiences means that each time people interact with others they need detailed background information. In low-context cultures, the verbal message contains most of the information and very little is embedded in the context or the participant's nonverbal activity. This characteristic manifests itself in communication. For example, the Asian mode of communication (high-context) is often vague, indirect and implicit, whereas Western communication (low-context) tends to be direct and explicit. Americans depend more on spoken words than on nonverbal behavior to convey messages. They think it is important to be able to "speak up" and "say what's on their mind". They admire a person who has a large vocabulary and who can express himself or herself clearly and cleverly.

The following figure shows cultures arranged along the high-context and low-context dimension found by Edward Hall.

Source: Hall. *Beyond Culture*. NY: Doubleday, 1976: 91.

From the figure we can see Asian cultures incline towards high-context communication that emphasizes role hierarchy and relations rather than the expression of self through direct communication. The high-context nature of Asian cultures is a result of Confucian philosophy.

Direct and Indirect Communication

An important difference between high-context and low-context communication is that with high-context communication, the burden of interpreting the meaning falls on the listener, while with low-context communication the speaker has the responsibility for making the meaning clear.

In the low-context cultures, such as American and British cultures, people are usually from diverse background and do not share much common information. So the way Westerners communicate tends to be relatively explicit and direct. In other words, Westerners tend to put most of their ideas and feelings into words, and then state these ideas and feelings plainly and openly. It is generally considered a good thing to "get to the point" to ensure that his/her message is stated in a way that is clear and easy to understand. They expect others to "take them at their word", i.e. to believe that what they say is what they mean.

Collectivist cultures are usually high-context cultures. In these cultures, such as Japanese, African-American, and Latino cultures, people are very homogeneous and share much background information. Therefore, it is not necessary to articulate every detail of the information explicitly. High-context communication style is more indirect and subtle, and listeners are expected to take more responsibility for interpreting messages correctly. People are expected to pay much attention to the context in which communication takes place—who the speaker is, where and why the conversation is taking place, body language, and so forth— and when people interpret what others mean, they often give more weight to the context than to the actual words said. In fact, people in high-context cultures often view direct, explicit communication as unsophisticated or even rude.

Differences in communication styles sometimes cause misunderstandings between Chinese and Westerners. Often in China when someone answers, "We must give it more thought" to a request, he/she is refusing a request that cannot be met. The speaker does not want to disrupt the relationship with the person making the request and expects the other person to interpret the answer as a polite refusal. The Westerners may assume that there is a good chance that the answer will be "yes" (in fact, there is a better chance that the implied answer is "no"). In a similar situation many Westerners would not hesitate to say, "Sorry, it can't be done."

Differences in communication styles may also cause bad feelings between Chinese and Westerners. Westerners tend to dislike indirect communication, and often feel that Chinese "beat around the bush" too much rather than being direct. In contrast, Chinese often find Westerners too blunt and direct.

It is important to note that Westerners are not all equally direct in their communication styles. For example, the direct low-context communication style described above is more typical of Western men than of Western women. Furthermore, even in Western culture it is generally not considered good to communicate so directly and bluntly that you hurt other people's feelings, offend them, or create conflicts.

Silence is often regarded as a very important nonverbal code highly valued by people in high-context cultures. Just as a proverb says, "Empty cans clatter the loudest," high-context people may perceive talkative low-context people as less credible. However, in the eyes of people in low-context cultures, who hate ambiguity and value clarity, silence is usually associated with negative meanings such as indifference, anger, hostility, disagreement, shyness, embarrassment, ignorance, boredom or coldness.

In-groups and Out-groups

In addition to differences in communication styles, the differences between in-groups and out-groups is another manifestation of high-context and low-context cultures. "In-groups" are the groups that people have the most in common with and identify most closely with, such as their family, classmates, or co-workers. They also have larger in-groups such as people who are from their own region, religious group, ethnic group, or nation. In contrast, "out-groups" are the groups that people do not identify with, people from other families, regions, ethnic groups, or nations.

In high-context cultures, people make a clear distinction between in-group members and out-group members. The way people relate to in-groups tends to differ from how they relate to out-groups in a number of ways. They generally have more positive feelings toward members of their in-groups than they do toward outsiders. When they are with their in-groups, they have a relatively strong sense of belonging and familiarity, and also usually feel more at ease and comfortable. They also usually trust other in-group members more than they trust outsiders. They tend to have a stronger sense of obligation to insiders than to outsiders. They tend to judge in-groups and out-groups by different standards. They are usually biased in favor of their in-groups and more generous in the ways they judge the behavior of in-group members. Toward outsiders, they tend to be more critical, suspicious, and willing to pass harsh judgments.

In high-context cultures, the commitment between people is very strong and deep, and loyalties to families and friends are long-lasting and unchanging. Long-term relationships, in turn, strengthen the high-context communication between in-groups. In low-context cultures, the bonds between people are, by comparison, quite fragile. Group membership changes rapidly. The extent of involvement and commitment is low. Therefore, the distinction between in-groups and out-groups is not clear-cut. To be explicit and articulate is always emphasized as an important skill in communication.

📝 Exercises for Understanding

1. Answer the following questions according to the passage you have just read.

(1) What is high-context culture and what is low-context culture?

(2) What are the differences between high-context communication and low-context communication?

(3) The proverb "Empty cans clatter the loudest" is used to illustrate the point that people in low-context culture may be perceived as less credible by high-context people. Can you think of some Chinese proverbs or sayings concerning Chinese people's view on silence or eloquence?

(4) According to the passage, who are one's in-group members?

(5) What are the differences in the way people relate to in-group and out-group members in high-context cultures?

2. Choose the most appropriate answers to the following questions.

(1) Which of the following expressions demonstrates the Western communication style?

A. Say what you mean.

B. Don't beat around the bush.

C. Get to the point.

D. All of the above.

(2) Which of the following sayings demonstrates the high-context communication in Chinese culture?

A. What I have said or written does not convey all I have on my mind.

B. Meaning beyond words, or hidden meaning between the lines.

C. The subtlety is beyond description though it can be sensed.

D. All of the above.

(3) According to Edward Hall, the following countries incline toward high-context culture EXCEPT _____.

A. Germany

B. China

C. Japan

D. Korea

(4) According to Edward Hall, the following countries incline toward low-context culture EXCEPT _____.

    A. Germany

    B. China

    C. the United States

    D. France

(5) People from all cultures communicate in high-context way in some situations. Which of the following are examples of high-context communication?

    A. Communication between close friends.

    B. Communication between husbands and wives.

    C. Communication between parents and children.

    D. All of the above.

3. Decide whether the following statements are true or false according to the passage you have just read. Write "T" for true or "F" for false.

_____ (1) Westerners tend to dislike indirect communication.

_____ (2) Westerners are all equally direct in their communication styles.

_____ (3) Collectivist cultures are usually high-context cultures.

_____ (4) In high-context cultures, the friendship between people is very strong and deep. Besides, people are more loyal to families.

_____ (5) In the mainstream American culture, the ideal form of communication includes being direct rather than indirect.

4. Case study.

    Learn about the popularity of the documentary *China* and discuss how to tell China's stories and convey China's voice effectively in different cultural contexts.

5. Small group task.

    In *Cross-Cultural Communication*, the authors listed the most common cultural patterns and their influences on behavior and communication in a table. Study the following table carefully and discuss in groups your understanding of the relationship between cultural patterns and communication styles.

Cultural Patterns	
Individualism vs. Collectivism	
Individualism (e.g., the US, Australia, Canada) * Focus is on the individual & self-promotion * Independency * Task dominates relationship * Social obedience through sense of guilt	Collectivism (e.g., ROK, China, Mexico) * Focus is on the group & self-criticism * Interdependency * Relationship dominates task * Social obedience through sense of shame
Egalitarian vs. Hierarchical (Power Distance)	
Egalitarian (e.g., Australia, Canada, the US) * Horizontal relationships * Subordinates consulted * Equality expected	Hierarchical (e.g., Mexico, India, ROK) * Vertical relationships * Subordinates informed * Inequality accepted
Low vs. High Uncertainty Avoidance	
Low Uncertainty Avoidance (e.g., India, the US) * Change is normal and good * Few behavioral protocols * Greater cultural diversity	High Uncertainty Avoidance (e.g., Japan, Spain) * Change is disruptive and disliked * Many behavioral protocols * Less cultural diversity
Low vs. High Context Communication	
Low Context (Direct) (e.g., Germany, the US) * Meaning reliant on verbal message * Nonverbal communication low importance * Silence is avoided	High Context (Indirect) (e.g., ROK, Japan) * Meaning can be derived from context * Nonverbal communication high importance * Silence is normal
Low vs. High Face Concerns	
Low Face Concerns (e.g. Canada, the US) * Conflict / disagreement is constructive * Concern for self-face	High Face Concerns (e.g., ROK, China) * Conflict / disagreement is threatening * Concern for mutual / other-face

Source: Samovar, Porter, McDaniel. *Cross-Cultural Communication.* 北京：北京大学出版社，2017.

 **Section C Case**

The Scenario

Scan and Listen

Scene 1: Two European American neighbors are having a conversation.

Jane: (knocks on her neighbor's open window) Excuse me, it is 11 o'clock already, and your high-pitched opera singing is really disturbing my sleep. Please stop your gargling noises immediately! I have an important job interview tomorrow morning, and I want to get a good night's sleep. I really need this job to pay my rent!

Diane: (resentfully) Well, this is the only time I can rehearse my opera! I've an important audition coming up tomorrow. You're not the only one that is starving, you know. I also need to pay my rent. Stop being so self-centered!

Jane: (frustrated) I really think you're being very unreasonable. If you don't stop your singing right now, I'm going to file a complaint with the apartment manager and he could evict you...

Diane: (sarcastically) OK, be my guest... Do whatever you want. I'm going to sing as I please.

Scene 2: Two Japanese housewives are having a conversation.

Mrs. A: Your daughter has started taking piano lessons, hasn't she? I envy you, because you can be proud of her talent. You must be looking forward to her future as a pianist. I'm really impressed by her enthusiasm—every day, she practices so hard, for hours and hours, until late at night.

Mrs. B: Oh, no, not at all. She is just a beginner. We don't know her future yet. We hadn't realized that you could hear her playing. I'm so sorry you have been disturbed by her noise.

📝 **Exercise**

Listen to the case above and answer the following questions.

(1) Why did Jane knock on her neighbor's window at 11 o'clock one night?

(2) What would Jane probably do if her neighbor insisted on singing at night?

(3) How did Mrs. A comment on Mrs. B's daughter's piano performance?

(4) How did Mrs. B interpret Ms. A's comments?

(5) Which dialogue exemplifies low-context communication? And which dialogue exemplifies high-context communication? Why?

Unit 5　Hofstede's Cultural Dimensions

▶ INTRODUCTION

● **Knowledge Objective:**

Guide students to master the four main dimensions of Hofstede's cultural dimensions theory (power distance, individualism & collectivism, uncertainty avoidance, masculinity & femininity) and their applications in intercultural communication.

● **知识目标：**

指导学生掌握霍夫斯塔德文化维度理论中的四个维度（权力距离、个人主义和集体主义、不确定性规避、男性主义和女性主义）的含义及其在跨文化交际中的表现形式。

● **Ability Objective:**

Guide students to recognize the psychological processes shared by people in a specific cultural environment, to identify the representative countries that are rated with respective dimension indexes and to apply the theory for effective intercultural communication.

● **能力目标：**

指导学生认知某一个具体文化环境下人们共同拥有的心理程序，识别四个文化维度指数的代表性国家，并运用文化维度理论有效地进行跨文化交际。

● **Educative Objective:**

Guide students to think about how foreigners report Chinese government's poverty alleviation endeavors in the documentary *China on the Move,* which can be used to interpret Hofstede's the power distance dimension and arouse students' patriotic enthusiasm. Guide students to understand that "In state-to-state relations, the principles of equality, mutual respect and mutual trust must be put front and center. We must advocate peace, development, equity, justice, democracy and freedom, which are common values of humanity, and encourage exchanges and mutual learning among civilizations to promote the progress of human civilization".

素质目标：

通过分析纪录片《行进中的中国》，引导学生思考外国人如何报道中国政府在脱贫攻坚中的创新举措，解读文化维度理论中的权力距离维度，激发学生的爱国主义热情。引导学生理解"国与国相处，要把平等相待、互尊互信挺在前面。要弘扬和平、发展、公平、正义、民主、自由的全人类共同价值，倡导不同文明交流互鉴"。

Section A   Video Clip Appreciation

I. Introduction to the movie *Monsoon Wedding*

It's a story set in the modern upper-middle class of India, where telecommunications and a western lifestyle mix with old traditions. Young Aditi accepts the arranged wedding when she ends the affair with a married TV producer. The groom, Hermant Rai, is an Indian living in Houston, Texas, US. All relatives from both families, some from distant places like Australia, come to New Delhi during the monsoon season to attend the wedding. The four-day arrangements and celebrations will see clumsy organization, family parties and drama, dangers to the happy end of the wedding, lots of music and even a new romance for the wedding planner Dubey with the housemaid Alice.

II. Introduction to the Video Clips

Clip 1

Aditi's father is calling P. K. Dubey, a wedding contractor, who is running far behind schedule.

Clip 2

The groom's family and guests begin to arrive, from all over India, US and Australia. The whole family comes together from all corners of the globe for the wedding.

Clip 3

The Verma family and guests are sitting around a table and chatting.

Clip 4

Pimmi Verma talks to her husband, hoping he could reconsider his decision to send their son to boarding school.

III. Script of the Video Clips

Clip 1

Lalit Verma: Dubey! Dubey!

Pimmi Verma: Not here.

Lalit Verma: Not here yet? He's an impossible fellow! Nearly 11:00. How to fix this? Pimmi, please bring the phone.

Video Clip 1

Pimmi Verma: Darling, you want something else? Tea? Nimbu pani?

Lalit Verma: No, no. That bloody bastard Dubey hasn't come yet. He wants money but doesn't want to work. Dubeyji? Lalit Verma, who else? Very kind of you to answer. What's going on? No sign of anyone.

Pimmi Verma: Alice? Alice? Fry the pakoras. Tea for the master. Hurry!

Shashi Chadha: Pimmi, I'm sorry to say. Lalit takes on too much tension. It's not good. You see all these young men getting heart attacks these days.

Ria's Mother: God forbid it! The wedding is so soon. And Lalit is doing everything single-handedly. Hundreds of things to get tense about.

Lalit Verma: The marigold gate is falling apart. The flowers are everywhere. What's going on?

P. K. Dubey: No need to get so upset, sir. Flowers? What's a few flowers? For you, I'll bring Kashmir's Mughal garden. Just say the word. I'm stranded in a traffic jam.

Lalit Verma: Enough! Get here on the double.

P. K. Dubey: Ten minutes, exactly and approximately. I can't phone and drive.

Lalit Verma: What's the idiot up to? Left, left, you idiot! Stop the car! You'll spoil the decorations also. Don't you even know how to drive?

Rahul Chadha: I've only got one hand to drive with.

Lalit Verma: Who told you to break your hand at this time, idiot? Where were you?

Rahul Chadha: I went to the airport to get your sister and her husband.

Lalit Verma: Where are they?

Rahul Chadha: I didn't see them.

Lalit Verma: You are incredible. What do you mean, you didn't see them?

Rahul Chadha: I don't even know what they look like.

Lalit Verma: Hold up a placard: "Mr. and Mrs. Tej Puri from USA." They could have seen you. Why are you yawning so much?

Rahul Chadha: I've hardly slept. Not to mention I got back from Australia just yesterday.

Lalit Verma: You young people! What do you need to sleep so much for? What time is the flight coming?

Rahul Chadha: About 9:00.

Lalit Verma: Make sure you're there on time. And take this car, okay?

Rahul Chadha: Okay.

Lalit Verma: Don't run the AC when you're going to receive them. And only run the AC when you've received them. And park this car somewhere else!

Rahul Chadha: Chill.

Lalit Verma: And take off that stupid topi.

****

Pimmi Verma: Oh, God, Varun, what are you doing with that? Why haven't you got ready? Didn't you hear Papa? He's getting so angry.

Varun Verma: It's the last step! Coconut curry, Ma.

Pimmi Verma: No, no. Now, hurry up. Don't give me a hard time. And this TV, I'm so sick of it! Take this off. Hurry up.

Varun Verma: Ma, what are you doing? I'll do it myself.

Pimmi Verma: What "wear it yourself"? I'll wear it myself. The guests are on their way. Did you change your underwear?

Varun Verma: Ma!

Pimmi Verma: Did you? Out with the truth! Are you wearing dirty ones from yesterday? I just hope they're not smelling. You're such a silly little boy.

Varun Verma: "Little"?

Pimmi Verma: Oh, God!

Clip 2

[*In the garden*]

Lalit Verma: Pimmi, come on!

Alice: The groom! The groom is here!

Aditi Verma: Oh, shit.

Lalit Verma: Welcome, welcome. Congratulations, Mr. Rai!

Mohan Rai: Thank you, thank you.

Lalit Verma: This is Pimmi's brother from Muscat. Rahul, come here!

Hermant Rai: It's okay, it's okay.

Lalit Verma: So, excited? Soon to be in family way! So, you like India?

Video Clip 2

Hermant Rai: Yeah.

Lalit Verma: Better than Houston, no? Good, good, good. India needs young men like you. Yes, computer engineers are India's biggest export.

Varun Verma: Am I a coolie or what?

[*In the house*]

Lalit Verma: Bhai-sahab, what would you like to drink?

Mohan Rai: Scotch, please on the "rockiolis".

Lalit Verma: "Rockiolis" means ice?

Mohan Rai: Two lumps, exactly.

Lalit Verma: Exactly.

Saroj Rai: I'll have the same, thanks.

Lalit Verma: Rahul, two whiskies here. Two cubes of ice exactly.

Mohan Rai: Oh, my goodness. Look at you! How lovely you look.

C. L. Chadha: Rockioli, rockioli. Mrs. Rai over there.

Lalit Verma: Pay your respects to Grandmother.

Ria Verma: Hi. Congratulations.

Hermant Rai: Hi.

Grandmother: Look what I have for you. Know why God arranged your marriage in a hurry? I told him I had to see a great-grandson before dying. He heard me! How beautiful! So fair and lovely.

Pimmi Verma: Say hello to Hermant.

Hermant Rai: Hi. How are you?

Aditi Verma: Fine.

Shashi Chadha: Enough! Give them some privacy. I met C. L. only once, and we got married right away!

Ria's Mother: Don't you feel like getting married?

Lalit Verma: Rahul, idiot, come here. Come here and hold the camera. Listen. Come on, put it on. Camera on! On the ring!

D. L. Chadha: Sweeten your mouths, my dears.

Lalit Verma: Just in time! My dear brother-in-law! Look at hime.

Vijaya: This is Varun? He's almost a young man.

Lalit Verma: How did you manage? I sent Rahul to airport, told me flight was late.

Tej Puri: No, it was not late. Nobody was there at the airport, so we took a cab.

Lalit Verma: You had to take a cab?

Tej Puri: It's okay.

Lalit Verma: Rahul, you idiot, I sent you to the airport to receive them. You come back and tell me the flight was late? What a complete idiot!

Shashi Chadha: He's been working day and night. He doesn't know India.

Lalit Verma: But he's number one most stupid duffer.

Shashi Chadha: I'm sorry to say, but I don't like this! Calls my son an idiot, then calls him a duffer. Who does he think he is? I'm not coming back to India.

Lalit Verma: Bhai-sahab, this is Mr. Tej Puri, married to my sister Vijaya. After my older brother Surinder bhai-sahab passed away, Tej bhai has been the hero of the family. He has really looked after us. Come and meet Hermant.

Tej Puri: Yes. Excuse me.

Lalit Verma: Excuse me.

Vijaya: My naughty niece, couldn't you wait? You know how difficult it was to get tickets at this time of the year?

Lalit Verma: Difficult or not, we would have brought you here first-class if we had to. We couldn't have had the shadi without you, my darling sister.

Tej Puri: Nothing would have stopped us.

Tej Puri: Ria? Is that you? Come here, come here, come here. God bless. Very good.

Clip 3

Lalit Verma: Paaji, would you like a cigar?

Tej Puri: I quit.

Lalit Verma: America makes everyone quit smoking.

Video Clip 3

Vijaya: The Rais are so cultured.

Lalit Verma: Speak a little English and you become a very cultured family.

Lalit Verma: Tej bhai-sahab, I wanted to talk to you about Ria's plans. Ria, come here a minute, please. Ria wants to study in America.

Tej Puri: Is that so?

Lalit Verma: We're hoping you could give us some advice.

Vijaya: What do you want to do?

Ria Verma: I'm applying for creative writing programs.

Lalit Verma: She wants to be a writer.

Tej Puri: Very good.

Ria's Mother: Have you thought of the budget? Where will the money come from? My teacher's salary? Make her understand. Why can't she be like Aditi and do the right thing at the right time?

C. L. Chadha: Lots of money in writing these days. That girl who won the Booker Prize became an overnight millionaire!

Lalit Verma: Absolutely! Just one book. Who knows? It might happen.

Shashi Chadha: You must go to the States. You Know saada Umang is also there.

Tej Puri: You must give us his phone number.

Shashi Chadha: He's coming here tonight. We're hoping Ria and Umang will like each other.

C. L. Chadha: Two weddings in one!

Lalit Verma: Umang? What are the chances of getting hooked?

Ria Verma: Bad.

D. L. Chadha: I have another joke. Nonvegetarian!

Lalit Verma: Save the jokes for the sangeet. He'll be the MC at the sangeet.

E. L. Chadha: Let me start rehearsing, then.

Aditi Verma: Varun, out!

Varun Verma: What's your problem anyway?

Aditi Verma: Out! I can't have some privacy in my own house?

Lalit Verma: Varun, what happened to you?

Tej Puri: Okay, okay, I have an announcement to make. I'm thinking that if Ria wants to study in America... I will fund her entire education. No, no arguments. This is my family. I won't listen to you or Ria's mother. You see, Lalit, Ria is a sensible girl. If she wants to write, we must encourage her.

Lalit Verma: I can still work.

Tej Puri: This is final! We'll talk about it later, okay? Now you tell us what needs to be done for the wedding.

Vijaya: Absolutely. Now you don't have to worry about anything. We're here, we take care of everything.

Tej Puri: Anything.

Lalit Verma: My God, I don't know what to say. This is enough for me that we are all here together. My God! Pimmi, it's wonderful, no? After so many years. After Surinder bhai-sahab passed away... I think this is the fisrt time the whole family's here together. Ria, Ria, Ria. Don't cry. I know you are missing him. We are all missing your father. But he is here with us. Your papa is always blessing our family.

Clip 4

Pimmi Verma: I've been thinking, Lalit. I don't want to send Varun to boarding school.

Video Clip 4

Lalit Verma: Don't start again.

Pimmi Verma: I don't want to lose both my children.

Lalit Verma: Pimmi, don't start over again, huh? We've been through all this. He's going to boarding school, and that's final. He's wasting his life, staying here watching TV the whole day. There's no one here to discipline him. He doesn't listen. I give up. I don't know what to do.

Pimmi Verma: He also needs love and affection. He's such a sensitive boy and he's so wonderful with all these creative things.

Lalit Verma: Creative things like singing and dancing, cooking sesame chicken. Let's find him a nice boy.

Pimmi Verma: Don't say that. Why do you always look at everything like that?

Lalit Verma: You know what he told Tej bhai-sahab he wants to be when he grows up?

Pimmi Verma: What?

Lalit Verma: He said he wants to be a chef. I tell you. Our son will be a cook. A cook!

Pimmi Verma: He's just a kid. It doesn't mean anything.

Lalit Verma: He's a fool. My son will be a man when he grows up, understand? He'll be an educated professional. He won't be singing and dancing in people's shadis.

Varun Verma: Mama. Can you do this for me? Make a mucchi and on my eyes?

Pimmi Verma: Why, beta?

Varun Verma: For my dance with Ayesha tonight.

Pimmi Verma: Okay.

Lalit Verma: Why can't you do something useful? Like some exercise or reading your schoolbooks for a change. Look at you, a big huge hulk. Can't spend your whole life singing and dancing.

Varun Verma: Why not?

Lalit Verma: What do you mean, why not? You want to be an entertainer? You don't do any exercise. You don't even play cricket. You don't read a book. Just sleeping all day and watching TV... and now this new nonsense, dancing!

Varun Verma: Why? You also took Mama's dupatta and danced the night.

Lalit Verma: Don't compare yourself with me. You're just a kid.

Varun Verma: But right now you said I'm big now.

Lalit Verma: That's it. You're going to boarding school. Decided!

Varun Verma: Since when?

Pimmi Verma: Beta, Papa and I are only talking about it.

Lalit Verma: No, I have made up my mind. We are not...

Pimmi Verma: Let me talk to him. It's going to be good for you. Soon Aditi's going away. You'll be so lonely at home. So we thought you'd go to boarding school. You'll have so much fun.

Varun Verma: You also have been trying to send me away to boarding school.

Pimmi Verma: No, beta. Nothing has been decided. That school is much better than this school. We thought you'll go there and there'll be so many boys your age. You'll really enjoy yourself.

Varun Verma: No, I don't want to go. I won't go. You do what you want.

Lalit Verma: We're just doing this for your own good. It'll make you a bit tougher. It'll be good for you.

Varun Verma: I hate you! I hate you both! You don't even understand one thing about me.

Lalit Verma: Don't you talk to me like that!

Varun Verma: Fine! I just won't talk to you at all.

Pimmi Verma: Varun.

Varun Verma: No.

Pimmi Verma: Please, son. Listen to me.

Varun Verma: Leave me alone!

Pimmi Verma: Happy now? Happy with what you've done?

Lalit Verma: I didn't mean to upset him like that. Why couldn't you say something?

Pimmi Verma: Don't talk to me, okay? Just don't talk to me.

New Words

monsoon （南亚地区的）雨季
contractor 承包商，承包公司
pakora （南亚）油炸辣肉菜片
strand 使滞留

placard 标语牌，广告牌

topi 遮阳帽

lump 块

sesame 芝麻

hulk 身躯巨大且笨重的人

dupatta 围巾，头巾

Phrases and Expressions

nimbu pani 柠檬水

AC 空调

MC 司仪，仪式主持人

Notes

marigold flower 万寿菊，金盏花

IV. Exercises for understanding

1. Decide whether the following statements are true or false according to the video clips you have just watched. Write "T" for true or "F" for false.

_____ (1) The wedding contractor was driving when he got Lalit's phone call.

_____ (2) The young man Rahul came back from America for the wedding.

_____ (3) Lalit's sister and brother-in-law had to take a taxi because their flight was late, and nobody was at the airport to meet them.

_____ (4) Lalit wanted to talk to his brother-in-law about the wedding preparation.

_____ (5) Varun wanted to be a chef when he grew up, but his parents didn't like the idea.

2. Put the following sentences in the right order according to the video clips you have just watched.

_____ (1) Lalit's brother-in-law proposed to fund Ria's education in America.

_____ (2) The groom's family came to the bride's house for the engagement ceremony.

_____ (3) Lalit was angry about the wedding contractor for not doing his job properly.

_____ (4) Lalit wanted to send his son to boarding school after his daughter's wedding.

_____ (5) The bride and groom met each other's family members and exchanged wedding rings in the presence of both families and guests.

3. Explore interculturally.

(1) Why did Lalit say that his brother-in-law had been "the hero of the family" since Lalit's older brother passed away? What does this tell us about the value of family in this culture?

(2) In the movie, who might have the final say over whether to send Varun to boarding school? Why do you think so? Why did Lalit want his son to be an educated professional instead of a chef or an entertainer? What does this tell us about Lalit's idea about the role of boys in society when they grow up?

Section B Reading

微课

In the 1970s, Dutch researcher Geert Hofstede conducted opinion surveys of employees of IBM, a large multinational business organization around the world. He then used statistical methods to analyze the responses to the surveys. From the analysis he identified four pairs of contrasting values that he used to compare values across cultures. He found a way to assign each country a score for each pair of contrasting values, and a rank was assigned according to the scores. Hofstede's study was later expanded by replication studies of the IBM research and the extended IBM models: the Chinese Value Survey and the World Values Survey. In this unit, the data about the ranks of the countries and regions are based on the IBM research and its replications, which give scores for seventy-six countries and regions.

The four pairs of contrasting values Hofstede identified are: individualism vs. collectivism, high and low power distances, masculinity vs. femininity, strong and weak uncertainty avoidance. Hofstede used the term "dimension" to refer to the contrasting values. A dimension is an aspect of a culture that can be measured relative to other cultures. More recently abundant research has shown that Hofstede's dimensional model applies not only to work-related values but also to cultural values in general.

Individualism vs. Collectivism

In Hofstede's research there are two pairs of contrasting values to describe social relationships: power distance and individualism vs. collectivism.

According to Hofstede, individualism pertains to societies in which the ties between individuals are loose: everyone is expected to look after himself or herself and his or her immediate family. Collectivism as its opposite pertains to societies in which people from birth onward are integrated into strong, cohesive in-groups, which throughout people's lifetime continue to protect them in exchange for unquestioning loyalty.

According to Hofstede's research, Western cultures tend to be individualist, and the countries in Hofstede's study that received the highest scores for individualism were (in order): the United States, Australia, Great Britain, Canada, Hungary, the Netherlands, and New Zealand. In contrast, the cultures of Asian countries such as China, Singapore, Thailand and Vietnam (all the four countries had an index of 20 and ranked No.58 out of 76 countries and regions) ranked much lower on the individualism scale, so were considered much more collectivist.

A minority of people in our world live in societies in which the interests of the individual prevail over the interests of the group, societies that we call individualist. An individualist culture is one in which people tend to view themselves as individuals and to emphasize the needs of individuals. It has the following components. First, the individual is the single most important unit in any social setting. Westerners tend to believe that individuals should make decisions for themselves, and that individuals should take credit and responsibility for what they have personally done. Second, independence rather than interdependence is stressed. Westerners tend to believe that people should rely on themselves as much as possible—and they usually expect other people to do the same. Third, individual achievement is rewarded. Lastly, the uniqueness of each individual is of paramount value. A person's rights and privacy prevail over group considerations in an individualistic culture. Westerners generally feel that the rights of individuals should not be subordinated to the needs of a large group, or at least that individuals should have the right to decide for themselves whether to sacrifice their personal benefit for the sake of the group. Individualists are likely to belong to many groups but retain only weak ties, changing membership when desired.

The majority of the world's population live in societies in which the interests of the group prevails over the interests of the individual. We call these societies collectivist. A collectivist culture is one in which people tend to view themselves as members of groups (families, work units, tribes, nations), and usually consider the needs of the group to be more important than the needs of individuals. In collective cultures, relationships form a rigid social framework that distinguishes between in-groups and out-groups. People rely on their in-groups (e.g. family, tribe, clan, organization) to look after them, and in exchange they believe they owe loyalty to that group. In collective cultures, the individual is emotionally dependent on organizations and institutions, and group membership is emphasized. The importance of the group in collective societies is shown by a Chinese proverb: "No matter how stout, one beam cannot support a house."

The individualism-collectivism dimension produces variations in family structures, how classroom activities are conducted, the way organizations manage work groups, and even how the individual conducts social relations. In a learning environment, a collective classroom will stress harmony and cooperation rather than competition.

There are two very important things we need to remember about the difference between individualist and collectivist cultures. First, saying that Western culture is individualist does not mean that all Westerners are always individualist. For example, in many Western countries there is a strong emphasis on teamwork, and we can see this in the popularity of team sports, through which young people are taught to work together and make sacrifices for the good of the team. So, while it is generally true that Westerners think and act in individualist ways more than people in collectivist cultures do, the difference between individualist and collectivist cultures is relative rather than absolute. Second, not all Western countries are equally individualist, and some Western countries tend to be more individualist than others. Likewise, while the cultures of East Asia all tend to be more or less collectivist, they also differ from each other in many important ways.

Power Distance

Another cultural values dimension about social relationship revealed by Hofstede's research is power distance, which classifies cultures on a continuum of high and low power distance. Every society has hierarchy to some degree. In other words, some people have a higher rank and more power than others. Power distance is concerned with how societies manage the fact that people are unequal. According to Hofstede, power distance refers to the extent to which the less powerful members of institutions and organizations within a country expect and accept that power is distributed unequally. In this sense, institution refers to family, school, and community, while organizations are the places where people work. So power distance is described based on the value system of the less powerful members. The way power is distributed is usually explained from the behavior of the more powerful members, the leaders rather than those led.

According to Hofstede's research, among the countries that received the highest scores for power distance were (in order) Malaysia, the Philippines, Russia, Mexico, China (ranked No.14), Indonesia, India, and Singapore. The countries that received the lowest scores for power distance included Ireland, Switzerland, New Zealand, Denmark, Israel and Austria, with Austria at the lowest end.

Individuals from high power distance cultures accept power as part of society. Superiors consider their subordinates to be different from themselves and vice versa. People in high power distance countries or regions believe that power and authority are facts of life. Both consciously and unconsciously, these cultures teach their members that people are not equal in this world and that everybody has a rightful place which is clearly marked by countless societal hierarchies. In organizations in high power distance cultures, there is a greater centralization of power, more recognition and use of rank and status, and adherence to established lines of authority.

Low power distance countries or regions hold that inequality in society should be minimized. Cultures referred to as "low power distance" are guided by laws, norms, and everyday behaviors that make power distinctions as minimal as possible. Subordinates and superiors consider each other as equals. People in power, be they supervisors, managers, or government officials, often interact with their constituents and try to look less powerful than they really are. In low power distance work centers, you might observe decisions being shared, subordinates being consulted, bosses relying on support teams, and status symbols being kept to a minimum.

We can observe signs of power distance dimension in nearly every social setting, for example, in family, at school and in the workplace. In the high-power-distance situation, children are expected to be obedient toward their parents while in the low-power-distance situation, children are more or less treated as equals as soon as they are able to act. In the high-power-distance situation, teachers are treated with respect, and seldom publicly contradicted or criticized, while in the low-power-distance situation, teachers are supposed to treat the students as basic equals and expect to be treated as equals by the students.

In North American companies there are always differences in position and power, but in daily conversation many North Americans try to interact as if there were no such differences. So, for example, in many US organizations the norm is for people to address each other by first names, thus minimizing the appearance of rank differences. Also, a boss is generally more liked by employees if he or she acts like "one of the guys" and doesn't "pull rank" too often.

Masculinity vs. Femininity

According to Hofstede, the words masculinity and femininity refer to the degree to which masculine or feminine traits are valued and revealed. His rationale is that many masculine and feminine behaviors are learned and mediated by cultural norms and traditions. For better understanding, we can use the terms "career success" and "quality of life" to convey the meaning behind this dimension.

According to Hofstede's research, the countries that received the highest masculinity-index scores were (in order): Slovakia, Japan, Hungary, Austria, Venezuela, Switzerland, Italy, Mexico, Ireland, Jamaica, China (ranked No.11 out of 76 countries), Germany, Great Britain, and the Philippines. The countries with the lowest masculinity-index scores were Denmark, the Netherlands, Latvia, Norway and Sweden, with Sweden at the lowest end.

Masculinity is the extent to which the dominant values in a society are male-oriented. A society is masculine when emotional gender roles are clearly distinct: men are supposed to be assertive, tough, and focused on material success, whereas women are supposed to be more modest, tender, and concerned with the quality of life. Masculine or career success oriented cultures have highly defined gender roles and promote achievement in the workplace. Assertiveness and the acquisitive of money are emphasized and often take precedence over interpersonal relationships.

Cultures that value femininity as a trait stress nurturing behavior. A society is feminine when emotional gender roles overlap: both men and women are supposed to be modest, tender, and concerned with the quality of life. A feminine worldview maintains that men need not be assertive and that they can assume nurturing roles. It also promotes sexual equality and holds that people and the environment are important. Interdependence is ideal and people sympathize with the less fortunate.

In all cultures, men and women adopt distinct norms of socialization and tend to play differentiated roles in society. However, different cultural expectations of male and female occur across cultures. We can observe signs of masculinity-femininity dimension in family and school settings.

In the family, the stability of gender role patterns is almost entirely a matter of socialization. Socialization means that both girls and boys learn their place in society, and once they have learned it, the majority of them want it that way. Boys in a masculine society are socialized toward assertiveness, ambition, and competition. When they grow up, they are expected to aspire to career advancement. The family within a feminine society socializes children toward modesty and solidarity, and in these societies both men and women may or may not be ambitious and may or may not want a career.

In feminine cultures, teachers will rather praise weaker students, in order to encourage them, than openly praise good students. As Hofstede noticed in his own teaching experience with students from all over the world, students from masculine countries may ask to take an exam again after passing with a mediocre grade, while Dutch students almost never do so.

He concluded that in the more feminine cultures, the average students are considered the norm, while in more masculine countries, the best students are the norm. Parents in these masculine countries expect their children to try to match the best. The "best boy in class" in the Netherlands is a somewhat ridiculous figure.

Uncertainty Avoidance

All human beings have to face the fact that we do not know what will happen tomorrow: the future is uncertain. However, cultures vary in their ability to tolerate ambiguity and unpredictability. As the term is used in Hofstede's research, uncertainty avoidance refers to the extent to which the members of a culture feel threatened by ambiguous or unknown situations.

According to Hofstede's research, the countries that received the highest uncertainty avoidance index scores included Greece, Portugal, Belgium, Russia, Poland, Japan. Countries with the lowest uncertainty avoidance index scores included the United States, the Philippines, India, Malaysia, Great Britain, Ireland, China (ranked No.70 out of 76 countries), Vietnam, Sweden, Denmark, Jamaica and Singapore, with Singapore in the lowest end. High uncertainty avoidance cultures endeavor to reduce unpredictability and ambiguity through intolerance of deviant ideas and behaviors, emphasizing consensus, resisting changes, and adhering to traditional social protocols. These cultures are often characterized by relatively high levels of anxiety and stress. People with this orientation believe that life carries the potential for continual hazards, and to avoid or mitigate these dangers, there is a strong need for laws, written rules, planning, regulations, rituals, ceremonies, and established societal, behavioral, and communication conventions, all of which add structure to life. Social expectations are clearly established and consistent. For example, Japan is a high uncertainty avoidance culture with many formal social protocols that help to predict how people will behave in almost every social interaction.

Low uncertainty avoidance cultures more easily accept the uncertainty inherent in life, tend to be tolerant of the unusual, and are not as threatened by different ideas and people. They prize initiative, dislike the structure associated with hierarchy, are willing to take risks, are flexible, think that there should be as few rules as possible, and depend not so much on experts as on themselves. As a whole, members of low uncertainty avoidance cultures are less constrained by social protocol.

Every human society has developed ways to alleviate anxiety from uncertainty, including technology, law and religion. Technology helps people to avoid uncertainties caused by nature. Laws and rules try to prevent uncertainties in the behavior of other people. Religion is a way of relating to the transcendental forces that are assumed to control people's personal future. Religion helps followers to accept the uncertainties against which one cannot defend oneself. The difference between strong and weak uncertainty avoidance sentiment can be summarized as "What is different is dangerous" versus "What is different is curious".

As with other value dimensions, differences in uncertainty avoidance influence communication and activities in varied contexts. In a classroom composed of children from a low uncertainty avoidance culture, such as Britain, you would expect to see students feeling comfortable dealing with unstructured learning situations, being rewarded for innovative approaches to problem solving, and learning without strict timetables. A different behavior is the case in high uncertainty avoidance cultures like Germany, where you find that students expect structured learning situations, firm timetables, and well-defined objectives.

As we discuss the above four value dimensions, it is important to keep in mind that Hofstede's work measured cultural dimensions at a national rather than individual level, which means that his value dimensions characterize the dominant culture in that society. Within every culture you will find individuals all along a particular value continuum. For example, in the United States, some members of the dominant culture possess strong collective tendencies. Conversely, in a group-oriented culture such as ROK, you can find individuals that assert individuality. Therefore, in any intercultural encounter, you must be mindful that the other person or persons may not adhere to the norm for their culture.

📝 Exercises for Understanding

1. Answer the following questions according to the passage you have just read.

(1) What does the proverb "No matter how stout, one beam cannot support a house" mean in Chinese? Can you think of other Chinese proverbs that demonstrate the collective sense in Chinese culture?

(2) Can you explain in your own words the contrasting values of individualism vs. collectivism identified in Hofstede's research? Illustrate with examples across countries to support Hofstede's findings.

(3) Explain in your own words the contrasting values of high and low power distance identified in Hofstede's research. Can you find examples across cultures to support Hofstede's findings?

(4) According to Hofstede, what is meant by the contrasting values of masculinity vs. femininity? What are the characteristics of a masculine culture?

(5) According to Hofstede, what does uncertainty avoidance mean? How do high uncertainty avoidance cultures deal with unpredictability and ambiguity?

2. Choose the most appropriate answers to the following questions.

(1) Which of the following demonstrates the characteristics of a collectivist culture?

　　A. People are supposed to take care of only themselves and their immediate families.

　　B. Asking for advice and help from one's supervisors is usually regarded as evidence of lack of competence.

　　C. People have a high sense of loyalty and obligation to their in-groups.

　　D. Friendships are often established rather quickly, and also end rather easily—most are not permanent.

(2) Which of the following demonstrates the characteristics of a high power distance culture?

　　A. People believe inequality in society should be minimized.

　　B. People believe that power and authority are part of society.

　　C. A boss is generally more liked by employees if he acts like "one of the guys".

　　D. Teachers are supposed to treat the students as basic equals and vice versa.

(3) Which of the following is NOT true according to Hofstede's research on uncertainty avoidance?

　　A. This dimension refers to the extent to which the members of a culture feel threatened by ambiguous or unknown situations.

　　B. High uncertainty avoidance cultures endeavor to reduce unpredictability and ambiguity.

　　C. People in high uncertainty avoidance cultures depend not so much on experts as on themselves.

　　D. Low uncertainty avoidance cultures more easily accept the uncertainty inherent in life, and tend to be tolerant of different ideas and people.

(4) Which of the following is NOT true according to Hofstede's research on masculinity vs. femininity dimension?

　　A. A society is feminine when emotional gender roles overlap.

　　B. Masculine oriented cultures have highly defined gender roles and promote achievement in the workplace.

　　C. A feminine worldview maintains that men need not be assertive and that they can assume nurturing roles.

　　D. Boys in a feminine society are socialized toward assertiveness, ambition, and competition.

(5) Which of the following is NOT a drawback of applying Hofstede's theory?

    A. Hofstede's theory of cultural differentiation can be used when analyzing a country's culture.

    B. The dimensions cannot be used for comparing the values of individuals.

    C. The list of countries examined in Hofstede's research was not exhaustive.

    D. The dominant culture of a country may change over a long period of time because of various internal and external forces.

3. Decide whether the following statements are true or false according to the passage you have just read. Write "T" for true or "F" for false.

_____ (1) Individualism is often regarded as the fundamental value held by Westerners.

_____ (2) In a collectivist culture, people usually consider the needs of individuals to be more important than the needs of the group.

_____ (3) Hofstede's work measured cultural dimensions at a national rather than individual level.

_____ (4) In a feminine society, interdependence is ideal and people sympathize with the less fortunate.

_____ (5) Japan is a low uncertainty avoidance culture with many formal social protocols.

4. Case study.

    Learn to use Hofstede's power distance dimension to illustrate foreigners' applause of China's poverty alleviation endeavors in the documentary *China on the Move*.

Section C Case

The Scenario

Scan and Listen

Chinese Culture Is Built into the Furniture

As an American teacher at a Chinese university, I find the arrangement of classrooms a problem. Most of them have large raised podiums with students sitting in rows below and in front. This design reinforces the authority of the teacher and encourages a teacher-centered style of learning. I prefer classrooms with movable tables and chairs that would make it easier to arrange the students into work groups. I would like to move among the groups monitoring their work and offering advice as needed. As a teacher I prefer the role of facilitator, a person who defines tasks and goals and arranges activities to achieve them. I am not the main source of knowledge for the students but the leader of their learning activities. I do not want students to sit below and in front of me listening to what I have to say, at least not all the time. I want the students to learn cooperatively with each other and to depend on peers as much as the teacher as resources for their learning. To do this in China, I have to work against the physical structures.

Exercise

Listen to the case above and answer the following questions.

(1) What does the author do in China?

(2) What's the arrangement of Chinese classroom like according to the author?

(3) What kind of classroom arrangement does the author prefer? Why?

(4) What does a facilitator do in a classroom?

(5) Why does the author prefer to play the role of a facilitator in a classroom?

Module 3
Verbal Communication

Unit 6 Language and Culture

INTRODUCTION

● **Knowledge Objective:**

Guide students to master the definition and importance of language in communication, the relationship between language and culture, and the differences between denotations and connotations in language.

● **知识目标：**

指导学生掌握语言交际的定义及其重要性、语言和文化的关系以及语言中指称意义和内涵意义的区别。

● **Ability Objective:**

Guide students to identify the cultural significance behind language and communicate effectively, and to conduct case analysis in English.

● **能力目标：**

指导学生辨识语言背后的文化意义并进行有效交际，同时用英文进行案例评述。

● **Educative Objective:**

Guide students to think about the documentary *Du Fu: China's Greatest Poet* to understand the power of language in conveying Chinese culture with distinctive characteristics and in reflecting the world's perception of China. Guide students to learn to "promote and unpack to the world more excellent culture with Chinese characteristics, reflecting Chinese spirit and containing Chinese wisdom".

● **素质目标：**

通过分析英文纪录片《杜甫：中国最伟大的诗人》，引导学生体会语言的力量，传递中国特色文化，折射世界眼中的中国。引导学生"向世界阐释推介更多具有中国特色、体现中国精神、蕴藏中国智慧的优秀文化"。

Section A Video Clip Appreciation

I. Introduction to the Movie *The King's Speech*

At the official closing of the British Empire Exhibition at Wembley Stadium, Prince Albert, Duke of York, the second son of King George V, addresses the crowd with a strong stammer. His search for treatment has been discouraging, but his wife, Elizabeth, persuades him to see the Australian-born Lionel Logue, a non-medically trained Harley Street speech defects therapist. "Bertie", as he is called by his family, believes the first session is not going well, but Lionel, who insists that all his patients address him as such, has his potential client recite Hamlet's "To be, or not to be" soliloquy while hearing classical music played on a pair of headphones. Bertie is frustrated at the experiment but Lionel gives him the acetate recording that he has made of the reading as a souvenir.

After Bertie's father, King George V, broadcasts his 1934 Royal Christmas Message, he explains to Bertie that the wireless will play a significant part in the role of the royal family, allowing them to enter the homes of the people, and that Bertie's brother's neglect of his responsibilities make training in it necessary. The attempt at reading the message himself is a failure, but that night Bertie plays the recording Lionel gave him and is astonished at the lack of stutter there. He therefore returns for daily treatments to overcome the physical and psychological roots of his speaking difficulty.

George V dies in 1936, and his eldest son David ascends the throne as King Edward VIII. A constitutional crisis arises with the new king over a prospective marriage with the twice-divorced American socialite Wallis Simpson. Edward, as head of the Church of England, cannot marry her, even if she receives her second divorce, since both her previous husbands are alive.

At an unscheduled session, Bertie expresses his frustration that, while his speech has improved when speaking to most people, he still stammers when talking to David. When Lionel insists that Bertie himself could make a good king, Bertie accuses Lionel of speaking treason and quits Lionel in anger. Bertie must now face the Accession Council without any assistance.

Bertie and Lionel only come together again after King Edward decides to abdicate in order to marry. Bertie ascends the throne as King George VI and visits Lionel's home with his wife before their coronation.

Bertie and Lionel's relationship is questioned by the King's advisors during the preparations for his coronation in Westminster Abbey. It comes to light that George never asked for advice from his advisors about his treatment and that Lionel has never had formal training. Lionel explains that at the time he started with speech defects there were no formal qualifications and that the only known help that was available for returning Great War shell-shocked Australian soldiers was from personal experience.

As the new king, Bertie is in a crisis when he must broadcast Britain's declaration of war with Nazi Germany in 1939. Lionel is summoned to Buckingham Palace to prepare the king for his address to Britain and the Empire. He delivers his speech with Logue conducting him, but by the end he is speaking freely.

As the Royal Family step onto the palace balcony and are applauded by the crowd, a title card explains that Logue was always present at King George VI's speeches during the war and that they remained friends for the rest of their lives.

The King's Speech is a 2010 film about King George VI of Britain, his impromptu ascension to the throne, and the speech therapist who helped the unsure monarch become worthy of it.

II. Introduction to the Video Clips

Clip 1

The film focuses on the professional and personal relationship between Prince Albert, (Bertie who later becomes King George VI), and Lionel Logue, his speech therapist. Structurally this scene signifies a key transition in Bertie's psychological journey to become an effective speaker. But beyond being an important scene, it is also a hugely entertaining moment seeing a King breaking into an emotional frustration anger that has been roiling around for years, just waiting to emerge. As a result, we then find Bertie sitting in the office of a speech therapist who's trying all sorts of unconventional ideas to cure his stutter.

Clip 2

In the movie's final scene, Logue steps into a broadcasting room with Bertie and helps him get through his first wartime speech. With the support of Lionel Logue and his family, the King will overcome his stammer and deliver a radio-address that inspires his people and unites them in battle. The end of the movie is about as heartwarming as it gets. Although Bertie hasn't exactly cured his speech impediment, he has learned to live with it in a more constructive way. A final goodbye tells us that Bertie and Logue would go on to be friends for the rest of their lives and that Logue would help Bertie with all of his wartime speeches.

III. Script of the Video Clips

Clip 1

Bertie: Strictly business. No... personal nonsense.

Elizabeth: Yes, I thought I'd made that clear in our interview.

Lionel: Have you got the shilling you owe me?

Bertie: No, I haven't.

Lionel: Didn't think so.

Bertie: Besides, you... you tricked me.

Lionel: Physical exercises and tricks are important. But what you're asking will only deal with the surface of the problem.

Elizabeth: Is that that's sufficient? Ah, no. As far as l see it, my husband has mechanical difficulties with his speech.

Bertie: I...

Elizabeth: Maybe just deal with that.

Bertie: I... I'm willing to work hard, Dr. Logue…

Video Clip 1

Lionel: Lionel.

Bertie: [*Stammering*] Are you... Are you willing to do your part?

Lionel: All right. You want mechanics? We need to relax your jaw muscles, strengthen your tongue, by repeating tongue twisters. For example, "I'm a thistle-sifter. I have a sieve of sifted thistles and a sieve of unsifted thistles. Because I am a thistle-sifter."

Bertie: Fine.

Lionel: And you do have a flabby tummy, so we'll need to spend some time strengthening your diaphragm. Simple mechanics.

Elizabeth: That's all we ask.

Lionel: All that's about a shilling's worth.

Bertie: Forget about the blessed shilling! Perhaps, upon occasions, you might be requested to assist in coping with... with some minor event. Would that be agreeable?

Lionel: Of course.

Elizabeth: Yes, and that would be the full extent of your services.

Bertie: Shall I see you next week?

Lionel: I shall see you every day.

Lionel: Feel the looseness of the jaw. Good. Little bounces. Bounces. Shoulders loose, shoulders loose. Beautiful, beautiful, beautiful. Now, loose.

Lionel: Take a nice deep breath. Expand the chest. Put your hands onto your ribs. Deeper. Good. How do you feel?

Bertie: Full of hot air.

Lionel: Isn't that what public speaking's all about?

Bertie: My wife and I are glad to visit this important...

Lionel: Take a good deep breath, and up comes Your Royal Highness. And slowly exhale, and down comes Your Royal Highness.

Elizabeth: You all right, Bertie?

Bertie: [*Groaning*] Yes.

Elizabeth: It's actually quite good fun.

Bertie: Mmm... Mother.

Lionel: Shorten the humming each time.

Bertie: Mmm... Mother. Mmm...

Bertie: ... manufacturing the district...

Lionel: Another deep breath. And Jack and Jill.

Bertie: Jack and Jill.

Lionel: Went up the hill.

Bertie: Went up the hill.

Lionel: Now, just sway. Perfect.

Bertie: ... will not permit us to...

Lionel: Loosen the shoulders.

Bertie: Ding dong bell, pussy's in the well. Who put her in? Little Tommy Tin.

Lionel: You have a short memory, Bertie. Come on.

Bertie: A cow, a cow...

Lionel: A... a king... Anyone who can shout vowels at an open window can learn to deliver a speech.

Elizabeth: 14, 15!

Lionel: Good. Deep breath, and...

Bertie: It is...

Lionel: Let the words flow.

Bertie: Mine doesn't bloody work.

Lionel: Come on, one more time, Bertie. You can do it.

Bertie: A sieve of thisted siphles. Gah! Mah! Bah!

Lionel: Father.

Bertie: Father.

Lionel: Father. Aim for the a-t-h. Father. Father. Father.

Bertie: Father. Father.

Clip 2

Man 1: Forty seconds, sir.

Bertie: Logue. However this turns out, I don't know how to thank you for what you've done.

Lionel: Knighthood?

Man 1: Twenty seconds.

Lionel: Forget everything else, and just say it to me. Say it to me as a friend.

Bertie: In this grave hour, perhaps the most fateful in our history, I send to every household of my (a-)peoples both at home and overseas this message spoken with the same depth of feeling for each one of you as if I were able to cross your threshold and speak to you

Video Clip 2

myself. For the second time in the lives of most of us, we are at... [*Lionel mouthing*] ... at war.

Lionel: [*Whisper*] Very good.

Bertie: Over and over again we have tried to find a peaceful way out of the differences between ourselves and those who are now our enemies. But it has been in vain. We have been forced into a conflict, for we are called to meet the challenge of a principle, which, if it were to prevail, would be fatal to any civilized order in the world. Such a principle, stripped of all disguise, is surely the mere primitive doctrine that might is right. For the sake of all that we ourselves hold dear, it is unthinkable that we should refuse to meet the challenge. It is to this high purpose that I now call my people at home and my peoples across the seas, who will make our cause their own. I ask them to stand calm and firm and united in this time of trial. The task will be hard. There may be dark days ahead, and war can no longer be confined to the battlefield. But we can only do the right as we see the right, and reverently commit our cause to God. If one and all we keep resolutely faithful to it, then, with God's help, we shall prevail.

[*Applause*]

Lionel: That was very good, Bertie. You still stammered on the "W."

Bertie: Well, I had to throw in a few, so they knew it was me.

Wood: Congratulations, Your Majesty. A true broadcaster.

Bertie: Thank you, Mr. Wood.

Man 2: Congratulations, Your Majesty.

Man 3: Sir.

Man 4: Congratulations, Your Majesty.

Bertie: Thank you.

Man 5: Congratulations, Your Majesty.

Bertie: Thank you.

Bertie: Ready. Good?

Man 6: Perfect, sir.

Lionel: Your first wartime speech. Congratulations.

Bertie: I expect I shall have to do a great deal more. Thank you, Logue. Well done. My friend.

Lionel: Thank you. Your Majesty.

Elizabeth: I knew you'd be good. Thank you... Lionel.

Bertie: Onwards.

Man 7: Congratulations, sir.

Man 8: Well done, sir.

Man 9: Couldn't have said it better myself, sir.

Man 10: Your Majesty, I am speechless.

Man 11: Congratulations, sir.

Bertie: Gentlemen.

Bertie: So how was Papa, Elizabeth?

Princess Elizabeth: Halting at first, but you got much better, Papa.

Bertie: Well, bless you.

Bertie: And how about you, Margaret?

Princess Margaret: You were just splendid, Papa.

Bertie: Of course I was.

Bertie: Are we all ready?

Elizabeth: Come on, girls.

New Words

thistle 蓟

sifter 筛子，负责筛选的人

sieve 筛子，过滤器

flabby 松弛的

tummy 肚子

diaphragm 横膈膜（位于肺和胃之间的肌肉，呼吸时起作用）

exhale 呼气

pussy 猫咪

knighthood （英国的）爵士称号及身份

threshold 门口

prevail 获胜

strip 剥离

disguise 掩饰

doctrine （尤指宗教的）信条，学说

cause 奋斗目标，事业

reverently 虔诚地，恭敬地

stammer 结结巴巴地说

Phrases and Expressions

in vain: 徒然，无效

be confined to: 局限于，限制于

IV. Exercises for understanding

1. Decide whether the following statements are true or false according to the video clips you have just watched. Write "T" for true or "F" for false.

_____ (1) When Bertie and Elizabeth went to receive training from Lionel, they didn't want to talk about personal affairs.

_____ (2) Lionel thought that physical exercises and tricks could completely solve Bertie's problem of stammering.

_____ (3) Tongue twisters were one of the mechanical ways used by Lionel to improve Bertie's speaking skills.

_____ (4) Bertie promised to give Lionel knighthood after he succeeded in delivering a speech against the Nazis.

_____ (5) Margaret thought that his father Bertie gave a wonderful public speech without any halting.

2. Put the following sentences in the right order according to the video clips you have just watched.

_____ (1) Doctor Logue helped Bertie do mechanical practices.

_____ (2) The ministers congratulated Bertie on his successful speech.

_____ (3) Bertie delivered a public speech to encourage the British people to fight against the Nazis.

_____ (4) Bertie and Elizabeth paid another visit to Doctor Logue, seeking help to relieve Bertie's stammering.

_____ (5) Bertie and his family members went to the balcony to wave greetings to his subjects.

3. Explore interculturally.

(1) Do you think language is powerful? Why or why not?

(2) What do you think are the reasons for Bertie to make a successful public speech against the Nazis?

微课

Section B Reading

Language

Austrian philosopher Ludwig Wittgenstein once said that "The limits of my language are the limits of my world". Language is extremely important to human interaction because it is how we reach out to make contact with our surroundings. We may use language when we are first awake and say "Good morning!" to unite with the outside world. We may use words to share an unpleasant experience and to get support from others: "Let me tell you about the horrible dream I had last night." We use words so that we can exercise some control over the present: "Please pass the salt and pepper." We also use words to form images of the future: "I have to meet with Jane at work today, but I dread seeing her, because I know she's going to be upset about the changes I'm making in her work schedule."

Language reflects the environment we live in. We label things that are around us. For example, in the Amazon area, snow is not part of the environment. Therefore, people in the region do not have a word for snow. It simply does not exit. In areas where it snows occasionally, people have a word for snow, but it may just be one word without any differentiations. Most Americans, for example, use terms such as *snow, powder snow, sleet, slush, blizzard, ice*. That's the extent of most people's snow vocabulary. People who live in an environment where it snows during most months of the year may have a much more differentiated terminology for snow.

Language reflects cultural values. Hall once pointed out that the Navajos do not have a word for *late*. Time does not play a role in Navajo life. There is a time to do everything, a natural time rather than the artificial clock time that industrial countries use. As a result, the Navajos do not have the differentiated vocabulary connected with time and clock that Americans have. Time and the passing of time are things one can't control. Therefore, one should not worry about wasting time and setting schedules. One of the problems in dealing with people from other cultures is that we transplant concepts from foreign languages and culture with words that fit our priorities. For example, businessmen in the United States are typically frustrated with the *manana* mentality of Spanish-speaking countries. For Americans, *tomorrow* means midnight to midnight, a very precise time period. To Mexicans, on the other hand, *manana* means in the future, soon. A Mexican businessman speaking with an American may use the word *tomorrow* but may not be aware of or may not intend the precise meaning of the word. This vague terminology is not precise enough for American emphasis on efficiency. The difficulties over the word *manana* are at least as much an American problem as a Mexican problem.

Language shapes our lives. The advertising world is a prime example of the use of language to shape, persuade, and dissuade. "Weasel words" tend to glorify very ordinary products into those that are "sparkling" or "refreshing". In the case of food that has been shaped of most its nutrients by the manufacturing process, we are told that these products are now "enriched" and "fortified". A foreigner in the United States once remarked that in the United States, there are no "small" eggs, only "medium" "large" "extra-large" and "jumbo". Euphemisms—or telling it like it isn't—abound in American culture where certain thoughts are taboo or certain words connote something less than desirable. Garbagemen are "sanitary engineers"; toilets are "rest rooms"; slums are "substandard dwellings". Even a common word like "family" has for some social scientists been replaced by a "micro cluster of structured role expectation".

Language and Culture

The language we use and the culture in which we live are intertwined and shape each other. Language is not a matter of neutral codes and grammatical rules. Each time we select words, form sentences, and send a message, either oral or written, we also make cultural choices. Some scholars compare language and culture to a living organism: language is flesh, and culture is blood. Without culture, language would be dead; without language, culture would have no shape. In other words, they cannot be separated and exist alone. Some other scholars consider language and culture as two sides of the same coin. Language embodies the products, perspectives, communities, and persons of a culture.

To fully reveal culture, we must examine language. Language is a product of culture, as any others, but it also plays a distinct role. Members of the culture have created the language to carry out all their cultural practices, to identify and organize all their cultural products, and to name the underlying cultural perspectives in all the various communities that comprise their culture. Language, therefore, is a window to culture.

To practice culture, we also need language. We need to be able to express ourselves and to communicate with members of the culture as we engage with them in the myriad practices and products that make up their way of life. Moreover, we need to do this appropriately, using the right language in the right way, according to the expectations of the members of the culture. This is the language of self-expression, communication, and social interaction.

Denotations and Connotations

The words in a language have meanings. When we use words, sometimes we use their denotative meanings, that is, the basic meaning of the words. Denotation is more aligned with the literal definition. Yet, sometimes, we use the implied meaning of words. This kind of implied meaning is also known as the connotation. Connotations are in general closely related to the culture they are rooted in. Connotation refers to the negative and positive relations that a word may have connected with it. These associations are emotional and often not literal.

For example, the denotation of the word *timid* is "lacking in courage or self-confidence". The connotation of *timid* is generally a negative one, particularly if you compare it to the word *reserved* or the word *apprehensive*, which have a more positive connotation. Another example is the photo of Marilyn Monroe. At the denotative level, this is a photograph of the movie star Marilyn Monroe. At a connotative level, we associate this photograph with Marilyn Monroe's star qualities of glamour, sexuality, beauty—if this is an early photograph—but also with her depression and untimely death if it is one of her last photographs.

When we learn about another culture or communicate with people from another culture, the "culturally loaded" aspect of the words they use require our special attention. More often than not, the problem is that the seeming equivalents in two languages may have the same denotations, but their connotations differ greatly. For example, the word "dog" in English has positive connotations. The expressions like "Love me, love my dog" "Every dog has his day" and so on convey Westerners' special love of dogs. This is totally a different picture in China. In Chinese, "dog" has a lot of negative connotations like "狗急跳墙" "狼心狗肺" "狗仗人势" "狗皮膏药" "狗头军师" "狗血喷头" "狗尾续貂" "丧家之犬" and so on.

Words of color also connote differently. To Chinese, Japanese, and Koreans, red represents a color of longevity, splendor, and wealth. In China and parts of India, red is a wedding color, but suggests impurity (a "scarlet woman") at a US wedding. The color black is very much welcome in the Caribbean and Africa. Yellow is a noble color for Chinese and

Indian. White is a wedding color in the United States, but a funeral color in India.

Besides, Chinese kinship terms are so complicated that they are beyond the understanding of foreigners. Mostly, they don't have equivalents in English. *Uncle* in English is used to indicate all of the father's and mother's brothers. It could refer to what we call "叔叔" "伯父" "舅舅" "姨夫" and so on. In the same way, *aunt* is used to refer to all of father's and mother's sisters. The difference is not only linguistic but also fundamentally cultural.

Clyde Kluckhohn once said that every language is a special way of looking at the world and interpreting experiences. It is impossible to master the connotation of every word when we communicate with people from different cultures. However, we should at least be aware that the words we choose to use may lead to misunderstandings and misinterpretations. To achieve successful intercultural communication, we should certainly NOT overlook cultural connotations.

📝 Exercises for Understanding

1. Answer the following questions according to the passage you have just read.

(1) How do you understand Ludwig Wittgenstein's saying that "The limits of my language are the limits of my world"?

(2) What is the metaphor that is used to describe the relationship between language and culture?

(3) What are the functions of language when practicing culture?

(4) Can you list 5 other examples of the use of English weasel words?

(5) What is the difference between denotative and connotative meaning?

2. Choose the most appropriate answers to the following questions.

(1) The word "blizzard" is used frequently in the following countries EXCEPT _____.

A. America

B. Russia

C. Brazil

D. Australia

(2) Which of the following people are not likely to use artificial clock time?

A. Navajo

B. French

C. American

D. Canadian

(3) Which of the following is the most representative weasel word when referring to the size of an egg?

A. Medium

B. Jumbo

C. Large

D. Extra-large

(4) The positive connotation of the word "timid" is probably _____.

A. reserved

B. fearful

C. cowardly

D. faint-hearted

(5) What is one of the connotations of "red" in the United States?

A. Wealth

B. Impurity

C. Splendor

D. Longevity

3. Decide whether the following statements are true or false according to the passage you have just read. Write "T" for true or "F" for false.

_____ (1) To Mexicans, tomorrow means 12 : 00 a.m. of one day to 12 : 00 a.m. of the day next.

_____ (2) Garbagemen is the euphemism of sanitary engineers in America.

_____ (3) Language and culture can sometimes be separated from each other.

_____ (4) The implied meaning of a word is called denotation.

_____ (5) Culturally-loaded words usually have rich connotations.

4. Case study.

Watch the documentary *Du Fu: China's Greatest Poet* and discuss the power of language in conveying Chinese culture with distinctive characteristics and in reflecting the world's perception of China.

5. Fill in the following blanks with the appropriate color terms. Each term can be used more than once.

black blue brown green red white yellow

(1) He is just a _____ recruit fresh from college.

(2) I tried to call her many times but she was in a _____ study and didn't hear me.

(3) One day, out of the _____, a girl rang up and said she was my sister.

(4) The new office block has unfortunately become an expensive _____ elephant.

(5) Mary was always regarded as the _____ sheep of the family.

(6) You'd better do something to prove you are not _____.

(7) Can you see the _____ in her eyes?

(8) The mere thought of her husband with the female secretary made her see _____.

(9) I got some _____ looks from the shopkeeper when I canceled my order.

(10) When I am feeling _____, all I have to do is to take a look at you and then I am not so sad.

(11) Don't tell me any _____ lie to make me feel good.

(12) It may cost over a week to go through all the _____ tape to get the permission.

(13) His type of humor is a bit too _____ for my tastes.

(14) Are you all right? You look absolutely _____.

(15) He based his judgment on headline and _____ journalism.

6. Find the connotations of the following words and phrases.

(1) lover	(2) busboy
(3) busybody	(4) dry goods
(5) heartman	(6) blind date
(7) dead president	(8) sweet water
(9) confidence man	(10) criminal lawyer
(11) dressing room	(12) horse sense
(13) familiar talk	(14) black stranger
(15) white man	(16) yellow book
(17) red tape	(18) blue stocking
(19) American beauty	(20) English disease
(21) Indian summer	(22) Greek gift
(23) Spanish athlete	(24) French chalk

7. Small group task: Analyze the following cases in groups.

Case 1: Scandinavian vacuum cleaner manufacturer Electrolux raised more than a few eyebrows when one of its most expensive marketing efforts in the US market was spearheaded by an ad claiming that "Nothing Sucks Like an Electrolux!"

Case 2: Catering to the needs of small farmers (farmers of small-size farms), a farming implement plant carried out a large scale advertisement campaign in the US, while it didn't enjoy the same popularity in Europe. Why?

Case 3: When the salesperson of General Motors promoted the latest model Chevrolet Noya in Puerto Rico, there wasn't the expected attention to this model.

Section C Case

The Scenario

Scan and Listen

Practicing English

One night, a Chinese student majoring in English sat on the steps of the foreign student's residence and talked with two young male foreign students, one German and one American. They didn't speak a word to her on their own initiative, but she asked many questions to get a conversation started. Every time they answered her with only one or two words. But she was determined to practice her English so she tried to keep the conversation going.

"How do you spend you weekend?" she asked.

The German boy answered immediately, "Fishing," and the two boys looked at each other meaningfully.

"Fishing?" She was really confused. "But where do you fish?" she asked.

"Fishing has two meanings. One is the literal meaning. The other is just sitting here and walking on the street and waiting for some girls to come up to us." Then they both burst out laughing.

She was annoyed. She sat there silently and then suddenly stood up and walked without saying goodbye.

Exercise

Listen to the case above and answer the following questions.

(1) Why did the Chinese student sit on the steps of foreign students' building?

(2) Were the two foreign students eager to talk with the Chinese student? Why or why not?

(3) Why was the Chinese student determined to keep the conversation going?

(4) What is the connotation of fishing?

(5) What cultural differences are shown in this case?

Unit 7 Norms of Social Interaction

INTRODUCTION

- **Knowledge Objective:**

  Guide students to master the definition, classification and role of body language in intercultural communication contexts and master the influence of culture on daily social rules such as addressing, greeting, saying goodbye, showing gratitude, and giving gifts.

- **知识目标：**

  指导学生掌握肢体语言的定义、分类和在跨文化交际语境中的作用，掌握文化对日常社交规则如称呼、问候、道别、道谢、送礼等方面的影响。

- **Ability Objective:**

  Guide students to identify and analyze different social rules in different countries through case study and to abide by proper social rules in intercultural contexts, being polite and courteous without being humble or arrogant.

- **能力目标：**

  指导学生通过案例识别和分析各国不同的社交规则，在跨文化商务情境中遵守社交规则，不卑不亢、有礼有节。

- **Educative Objective:**

  Guide students to observe and reflect on the daily social rules in the era of the Internet and think about how to help Chinese enterprises comply with international business norms in the process of "going global". Analyze the gifts prepared by the Beijing Winter Olympics Organizing Committee for athletes from various countries and learn how to give proper gifts in international communication.

● **素质目标：**

　　引导学生观察和思考互联网时代的日常社交规则，思考如何助力中国企业在"走出去"的过程中遵守国际通用的商业规范。分析北京冬奥组委会为各国运动员准备的礼物，学习如何在国际交流中赠送合适的礼物。

Section A Video Clip Appreciation

I. Introduction to the Movie *My Big Fat Greek Wedding 2*

In *My Big Fat Greek Wedding 2*, Toula and Ian are still happily married and still live right next door to Toula's family, and are in fact now sandwiched by the clan. The couple's daughter, Paris, is now 17 and ready to go off to college, and her heart is set on any school that can get her hundreds, if not thousands, of miles away from her overbearing Greek family. The economic downturn has forced Toula to abandon her travel agency business, but the family restaurant is still going strong. The family schemes to find a way to make Paris stay close to home rather than travel for college. Another important thing in the movie is that Toula's father Gus makes a shocking discovery: he's not actually married to

Maria, the woman he has called "wife" for half a century. They plan on "officially" tying the knot, but only if Gus will properly court her, ask for her hand in marriage, and put on a big fat Greek wedding. But do they still share that spark they need for happily-ever-after, and can the ceremony go off without a hitch?

II. Introduction to the Video Clip

It's a cold, fall morning in Chicago. We are introduced to the Portokalos family one by one as Gus, the grandfather, picks up his grandchildren to take them to school. Gus harps on Paris to get married before she gets too old and tells his daughter, Toula, to find Paris a Greek boyfriend. After stopping at his daughter's house, he drives to two other houses which belong to Toula's brother Nick and Toula's sister Athena. When Athena gets to the car, she tells Paris to come by the family restaurant and then criticizes Toula for letting Paris wear too much mascara. A few minutes later, Gus drops all the kids off at school and as Paris jumps out, Gus tells her to find a nice Greek boy and have babies. As Gus drives through Greektown, Toula realizes that she is now taking care of her parents instead of her daughter. Paris gazes out the hallway window alone, as other students talk together. She runs into her dad, Ian, at the library. Ian is concerned that she's not in class and Paris goes off on him for being another family member that smothers her. Toula is volunteering at the College Fair where the whole family comes around, including Maria, Gus, Uncle Taki, Aunt Voula, Angelo, Nikki, and all the kids and cousins. Gus and Uncle Taki run through available Greek boys for Paris. Paris then tells her family that she's applying to schools that are far away from them and storms off. Gus argues that everyone is a descendent of Alexander the Great and that he is determined to find Paris a Greek boyfriend.

III. Script of the Video Clip

Gus: You better get married. You're starting to look old.

Toula: Dad! You can't say that to her!

Paris: Pappou!

Video Clip

Toula: That's a family tradition. My dad used to say that to me, and now he just said it to my daughter. She's 17. My family worries about each other because we're close. Very close. Extremely close. We see no difference between hugging and suffocation.

Gus: Toula, find your daughter a Greek boyfriend before she does what you did.

Toula: What the...

Gus: You married a kseno.

Toula: My husband!

Gus: He's a nice boy, very nice, but not Greek, a kseno.

Toula: How can you say that?

Paris: Please stop!

Toula: Do I speak for all mothers of teens when I ask, "Does it ever get better?"

Nick: Hey, hey, hey. Ela, Costa!

Gus: Nicko.

Nick: Hey, Dad, pop the trunk. I'm freezing my nads off.

Costa: Too much makeup.

Maria: We're gonna have a nice day. And we'll paint, and we'll do nice things. Gus, I put your pills by your coffee.

Gus: Yeah, yeah, yeah. Costa, did you finish drawing Alexander the Great?

Costa: Uh-huh. And I sculpted a Parthenon out of soap.

Gus: Very good, very good. Oh, no. Spell check corrected "spanakopita" to "spina bifida".

Nick: Kisses. Ela.

Toula: Aw, kisses from your child. That's over. My sister did it right. When her sons became possessed by the *Teen Wolf* hormones, she popped out another one. And another one.

Anna: Let's go!

Angelo: Put on your hat.

Anna: Paris, you should come and help at the restaurant sometime.

Aristotle: You should butter the garlic bread.

Paris: Can't wait.

Anna: Come here, darling. Toula, you and Ian seen these eyes? You better fix this.

Gus: Okay, bye, bye.

Anna: After school you have hockey. Your brothers are coming, so you make sure you score.

Gus: You will score. The Greeks invented hockey.

Costa: Yes, because what do you play hockey on? Ice.

Aristotle: What is the Greek word for ice? Pago.

Costa: Pago, puck. There you go.

Aristotle: There you go.

Gus: There you go. Now, give me a word, any word... and I will show you how the root of that word is Greek.

Costa: Uh, Facebook.

Gus: Huh. The Greeks invented Facebook. We called it the telephone.

Aristotle and Costa: Bye-bye! Bye, Pappou!

Gus: Paris. Keep your eyeballs open now for a nice Greek boy so one day you can make babies. Don't waste your eggs.

Paris: Outstanding.

Toula: Paris! Pappou didn't mean to say anything hurtful. You're beautiful, so beautiful. Of course you don't look old. He just says stuff like that. To me, too. You don't need a boyfriend, you don't need to get married and make babies!

Girl 1: Oh, my God.

Guy 1: The lady's back again.

Paris: Mother. When did my name change from... Mommy! to... Mother!

Tommy: Drama.

Paris: Shut up, Tommy.

Toula: I guess when my daughter started to pull away, I should have retreated. But I stayed too close. I kept volunteering at her school. I wanted her to think I was cool again.

Guy 2: Loser!

Toula: Then I remembered I've never been cool.

Tommy: Here comes the principal.

Toula: My husband has always been cool. He just has it. And he always knows the perfect thing to say.

Ian: You okay, babe?

Toula: Okay, so just when my daughter doesn't want me around anymore, my parents need me more than ever. So I go with them to get groceries, to their doctors, and to physical therapy.

Woman 1: The old guys suck the chocolate off those nuts.

Toula: I loved being a travel agent, but in a tight economy, the first things to go are luxuries like travel and dry cleaning. Well, luckily, people still eat. Hold up, Dad.

Toula: My sister and brother have young children so I help at the restaurant. It's what we do. Because families that are close like mine, we make it through bad economies and sickness and even wars because we stick together. But some of us just get stuck.

Ian: Hey, Paris. Hey.

Paris: Dad, do not talk to me. People think I'm a narc!

Ian: Well, shouldn't you be in class right now?

Paris: You track me all day. Mom's needy, Pappou wants to marry me off, Yiayia constantly tells me to never ever let a boy touch my poulaki because "once he feels it, he wants it"! This family.

Tommy: Hey! Save it for the shrink.

Paris: Shut up, Tommy.

Ian: Honey, your mom felt the same way about being Greek.

Paris: Dad, that's obtuse. Why would I have an issue being Greek? I can't take that everyone is always in my business. Give me some air. I'm not a kid. I can be late to a class. There won't be a spasmodic catastrophic ripple in the space-time continuum. And, yes, four of those words are Greek.

****

Toula: Hi.

Woman 2: Hi.

Parent Volunteer 1: Where were you when we set up?

Toula: I'm so sorry. My pipes froze.

Parent Volunteer 2: And decorated the gym.

Toula: So I had to plunge my sink.

Parent Volunteer 1: You're on clean-up.

Toula: Thank you.

Ian: Hi.

Toula: Hi.

Ian: You can say no to them.

Toula: Oh, yeah, sure.

Ian: Been a long time since those two made fun of your lunch.

Toula: They called it moose-caca.

Ian: Eh, come on, don't let them boss you around.

Toula: There's Paris.

Ian: If she goes to Northwestern, she'll stay in Chicago.

Toula: Please, oh, please. Let's go over there.

Ian: No.

Toula: Right.

Maria: There she is!

Ian: Did you invite the family?

Gus: Paris!

Toula: I told my ma.

Toula: Hold on. Hey! Hey!

Taki: We're just in time. We're here!

Maria: I want you to be a dental hygienist. A mother working two days a week, perfect!

Cousin Nikki: Paris, be a hairdresser. Like me!

Gus: Ian, look. Everybody has boys. You vegetarian. One girl. Slow sperm.

Maria: That's Theia Voula on the FaceTimes.

Aunt Voula: Maria, I'm on my way. I was at Zumba.

Maria: Who is Zumba?

Toula: Sorry.

Gus: We need to find a boyfriend for Paris.

Taki: How about Ariana Skoufis' boy, huh?

Gus: Everybody on that island has six toes.

Taki: Let's wait until summer. We check his feet.

Aunt Voula: I see you. I don't see you. I see you. I don't see you. I see you. I don't see you. I see you!

Ian: I see her.

Aunt Voula: Look at this app. Ten thousand steps, I met my goal. Where's Taki? He never answers the phone.

Maria: Why stand when you can sit?

Gus: Look tired so they leave us alone.

Nick: Hey, Angelo. You get my flat-screen TV?

Angelo: Yeah, I got it right here.

Nick: You can't breathe. You can't breathe.

Ian: Guys!

Mike: All right, break it up. Break it up. You're coming with me.

Ian: Hey, Mike?

Mike: Hey, buddy.

Ian: You miss working here?

Mike: No. Way too scary for me. Hey, sorry we're late.

Mrs. White: Yeah, we had to stop and pick up Mana-Yiayia. Wait, where is she?

Family Members: Mana-Yiayia? Mana-Yiayia?

Mike: Look low, everybody.

Mana-Yiayia: Spanakopita!

Family Members: Let me in there! I want a piece. Easy. Guys. Easy.

Aunt Voula: Take a picture.

Family Members: Ooh, that's good.

Aunt Voula: Hey, come.

Toula: No, no, honey. You don't have to do that. Why don't you just...

Admission Officer: It's okay.

Cousin Nikki: Pull my neck back.

Family Member: Oh, yeah. And you do mine. Okay?

Mrs. White: Okay.

Cousin Nikki: One, two, three, pull!

Admission Officer: Okay.

Guy 3: Hey, Bennett.

Aunt Voula: Good?

Maria: Let me. I'll be the judge.

Cousin Nikki: Not bad.

Family Member: Oh, that looks good.

Toula: We should go.

Cousin Nikki: Why?

Toula: So Paris can speak with this gentleman and go to Northwestern.

Admission Officer: Well, if she gets in.

Nick: Come here. My niece wants to come to your school, you're gonna say, "Welcome." You got it?

Angelo: Come here, pal. And a tuition discount means a box of steaks for ya.

Admission Officer: Northwestern is very selective.

Gus: She's only coming there if you teach Greek history.

Admission Officer: Of course. We have an outstanding classics program. Greek, Italian.

Gus: The Greeks invented Italian.

Admission Officer: Actually, no.

Gus: Yes.

Admission Officer: Nope.

Gus: You Greek?

Admission Officer: No, sir. I'm a Sephardic Jew.

Gus: Then you Greek.

Admission Officer: No, my family is Spanish.

Gus: Alexander the Great went through Spain spreading his seed. You Greek.

Maria: This is not the time.

Admission Officer: And it's ridiculous.

Toula: Let's go!

Gus: The man doesn't know history. "Spreading his seed?"

Paris: Hey! Alabama, Florida, Texas, New York. These are the colleges I'm applying to, far, far away from here.

Toula: Why do you want to leave me?

Gus: Didn't I say, get your daughter a Greek boyfriend?

Toula: Dad!

Gus: And you, educate yourself. We are all descendants of Alexander the Great. I am for sure!

Maria: No, you're not.

Gus: Maria...

Maria: No, you're not.

Toula: It's okay.

Ian: He knows, he knows.

Toula: It's okay.

Admission Officer: Gracias.

****

Costa: Okay, give me a word. Any word.

Aristotle: Chimichanga.

Costa: Sure. "Chimi" comes from the Greek word "kima", which means "spicy beef". And "changa" comes from the Greek word "tsanda", which means "purse". So meat that is shaped like a purse. Chimichanga. There you go.

Gus: There you go.

Angelo: Quit setting me up.

Nick: Hey, just meet her. She's from Holland.

Angelo: Nah. I don't speak Hollandaise.

Family Member: Yeah, in the city.

Cousin Nikki: Exactly. It's ready.

Toula: Hey.

Paris: Hi.

Toula: Just because you don't want to be working here when you're my age doesn't mean you have to run off to college in another city. I just hope you applied to some local colleges, too.

Paris: Why do parents always say "dream big" when they really mean "not too big?" Like, "Fly, little birdy. Wait, no, let me hold your wings".

Gus: Payback.

Toula: What?

Gus: Office.

New Words

suffocation 窒息

Parthenon 帕特农神庙

hockey 曲棍球

therapy 治疗

narc 缉毒侦探

obtuse 迟钝的

spasmodic 间歇的

catastrophic 灾难的，毁灭性的

ripple 波纹，涟漪

hygienist 口腔保健员，牙科保洁员

sperm 精子

Sephardic（来自西班牙或葡萄牙的）赛法迪犹太人

Hollandaise 荷兰酱，荷兰汁

Phrases and Expressions

pop the trunk 打开后备箱

pop out 蹦出来

boss sb around 对某人颐指气使

Notes

Alexander the Great 亚历山大大帝，即亚历山大三世，马其顿王国国王，世界古代史上著名的军事家和政治家

IV. Exercises for Understanding

1. Decide whether the following statements are true or false according to the video clip you have just watched. Write "T" for true or "F" for false.

_____ (1) Gus urged Paris to get a Greek boyfriend and have babies soon.

_____ (2) Toula spent more time with her parents than with her daughter Paris as Paris was already a grown-up.

_____ (3) Gus was satisfied that his daughter Toula got married with a non-Greek man.

_____ (4) The admission officer finally admitted that he was kind of Greek as a descendant of Alexander the Great.

_____ (5) It seemed that Gus was able to trace every English word to Greek origin.

2. Put the following sentences in the right order according to the video clip you have just watched.

_____ (1) Toula accompanied Gus to the LAKEPORT physical therapy.

_____ (2) The Greek family went to the College fair where Paris selected her future university.

_____ (3) Gus and Toula picked up children of the Greek family and drove them to school in the morning.

_____ (4) Paris thought her father Ian tracked her in the library and felt kind of angry.

_____ (5) Gus argued with the Admission officer of Northwestern University that the officer should be a descendant of Alexander the Great.

3. Explore interculturally.

(1) What does Toula mean when she says that in her family there is no difference between hugging and suffocation?

(2) How does Paris comment on her parents?

 **Section B Reading**

微课

Norms of social interaction are beliefs about what is acceptable in a social context. They are socially accepted rules of behavior and conduct that are prescribed by society and expected of an individual by that society. Social norms are based on traditions, beliefs and values of a society and they may change from one society to another. These rules may be explicit or implicit. Human behavior is influenced by a perceived group norm. Individuals who do not conform to these rules are said to have deviated from social norms.

Much of the world's business is done while enjoying social events rather than in a bland office environment. Understanding the basics of social norms, that is, the type of behavior that others expect of you in both informal and formal settings is an important skill. It can instill an individual with confidence to handle almost any situation in any culture and allow a businessperson to concentrate on the deal at hand rather than worrying about such peripheral distractions as which fork to use or which hand to use for passing food. Without an understanding of social norms, you risk coming off as a boorish Neanderthal. You may even put your company's image at risk or risk potential failure in the formation of key business relationships that are vital to global success. Finally, a well-honed sense and appreciation of local customs, etiquette and protocol can make you stand out as a world-savvy individual in a competitive global market. The world may indeed be an oyster today for many businesses. The problem is that too many businesspeople are still, like Oscar Wilde, using the wrong fork. Like grammar, a system of norms specifies what is acceptable and what is not in a society or group.

Face-to-Face Greeting

The physical greeting you can expect from a foreign colleague and what type of greeting they can expect to receive from you are very important. Not everyone appreciates the back-slapping, death-grip handshake Americans are famous for. On the other hand, Americans may deem the traditional reserve of the Japanese greeting (a bow) as an indication of aloofness and mistrust. It is really up to the visitor to adapt and, in this case, when in Rome doing what the Romans do is the best course.

Each culture has its own form of acceptable greeting behavior, usually based on the level of formality found within the society. The rules of social distance etiquette vary by culture. Africans, for example, are far less structured in their greetings than Europeans. Expect a warm physical greeting, an extended hand-shake or a hand on the shoulder in most African cultures. Also expect to be asked how your trip was and how your family is doing. The tradition of long greetings stems from the time when Africans once walked miles to visit neighboring villages on social calls. The arrival and a gushing greeting were considered the least a villager could do for a traveler. Don't be impatient with such a long drawn-out exchange and don't hurry things along. Rather, get into the spirit and appreciate that the person you came to see is prepared to take the time to sincerely inquire about your welfare.

In Argentina, greetings are usually effusive with plenty of hugging and kissing, not unlike the French *faire la bise* (kiss on both checks). This is even the case in business meetings, unless they are of a highly formal nature. In Argentina, men kiss women, women kiss women, but men do not kiss men. By contrast the Chinese way of greeting shuns the physical. It is generally a nod or a slight bow. However, when dealing with individuals from cultures where more direct physical contact is the norm, e.g., a handshake, the Chinese will adapt and shake hands. Don't interpret a soft handshake or lack of eye contact as a sign of weakness or lack of aggression. It simply means that your Chinese colleague is not overly used to physical contact when greeting a stranger.

Dining Practice

The dining protocol includes what to eat, how to eat, when to eat, and where to eat, etc. Dining protocol in different cultures reflects different cultures' underlying values. The purpose of dining with business associates is not merely to eat or drink, but to extend the business meeting through the mealtime. It is an opportunity for an enjoyable interchange in association with the pleasure of eating or drinking.

Time and place of dining also vary in different cultures. In some parts of the world, the main meal is at noon while in others the main meal is in the evening. Lunchtime in many cultures is from noon to 2 p.m., but in Mexico, lunchtime is 2 p.m. to 4 p.m. and is the main meal of the day. In some cultures, business meals are eaten in private homes while in other cultures usually eaten at restaurants.

The manner of eating is widely diverse. You will have your own plate of food on a Western dinner table, while in China the dishes are placed on the table and everyone shares. Tahitian food is eaten with the fingers. In the Middle East, be prepared to eat with your fingers if your host does, but use the right hand only.

In Bolivia, you are expected to clean your plate. Egyptians, however, consider it impolite to eat everything on your plate. Dining in Japan, especially in Japanese homes, requires sitting in a kneeling position on a tatami mat. Men keep their knees 3 or 4 inches apart while women keep their knees together. Being able to lower yourself to a position and rise from it gracefully requires practice.

Strict Muslims do not consume pork or alcohol. Orthodox Jews eat neither pork nor shellfish. Hindus do not eat any beef because the cow is considered sacred. People from countries such as India are often vegetarians because of personal or religious beliefs.

Though each culture has its own peculiarities when it comes to dining customs, the following list of basic dining etiquette tips is valid for all cultures. The list is a mix of accepted universal custom and common sense. The way you behave at a meal will have an impact on the impression business colleagues have of you.

■ Place your napkin on your lap only after everyone has been seated. Be discreet, do not open the napkin with a mid-air snap or flourish but rather open it below table level and place it on your lap. If you must leave in mid-course, place your napkin on the chair or to the left of your plate. Never, never place it on your plate. When the meal is concluded, place the finished napkin to the right of your plate.

■ Never begin eating until everyone has been served, unless invited to do so by the hosts.

■ Forearms are OK on the table but elbows are not. In some cultures, particularly in Asia, it is considered rude to put your hands beneath table level.

■ It is common in Europe, Asia, and Africa for diners to keep the same flatware throughout a meal. It is acceptable to wipe them off with a piece of bread.

■ Do not point or gesticulate with your knife (or any other implement for that matter) while engaged in conversation at table. It is considered the height of rudeness and bad breeding.

■ In Europe and Africa, the salad is served after the main course. In America it is served at the start of a meal.

■ In most European and Middle Eastern cultures, coffee will be served after dessert and, in the case of Europe, after the cheese course which concludes the meal. In the United States, cheese is often served as an *hors d'oeuvre.*

■ When it comes to formal toasts, follow the lead of the hosts. In many Asian cultures only counterparts of equal stature may toast each other.

■ Always taste your food before adding any seasonings, including salt. It is rude to season without tasting and may actually reflect negatively on your character by implying that you are prone to making hasty decisions before checking out the facts.

Alcohol-Drinking Protocol

Drinking is always involved in many social entertainments. Different cultures have various attitudes towards alcohol drinking. In many cultures alcohol remains a great facilitator, the lubricant that loosens up the relationship and greases the social skids on the way to a successful business deal. While Muslims have a complete shunning of alcohol, most of the rest of the world still enjoys a tipple during lunch and at after-hours meetings in connection with business.

For example, in modern China, alcohol maintains its important role, despite many social changes. It still appears at almost all social activities, the most common occasions being business dinner, birthday parties, wedding feasts and sacrifice ceremonies in which liquor must be the main drink to show respect and express happiness.

In Russia and ROK, the ability to consume (or at least attempt to consume) great quantities of alcohol in short periods is still considered a measure of an individual's manhood or womanhood to a lesser extent. In several Asian cultures, especially China, and in Russia, formal toasts are still the norm (never propose a toast before the host—it is the height of *nyetkulturny*). Always be prepared with something cheery or witty to say. Avoid the profound phrase or statement or an attempt at a double entendre. Keep the language simple, and avoid subtle messages. This is supposed to be a joyous occasion, not a stage for hidden social comment.

Perhaps the best-known drinking culture in the world is Russia. Of course, no Russian meal is complete without vodka, which is a big business in the country. The white spirit alone accounts for 5 percent of all retail sales in Russia. And it is true that an open bottle must be consumed. But this has less to do with some deep-rooted Russian tradition than it does with the unavailability of screw tops and re-sealable bottles.

In many Asian cultures, as in Russia, it is almost impossible to avoid consuming large amounts of booze. In cultures such as ROK and Japan, alcohol helps to break down the strict social barrier between classes and allows for a hint of informality to creep in. It is traditional for host and guest to take turns filling each other's cups and encouraging each other to gulp it down.

For someone who does not imbibe (except for religious reasons), it can be rather tricky escaping the ritual of the social drink. Though loathe to admitting it, individuals in cultures where heavy drinking is acceptable probably don't entirely trust someone who is abstemious. They don't like doing business with strangers and social drinking is part of relationship building.

If you disapprove of alcohol, keep it to yourself. Displaying a superior attitude about society can be a relationship killer. Of course, nursing one drink throughout the evening is one way you may be able to escape but more expert trick is often necessary. More than one business person has been known to feign drunkenness after just one or two drinks to avoid the real thing. One British banking executive recalls how he repeatedly outfoxed his Russian colleagues by simply substituting water for vodka, drinking one shot of liquor for every three or four consumed by his Russian hosts without ever missing toast or appearing to be a non-participant. The switch became easier—there was less danger of being found out as the night dragged on.

Tipping

Tipping rules and etiquettes are always a hot-button issue and may spoil your fun-filled scenes. Imagine that you pay the bill after a scrumptious dinner and still get weird looks from your server, calling you a cheapskate for not leaving a tip. Alternatively, generous tipping might fetch the same reaction in some parts of the world.

Tipping culture is a brain-teaser for avid travelers because it may change sooner than the time zone. To tip or not to tip—that's the question, and the only question that matters while putting out a stack of notes in the cab or writing credit card receipts in the restaurant. Here's the gratuity guide to the rescue.

The US and Canada

The United States is the leading exporter of tipping culture. You're expected to pay about 15%–20% on the overall bill in restaurants, bars, and taxi rides. Putting $1–2 on each drink towards the bartender is customary. The same is true for hotel porters and housekeeping staff.

Here service charges are not generally included in the invoice. And waiters earn less than minimum wage unless supplemented with gratuity. Canada and most Caribbean islands are accustomed to the same rules.

Central and South America

The employees in the hospitality industry of countries like Mexico, Argentina, Brazil, and Colombia expect foreigners to tip. However, look out for cover charges in eateries to prevent double-tipping.

In Latin and South America, people favor staying at off-grid haciendas compared to hotels. So, you should make a pool—let's say $20–50—and hand it over to the host/maitre d'hotel at the checkout. You have to haggle for taxi fares beforehand, so tips can be easily avoided.

Europe

Unlike in the US, service charges are added to the quoted price. And the wait staff is well compensated. Still, you're encouraged to reward a modest tip if you feel flattered. It wouldn't be necessary at counter and takeout services.

One common tradition in Europe is to round up the bill to the next euro. It's true for cab drivers and chauffeurs as well. Hotel porters are an exception—feel free to offer € 1 for a bag. But the expected amount decreases as you visit the Balkans and overlooked Mediterranean countries.

Scandinavia

Norway, Denmark, Finland, Sweden, and Iceland make up the breathtaking Nordic region. These countries are known to be elegant and expensive, but not tip-crazed indeed. From busboys to the bellhops, no one looks forward to gratuity. Service charges already go into the wages of restaurant and hotel workers. But tipping concierge and cab drivers is at your discretion. You should give € 3–6 to tour escorts and slightly less to the drivers per day of their work.

Turkey and Russia

You must put aside 10%–15% for table service in Russia. The sit-down is not charged. Make sure to have some cash in the local currency because credit card facilities are not widespread.

The same goes for Turkey. Only a few upscale establishments charge baksheesh. Whereas attendants in Turkish Hammams expect tips, such is not the case with the Russian Banya—two can't miss sauna experiences! Also, the European rule of thumb to round up taxi fares might upset Russian drivers. They expect lavish tipping of around 200 rubles at the end of the trip.

The Middle East

The Arab holiday destinations are full of tipped professionals. You should give at least 10%–15% at the end of the meal or a taxi ride. Housekeepers and porters also reach out for farewell rewards. You can tip them a sum of $1–2 in equivalent local currency. However, dining spots and accommodations in Israel often incorporate gratuity. The Dubai government has also made these charges compulsory. But for the sake of all flashiness, servers would appreciate a couple of extra dirhams.

East and Southeast Asia

East and Southeast Asia include China, Japan, ROK, Cambodia, the Philippines, Malaysia, Singapore, Thailand, to name a few.

Travelers love soaking into the hidden cultures of Southeast Asia. This diverse region exhibits a nascent tipping tradition. But the status-quo is evolving due to the influx of tourists in China and neighboring island nations. Japan is the strongest advocate of the no-tipping policy, so much so that workers may even turn down the offer. Still, rounding up the fare is a common practice across the region.

There is no hard-and-fast rule in India. Giving 10% in restaurants and cafes is standard. Bear in mind not to tip everyone asking for it—mostly, they are street beggars. You may give about 50 rupees to housekeeping and coatroom staff. Porters flock to lift your luggage at airports and bus stations. Politely refuse the errand if you're unwilling to grant a tip. Letting tuk-tuk and taxi drivers keep the change will suffice. If someone goes out of the way, you should raise the bar.

Africa

Africa remains a hotbed of tourism thanks to the historical sites in Egypt, Morocco, Tanzania, South Africa, and the rest of the continent. You're supposed to leave a 10%–15%

tip for wait staff in restaurants, especially in the non-existence of separate charges. Porters and maids also appreciate gratuity since they're underpaid. If you don't consider tipping as borderline bribery, the hotel concierge might bring you a favor or two. Cab drivers in touristy areas are familiar with 10%–20% gratuity. Remember to make payments discreetly.

Oceania

The service industry in Australia and New Zealand doesn't skimp on finances. Naturally, tipping is not a big deal throughout the South Pacific. Although bonuses are highly welcomed, keep it under 10% for servers and $5 for housekeepers.

Rounding up a taxi fare to the nearest $5 is a warm gesture. But Australia is best explored by a private car. Hospitality is woven into the indigenous culture of Polynesian isles. So, don't take the locals' behavior as an indirect call for tips. Nonetheless, you should reward in proportion to the experience.

In a nutshell, globalization puts you closer to different cultures. You must understand and respect cultural sensitivities. Tipping is a form of "thank you note", thus never hold back to writing one whenever the situation warrants it. Make transactions in person according to the quality of service. For example, a bartender who stirs multiple ingredients with an umbrella peeking out of the cocktail glass deserves a higher tip than someone who just opens a beer bottle of the same price.

📝 Exercises for Understanding

1. Answer the following questions according to the passage you have just read.

(1) Why is it important to study the basics of social norms in business context?

(2) Why do Africans prefer long greetings?

(3) What are the diverse eating manners mentioned in the passage?

(4) How do you understand the word "*nyetkulturny*" when it comes to toast? How to toast properly according to the passage?

(5) Can you accept tipping culture? Why or why not?

2. Choose the most appropriate answers to the following questions.

(1) Which of the following is more likely the American way of greeting?

    A. Back-slapping

    B. Hugging and kissing

    C. Bowing

    D. Hongi

(2) According to the passage, what is the most appropriate way of napkin-placing?

    A. Open the napkin with a mid-air snap.

    B. Place the napkin to the right of the chair when leaving in the middle.

    C. Place the finished napkin on the plate when the meal is concluded.

    D. Open the napkin below table level and place it on lap.

(3) Which of the following groups has a complete shunning of alcohol?

    A. Russian

    B. Chinese

    C. Muslim

    D. Japanese

(4) Which country is a leading one with tipping culture?

    A. Norway

    B. America

    C. Russia

    D. Israel

(5) The advocate of no-tipping policy mostly likely happens in _____.

    A. Russia

    B. Japan

    C. China

    D. Turkey

3. Decide whether the following statements are true or false according to the passage you have just read. Write "T" for true or "F" for false.

_____ (1) In Argentina, it is common for men to greet men with kissing.

_____ (2) Japanese men and women kneel on tatami mat for dinner, with their knees 3 or 4 inches apart.

_____ (3) In most cultures, drinking is a way to build social relationship in which displaying a superior attitude can be a relationship killer.

_____ (4) Scandinavian countries are less tip-crazed than North American countries.

_____ (5) People usually tip when they enjoy Turkish Hammams and Russian Banya.

4. Case study.

    Analyze the gifts prepared by the Beijing Winter Olympics Organizing Committee for athletes from various countries and learn how to give proper gifts in international communication.

 **Section C Case**

The Scenario

Scan and Listen

What's True Friendship?

Yang Ruifang worked as a secretary in an Australian company in Melbourne. She became friendly with one of the Australian secretaries, a woman named Cathy Lane. The two usually ate lunch together and Yang Ruifang often asked Cathy for advice on problems she faced when adjusting to Australian society. Cathy gave her a lot of advice and helped her move from one apartment to another. Cathy went with Yang Ruifang to the Immigration Bureau several times to help sort out some problems. Yang Ruifang visted Cathy several times at home but did not invite Cathy to her apartment because she shared it with four other people. If they did not see each other over the weekend, they usually talked on the telephone. As Yang Ruifang was also preparing to take an English test, she was able to get a lot of help with English in this way.

However, something seemed to be going wrong. Cathy seemed to be getting impatient, even a little cold. She started going out by herself at lunchtime instead of eating with Yang and seemed reluctant to answer questions. Yang Ruifang was puzzled. She couldn't imagine what the problem was.

📝 Exercise

Listen to the case above and answer the following questions.

(1) What were Yang Ruifang and Cathy?

(2) What was the relationship like between Yang Ruifang and Cathy in the beginning?

(3) How did Cathy help Yang Ruifang with Yang's adjustment to Australian society?

(4) How did Cathy show her impatience with her relationship with Yang Ruifang?

(5) What advice would you give to Yang Ruifang for her to maintain the friendship with Cathy?

Module 4

Nonverbal Communication

Unit 8 Body Language

● **Knowledge Objective:**

Guide students to master the definition, classification, role and cultural differences of body language.

● **知识目标:**

指导学生掌握肢体语言的定义、分类、作用和文化差异。

● **Ability Objective:**

Guide students to identify different cultural interpretations of body language through case study and use body language appropriately in intercultural communication.

● **能力目标:**

指导学生通过案例分析识别不同文化对肢体语言的不同解读，并在跨文化交际中恰当、得体地使用肢体语言。

● **Educative Objective:**

Guide students to analyze the TED video *Your Body Language Shapes Who You Are* and study the body language of famous figures from ancient and modern times both at home and abroad. Guide students to reflect on the diversified worldviews and cultural values that are embedded in body language and feel China's rise on the international stage. Guide students to think about the important role of body language in daily communication and maintain positive body language as small posture adjustments can make significant changes. Guide students to think about how to "strive to create a trustworthy, lovable and respectable image of China".

● 素质目标：

通过分析 TED 视频《你的肢体语言塑造了你自己》，讲授古今中外名人的肢体语言案例，分析肢体语言所体现的世界观和价值观，感受中国在世界舞台上的崛起。引导学生思考肢体语言在日常交流中的重要作用，保持积极有力的肢体语言，因为小小的姿势调整可以带来大大的改变。引导学生思考如何"努力塑造可信、可爱、可敬的中国形象"。

Section A Video Clip Appreciation

I. Introduction to the TV Series *Lie to Me*

Lie to Me is an American crime drama television series. It originally ran on the Fox network from January 21, 2009 to January 31, 2011. In the show, Dr. Cal Lightman and his colleagues in The Lightman Group accept assignments from third parties and assist in investigations, reaching the truth through applied psychology: interpreting microexpressions and body language.

The show is inspired by the work of Paul Ekman, the world's foremost expert on facial expressions and a professor emeritus of Psychology at the University of California San Francisco School of Medicine. Dr. Ekman has served as an advisor to police departments and anti-terrorism groups and acted as a scientific consultant in the production of the series. He is also the author of 15 books, including *Telling Lies* and *Emotions Revealed*.

Season one opens with Cal and Gillian hiring a new associate: TSA officer Ria Torres, who scored extraordinarily high on Cal's deception-detection diagnostic, and is in turn labeled a "natural" at deception detection. Her innate talent in the field clashes with Cal's academic approach, and he often shows off by rapidly analyzing her every facial expression. She counters by reading Lightman and, when he least expects it, peppers conversations with quotes from his books.

It was gradually revealed that Dr. Lightman was driven to study micro-expressions as a result of guilt over his mother's suicide. She claimed to have been fine in order to obtain a weekend pass from a psychiatric ward, when she was actually experiencing agony.

For a small number of the early episodes, Lightman would team up with Torres to work on a case, while Foster and Loker would team up on a separate case. Occasionally, their work would intertwine, or Foster and/or Lightman would provide assistance on each other's cases. As the first season progressed, the cases became more involved, and all four of the main characters would work together on one case for each episode.

In addition to detecting deception in subjects they interview, Lightman and his team also use various interviewing and interrogation tactics to elicit useful information. Rather than by force, they use careful lines of questioning, provocative statements, theatrics and healthy doses of deception on their own part. In the show's pilot episode, Lightman is speaking to a man who is refusing to speak at all, and is able to discern vital information by talking to him and gauging his reaction to each statement.

II. Introduction to the Video Clip

What you have here is Dr. Cal Lightman, looking at human behavior, facial tics and body gestures which will ultimately be used for investigative purposes. He is known for looking at his subjects quite intensively which makes them feel uncomfortable. In this scene, a woman named Jane is being questioned on the topic of her relation with John Stafford and the group S. R. P. Dr. Cal Lightman clearly sees the evasiveness in her answers and tells her that he knows she is lying about everything. A few associates also watch each and every sign of hesitation and nervousness by analyzing her eye contact and the coherence of her answers in the next door. Dr. Cal Lightman uses his power of unconventional mentalist to get the facts right and the ultimate truth.

III. Script of the Video Clip

Jane: Whatever people may feel personally about John Stafford and S. R. P., it's been a great help in my life, and in a lot of people's lives. And John would never hurt anyone.

Gillian: But you left S. R. P. Why?

Jane: You can leave whenever you want. When your course work is finished, it's time to move on.

Video Clip

Ria: Broken eye contact, hesitation.

Dr. Lightman: That's a straight up lie, Jane.

Jane: No, it's not. I still embrace the precepts, but I choose to live my own life now.

Dr. Lightman: Precepts?

Ria: Defensive.

Terres: She feels attacked.

Dr. Lightman: I'm not trying to attack you, but from the look in your eye, you got a story to tell.

Ria: He's in.

Jane: I knew John... in the beginning. S. R. P. started off as... a beautiful thing, just a few of us exchanging ideas on how we could change our lives. People got interested and more people came. We were doing something special. We were helping them.

Gillian: And then what happened?

Dr. Lightman: Money. And more money, eh? You hate the money, don't ya? Ruined everything.

Jane: It changed John. He appointed himself our leader. My boyfriend at the time, Martin, he was the first one to leave.

Gillian: So, where's Martin now?

Jane: There was a fire. The police said it was an accident. John said it was Martin's own negativity that lit the fire that killed him.

Gillian: You blame stafford.

Dr. Lightman: You blame mine.

Jane: Blame is a very negative term.

Gillian: You blame yourself.

Jane: I blame no one.

Dr. Lightman: You blame everyone.

Ria: Head down, eyes down, blocking the eyes with the hand.

Terres: Shame.

Gillian: Were you what they call an initiate?

Jane: What are you suggesting?

Dr. Lightman: You're the one who's doing that, darling. You still love him.

Jane: I will always love Martin.

Dr. Lightman: I'm not talking about Martin and you know that. Stafford's done with you though, right? He's through. How old are you?

Jane: I'm 37.

Dr. Lightman: You're outraged at the fact that you're being replaced by younger women, right? You ever thought of suicide?

Ria: Shame again.

Dr. Lightman: Send this one on to Florida before she goes running back to Stafford.

Gillian: Stafford's a narcissist. He's his own weak spot and we just have to wait and he'll trip himself up.

Dr. Lightman: There's no time for that. He had his thugs break into my house.

Gillian: I called him a narcissist and you make this about you?

Dr. Lightman: Oh, that reminds me. I want a big wanky picture of myself to put up in my office.

Gillian: Can you just wait until I get my purse?

****

John: You know, it's easy to be negative. Everything around us is designed to make us think negatively. But guess what? We ain't buying it. We ain't buying it. Go on, say it.

Crowd: We ain't buying it.

John: We ain't buying because we know the truth that can't be bought or sold. Young lady, would you come up here? Welcome.

Dr. Lightman: Mind your back. That's it.

John: How long have you been with us?

Girl: 11 months.

John: 11 months. And how's that going?

Dr. Lightman: Thank you.

Girl: I'm on the fourth transition.

Dr. Lightman: Where's Carol?

Ria: I don't know. No one's seen her.

Dr. Lightman: Right. Excuse me.

Girl: S. R. P. is the best thing I've ever done.

John: Come on, you can say it. It's OK, you're with family now.

Girl: S. R. P.'s the best thing I've ever done.

Gillian: She's disappeared?

Dr. Lightman: Yeah, you noticed it?

****

Gillian: Dr. John.

Dr. Lightman: Carol Ashland? Any news?

John: Would you excuse me? Um... I don't know where Carol Ashland is. That's the truth and you know it.

Dr. Lightman: You want to know why you get on my nerves? I'm going to tell you anyway. Although I don't see any lies on your face, also, I can't see any truth.

John: Look, I'm sure you thought you were helping Carol by coming here, Dr. Lightman.

Dr. Lightman: Any fear for her safety? I can't even see that, can you?

John: Maybe Danielle knows something.

Gillian: Carol's daughter, Danielle? It's just the way you said Danielle's name just now, you seem more familiar with her than her own mother does.

Dr. Lightman: See, you know, even though I don't get sweet F. A. from your face... huh? That's a classic, that is.

****

Gilliana: Were you ever a member of S. R. P.?

Dr. Lightman: Not really a question, that one, love. So... on you go.

Danielle: How did you find out?

Dr. Lightman: Stafford.

Danielle: He told you?

Dr. Lightman: In a manner of speaking, yeah.

Danielle: I was in S. R. P. until a few months ago. It just wasn't for me.

Dr. Lightman: What did he do to you?

Danielle: I was in the core group, an initiate. We had sex every day for nearly a year. I'd be in the middle of something and someone would say John wanted to see me, so I'd go. Anytime, night or day. Sometimes you wouldn't even know where you were going. They'd send a jet and fly you back in the morning. At first I liked it. I was proud of myself. I felt like I was better than the rest of the women. But then I saw myself... what I was really doing. It got bad... really bad. Some nights... I would just... scratch myself. My face. I wanted to be ugly. I didn't want him to touch me.

Dr. Lightman: But you didn't leave.

Gillian: You couldn't.

Danielle: It feels like there's no world outside S. R. P.

Dr. Lightman: So, you come to see us about your mum? But it's not just her.

Danielle: I want to kill him.

Dr. Lightman: Well, it could cost you a little extra. What are you so excited about?

Ria: John Stafford loves a close-up. Everything's right here. He's just hard to pin down, all these stored microexpression. So I isolated the most obvious examples.

Dr. Lightman: Stop. Pan on the left. Go back. All right, there. Subcutaneous muscle damage. No wonder we couldn't get a read on him. Do you care to take a guess?

Ria: Surgery. I was already there.

Dr. Lightman: All right, well, calm down, because this is the first time I've seen these.

Ria: Do you want to see what he looked like before?

Dr. Lightman: Yeah, fire away.

Dr. Lightman: Blimey, no wonder we couldn't get a read on him.

Ria: Meet Carl Weatherly from Ontario. Wanted by the R. C. M. P. since 1989 for vehicular manslaughter. Leaving a wife and a kid.

Dr. Lightman: John Stafford is not John Stafford.

New Words

precept 准则，规范

ruin 毁坏，糟蹋

initiate 开始，新加入者，接受初步知识者

outraged 震怒的

suicide 自杀

narcissist 自我陶醉者

thug 暴徒，恶棍，刺客

wanky 蠢的，劣质的

subcutaneous 皮下的

close-up 特写镜头

vehicular 车辆的，交通的

blimey 天啊（表示吃惊或恼怒）

manslaughter 过失杀人

Phrases and Expressions

trip up （使）犯错，（使）失误

get on one's nerves 使人不安

pin down 确定

IV. Exercises for Understanding

1. Decide whether the following statements are true or false according to the video clip you have just watched. Write "T" for true or "F" for false.

_____ (1) Broken eye contact was a sign of shame according to Ria and Terres.

_____ (2) The relationship between John Stafford and Jane broke up because they didn't love each other anymore.

_____ (3) According to Jane, John Stafford said that it was Martin's own negativity that caused him to light fire that killed him.

_____ (4) John Stafford's preference of close-ups showed that he was a narcissist.

_____ (5) John Stafford once received a facial surgery so that Dr. Lightman could not get a read on John in the beginning.

2. Put the following sentences in the right order according to the video clip you have just watched.

_____ (1) John Stafford said to his followers in a speech that they would begin the greatest journey of their lives by having people around as family members.

_____ (2) Dr. Lightman went to visit John Stafford to check on the news of Carol Ashland.

_____ (3) Ria and Terres judged from Jane's body language that Jane was ashamed of herself.

_____ (4) Ria noticed from John Stafford's close-ups that he once underwent a facial surgery.

_____ (5) Danielle found out the negative truth of S.R.P. and felt guilty of herself.

3. Explore interculturally.

(1) How does Ria tell that Jane feels ashamed of her words?

(2) What kind of changes did Danielle undergo when she stayed with John Stafford as a member of S. R. P.?

Section B Reading

微课

Kinesics

The study of body language is known as Kinesics. Kinesic behaviors include gestures, head movements, facial expressions, eye behaviors, and other physical movements that can be used to communicate. No single type of behavior exists in isolation. Specific body movements can be understood only by taking the person's total behavior into account.

William Shakespeare emphasized the significance of body language by saying that "There is language in her eye, her cheek, her lip". E. M. Forster in *A Passage to India* wrote: A pause in the wrong place, an intonation misunderstood, and a whole conversation went awry.

According to a survey conducted by Grayson and Stein in 1981—First they filmed people walking in the streets of New York, then showed the films to prisoners, who indicated which walkers appeared vulnerable to attack—people who walked confidently with swinging foot movements were less likely to be selected as victims.

Importance of Body Language

Consciously or unconsciously, intentionally or unintentionally, we make important judgments and decisions concerning the internal states of others—states they often express without words. Body language is so subtle that a shifting of body zones can also send a message. Body language is important because we use the actions of others to learn their affective or emotional states. If we see someone with a clenched fist and a grim expression, we do not need words to tell us that this person is not happy. Body language is also significant in human interaction because it is usually responsible for first impressions. Think for a moment how often your first judgments are based on the color of a person's skin or the manner in which he or she is dressed. More importantly, those initial messages usually influence the perception of everything else that follows. Body language has value in human interaction because many of our nonverbal actions are not easily controlled consciously. This means that they are relatively free of distortions and deception.

Categories of Kinesic Behaviors

In 1969, Paul Ekman and Wallace Friesen suggested that there are five categories of kinesic behaviors. They are emblems, illustrators, affect displays, regulators, and adaptors.

Emblems are nonverbal behaviors that have a direct verbal translation. They are direct replacements for words (e.g. the peace sign).

Illustrators are nonverbal behaviors directly tied to or accompanying the verbal message (e.g. a circular hand movement to describe a circle).

Affect displays are facial and body movements that show feelings and emotions (e.g. hugging to express love, and smiling to express happiness).

Regulators are nonverbal behaviors that maintain or regulate turn-taking conversations. They are used by speakers to indicate whether others should take a turn and by listeners to indicate whether they wish to speak or would prefer to continue listening (e.g. raising your hand when you want to speak).

Adaptors are personal body movements that occur as a reaction to an individual's physical and psychological state (e.g. chewing your fingernails or twirling your hair).

Examples of Body Language around the World

Body language is very important in that it is estimated that less than 10% of the whole message understood by an audience is the actual content, some 30% is attributed to the pitch and tenor or a person's voice, and 60% to other forms of nonverbal communication from body language to facial expressions to hand gestures. Body language says more than what words can say.

Arab men often greet by kissing on both cheeks. In Japan, men greet by bowing, and in the United States, people shake hands. In Thailand, to signal another person to come near, one moves the finger back and forth with the palm down. In the United States, people beckon someone to come near by holding the palm up and moving the fingers toward their body. The Tongans sit down in the presence of superiors; in the West, people stand up. Crossing one's legs in the United States is often a sign of being relaxed; in ROK, it is a social taboo. In Japan, gifts are usually exchanged with both hands. Muslims consider the left hand unclean and do not eat or pass objects with it. Buddha maintained that great wisdom arrived during moments of silence. In the United States, people talk to arrive at the truth.

Ten Body Language Mistakes

The following are several body language mistakes that are going to be tough to ditch. But if you're able to quit them, you'll definitely thank yourself later.

1. Fidgeting

If you've gotten into the habit of fidgeting, it can be difficult to snap out of it. However, it's important to take steps to reigning in this nervous habit. Fidgeting demonstrates nervousness and a lack of power.

2. Playing with hair

Leave your hair alone. Constantly running your hands across your scalp and twirling your locks is pretty distracting. Plus, it can damage your hair overtime. So try playing around a stress ball instead of your hair.

3. Adopting a defensive pose

Many people naturally cross their arms or hunch over a bit just because they don't know what to do with their hands. However, this posture can make you look uncomfortable, defensive, or untrustworthy. "You should always keep your hands in view when you are talking," Patti Wood, a body language expert and author of *SNAP: Making the Most of First Impressions—Body Language and Charisma* previously told *Business Insider*. "When a listener can't see your hands, they wonder what you are hiding."

4. Doing weird things with your hands

To gesture or not to gesture? That is the question. Some people keep too still while speaking, while others flail all over the place. As behavioral consultant Vanessa Van Edwards previously noted, using hand gestures while speaking is actually an effective way to engage your audience. The trick is, avoiding the hand gestures that will trip you up. Don't point, don't pretend to conduct an imaginary orchestra (seriously), and don't get too choreographed.

5. Shuffling instead of walking

Humans are pretty judgmental creatures. We think we can tell a lot about someone based on snap judgments over something as simple as their manner of walking. How we walk can actually determine our risk of being mugged. It can be hard to change up your walk once you've fallen into bad habits, but it's important to walk with confidence and coordination. Don't shuffle through life.

6. Forgetting to smile

Smiling demonstrates confidence, openness, warmth, and energy. It also sets off the mirror neurons in your listener, instructing them to smile back. Without the smile, an individual is often seen as grim or aloof.

7. Appearing distracted

There's nothing more irritating than talking to someone who's clearly not paying attention to you. Some people are just naturally distracted or busy, so it can be tempting to check your phone or watch at every available moment. Still, you've got to keep this impulse in check when you're around others. Otherwise, you'll just come across as a rude and uncaring person.

8. Slouching

Stand up straight. Terrible posture is easy to develop, especially if you're slouched over a desk for the majority of the day. Slouching doesn't just make you look unconfident. It's also bad for your back. Improve your health and the image you present to the world by standing up straight.

9. Nonexistent or aggressive eye contact

The ideal amount of eye contact should be a series of long glances instead of intense stares. Overly long stares can make whoever you're talking to pretty uncomfortable. On the other hand, averting your eyes indicates disgust or a lack of confidence.

10. Being too still

It's definitely good not to be jumping all over the place constantly. However, you don't want to be too eerily calm during conversation, which may make people feel uneasy or think that you're not interested in what they're saying. Instead, try to mirror the person you're speaking with. Don't mimic them—they'll probably get offended by that—but subtly copy some of their gestures and expressions. Mirroring will leave people perceiving you as positive and persuasive. It can be tough to break out of your poker face, especially if you're just naturally not that expressive—but it's worth trying, since it can improve how you're perceived.

Mismatching Verbal and Nonverbal Communication

You might be saying all the right things—but if your body language doesn't match up with your words, you might end up rubbing people the wrong way.

The body is never mute. Even when people come together and don't speak to each other, they communicate through their body language. Interlocked arms are as much a message as changing the position of the legs, but also the color of the blouse or a subtle perfume is a way of communication. Facial expressions, gestures, posture and clothing are important instruments of nonverbal communication, which is the oldest form of interpersonal communication. Unknowingly we send out powerful messages with our bodies, which reveal our real feelings.

Nonverbal behavior functions as a culturally rule-governed communication system. The rules are governed by culture, and the rules and nonverbal behavior differ among cultures. Besides, we should not forget that nonverbal behaviors seldom occur in isolation. Individual messages are but part of the total communication context. We usually send many nonverbal cues simultaneously and these cues are normally linked to both our verbal messages and the setting in which we find ourselves.

🖉 Exercises for Understanding

1. Answer the following questions according to the passage you have just read.

(1) What do kinesic behaviors generally include? What are the categories?

(2) According to the survey conducted by Grayson and Stein, who are less likely to be attacked?

(3) Why is nonverbal communication valuable in social interaction?

(4) What is the difference between emblems and illustrators?

(5) Can nonverbal messages be judged in isolation? Why or why not?

2. Choose the most appropriate answers to the following questions.

(1) The following statements tell the importance of nonverbal communication EXCEPT

_____.

   A. nonverbal communication helps learn people's emotional state

   B. nonverbal communication is responsible for first impressions

   C. nonverbal communication is reliable as it is free of distortion and deception

   D. nonverbal communication is valuable as it is usually conveyed consciously

(2) According to Paul Ekman and Wallace Friesen, which of the following is NOT a category of kinesic behavior?

   A. Emblems

   B. Illustrators

   C. Affect displays

   D. Gestures

(3) According to the passage, what's the percentage nonverbal communication occupies in daily life?

   A. 10%

   B. 30%

   C. 50%

   D. 60%

(4) According to the passage, the proper use of hands is to _____.

   A. hunch over with hands

   B. conduct an imaginary orchestra with hands when talking

   C. keep hands in view when talking

   D. cross arms with hands to show strength

(5) According to the passage, smiling is NOT a sign of _____.

    A. confidence

    B. openness

    C. arrogance

    D. energy

3. Decide whether the following statements are true or false according to the passage you have just read. Write "T" for true or "F" for false.

_____ (1) The survey conducted by Grayson and Stein in 1981 showed that people who shuffle are more likely to be mugged.

_____ (2) An unconscious shifting of body zone may send a message in communication.

_____ (3) Emblems are nonverbal behaviors that are directly tied to verbal messages.

_____ (4) In Thailand, people hold the palm up and move fingers toward the body when beckoning people to come near.

_____ (5) According to the passage, the ideal eye contact is to have a series of long glances instead of intense stares.

4. Case study.

In the animated film *The Simpsons* Montgomery Burns had a common gesture, known as the "spire gesture" by psychologists, where his hands touched with their fingers, pointing upwards to form a spire, which was a sign of confidence. Please watch the TED video *Your Body Language Shapes Who You are* and discuss how to use body language to create a trustworthy, lovable and respectable image of China.

5. Role-play the following demonstrations concerning handshakes.

The handshake is the most common and most meaningful physical contact you will have with people. Analyzing people's handshake may provide some clues into their characters and intentions. The following are some handshake basics.

■ A handshake in which an individual grips firmly but not too firmly, pumps your hand once or twice and looks you straight in the eye can signify an individual who is confident, sees you as an equal and intends an honest, up-front negotiation or discussion. If a person continues to hold onto your hand for longer than expected, he or she may be attempting to show sincerity.

■ If while shaking your hand, an individual tries to guide you into a room or toward a seat, it may indicate that that individual likes to be in control and insists on having his or her way. It can signal difficult talks if things do not go their way. In many Asian nations, however, such an action should be seen as a sign of respect and friendship, not a power play.

■ If someone grips your hand and then twists his/her hand so it is on the top, the signal is that of a competitive person who is saying that, although you may be starting out as equals, he or she will win in the end.

■ Most people have been the victim of a handshake where an individual attempts to crush your hand in a vice-like grip. This is an indication of a person who is competitive and plans to win at all costs but associates physical strength with acuity. Their bark (or, in this case, their handshake) is often much worse than their bite.

■ When offered by a Westerner, the limp handshake that resembles grabbing hold of a dead fish usually indicates someone with low energy and lack of enthusiasm and confidence. In Asia, such a handshake is common and is an indicator of equality, not deference. Some Southeast Asian societies will actually use their other hand to support their handshaking wrist. This is a sign of respect, not weakness.

Section C   Case

The Scenario

Scan and Listen

Whose Car Is It?

A joint venture in Beijing involved Chinese and American partners. American-recruited specialists were working together with Chinese specialists in establishing a factory. The American side of this project had provided most of the material and equipment necessary to start the plant, including a car. The use of this car became the focus of an on-going battle that was regularly raised at each semi-annual management meeting.

The Americans claimed that the car had been provided for project use during working hours and for private use for American project members outside office hours. They claimed that this implied that the American team members should be able to drive it. The Chinese felt that the car should only be driven by authorized Chinese drivers, which effectively limited its use by Americans but increased its use by senior Chinese project members.

The conflict centered on the registration. The car first has a registration that prevented its being driven by the Americans. Their aim was to change this registration. The Chinese were apologetic—it could not legally be done. The Americans cited the Memorandum of the Understanding that formed the legal basis of the project; they cited the Chinese law and precedents. All agreed that it was possible. The Chinese authorities answered with a number of practical difficulties, but conceded that the Americans had the right to drive the car and promised to look into this matter.

Six months later, nothing had changed. The matter was again raised at the semi-annual management meeting. The right of the Americans to drive the car was again acknowledged, difficulties mentioned and the action promised.

Exercise

Listen to the case above and answer the following questions.

(1) In establishing the joint venture, what did the American side provide?

(2) As to the use of the car, what did the Americans claim?

(3) What did the Chinese do to keep the car use right?

(4) How was the right of the Americans to use the car acknowledged?

(5) What did the conflict center on?

Unit 9　Time

▶ INTRODUCTION

- **Knowledge Objective:**

    Guide students to master the definition of chronemics, the characteristics of monochromic and polychromic time systems and the features of three time orientations, namely, past orientation, present orientation and future orientation.

- **知识目标：**

    指导学生掌握时间学的定义、多向计时制文化和单向计时制文化的特点以及三大时间取向（过去时间取向、现在时间取向和未来时间取向）的特征。

- **Ability Objective:**

    Guide students to effectively communicate across cultures in accordance with the conventions of different time systems regarding people's ways of thinking and acting, and be able to analyze the time concept of Chinese culture through case study.

- **能力目标：**

    指导学生根据不同时间体系中文化对人们思维方式和行为方式的约定进行有效的跨文化沟通，并通过案例分析中国文化的时间观。

- **Educative Objective:**

    Guide students to understand the courage and responsibility of the CPC to summarize historical experience in the course of over a century's struggle, unite and lead the people of all ethnic groups in China to achieve the second centenary goal by analyzing China as a representative culture of past time orientation. Guide students to analyze China's commitment to carbon peak and neutrality, which reflects China's future-oriented responsibility as a big country. Guide students to understand that "by learning from history, we can understand why powers rise and fall; through the mirror of history, we can find where we currently stand and gain foresight into the future".

● 素质目标：

　　通过分析中国作为过去时间取向文化的代表性国家，鉴往知来，引导学生领会中国共产党在百年奋斗历程中不断总结历史经验，团结带领全国各族人民实现第二个百年奋斗目标的勇气和担当。通过分析中国应对气候变化所提出的碳达峰和碳中和承诺，引导学生领会中国面向未来的大国担当。引导学生理解"以史为鉴，可以知兴替。我们要用历史映照现实、远观未来"。

Section A   Video Clip Appreciation

AMANDA SEYFRIED   JUSTIN TIMBERLAKE

IN TIME

LIVE FOREVER OR DIE TRYING

I. Introduction to the Movie *In Time*

In 2169, the physical aging of the human body stops when people turn to 25, after which the "watch" on everyone's forearm starts to click. A person dies when the countdown of the "watch," originally set for one year, reaches zero. No cash, credit cards, or any other kind of payment method is used at that time. Instead, people do their job to earn themselves more time, the only currency in circulation. The world is divided into different Time Zones according to the amount of time owned by the people in each district. Day after day, the rich are bored to death in the leisure brownstone area New Greenwich, while the poor struggle to survive in Dayton, where people rarely have over 24 hours left and what's worse, Minutemen murder for watches with more time. Will Salas, a poor young man living in Dayton, is accused of larceny and murder after he saves Henry Hamilton, who comes from New Greenwich and owns more than a decade in his watch, from a group of Minutemen led by Fortis. In his escape from the Timekeepers, Will meets Sylvia Weis, the daughter of a millionaire named Philippe Weis. They then start making their efforts to challenge or even destroy the existing time system.

II. Introduction to the Video Clip

Will Salas is a 25-year-old factory worker living in Dayton with his mother, Rachel Salas. It is Rachel's 50th birthday, so Will spends the time he earned last night buying his mother a bottle of decent champagne as a birthday present. Both of them decide to celebrate Rachel's birthday after she comes back home from work two days later. After a day's work in the time capsule factory, Will goes to the pub to meet his best friend Borel. Borel tells Will that there is a madman who has been buying drinks all night. The madman's name is Henry. Will notices that there is over a century in Henry's watch, so he tries to warn him of the dangers of flaunting his wealth in Dayton. Unfortunately, the time robbers, or Minutemen, come soon after they receive the message of Henry's visit to the pub and are about to clean his watch, leaving him to die alone. At this crucial moment, Will rescues Henry from being robbed and they escape from the Minutemen.

 ## III. Script of the Video Clip

Video Clip

Will: [*Monologue*] I don't have time. I don't have time to worry about how it happened. It is what it is. We're genetically engineered to stop aging at 25. The trouble is, we live only one more year unless we can get more time. Time is now the currency. We earn it and spend it. The rich can live forever. And the rest of us? I just want to wake up with more time on my hand than hours in the day.

Will: Hey, Mom.

Rachel: You got in late last night.

Will: I put in some overtime.

Rachel: Where'd it go?

Will: On you. They drink it in New Greenwich. Happy 50th!

Rachel: Fifty?

Will: That's right. Twenty-five for the 25th time.

Rachel: I was sure I'd have a grandchild by now.

Will: Here we go.

Rachel: Bela's daughter is always asking about you.

Will: Who has time for a girlfriend? Besides, what's the hurry? What do you got?

Rachel: Three days. Not even. We owe half that in rent. Eight for the electric and we're still late on that loan.

Will: I can make extra on the side, you know. I could...

Rachel: What, start fighting? Nobody wins.

Will: Yeah…

Rachel: Remember, I'm not here tonight. I got two days' work in the garment district.

Will: I know.

Rachel: Meet me at the bus stop tomorrow. After I pay off the loan, I won't have long.

Will: I'll be there.

Rachel: Will... I just wouldn't know what to do if I lost you.

Will: I'm late.

Rachel: Let me give you 30 minutes so you can have a decent lunch.

Will: I love you. Happy birthday, Mom. When you get back, we're going to celebrate.

Mya: Will! Will! You got a minute?

Will: What are you talking about, Mya? You have a whole year.

Mya: Not a year I can use yet. Come on, Will. I've got bills to pay.

Will: Here, take five minutes. Get out of here.

****

Will: Four minutes for a cup of coffee?

Borel: Yesterday, it was three.

Seller: You want coffee or you want to reminisce?

Will: Two coffees. How many shifts you got today, Borel?

Borel: Just the two. Really excited about it. If you had any of your father in you, we could make a fortune.

Will: I don't fight.

Borel: There's another one. Broad daylight.

Will: Whoa, what is this? Where's the rest?

Officer: Never met the quota.

Will: My units are up from last week.

Officer: So's the quota. Next.

Will: That's a joke, right?

Officer: Next.

Workers: Move it. You're taking forever.

Gambler: You in, Will?

Will: I don't have time to gamble anymore.

Gambler: Thank God. Because ever since you stopped playing, I started winning.

Will: You still owe me an hour. You seen Borel?

Borel: Will!

Will: Hey, man. Your wife's looking for you.

Borel: You're not gonna believe it. This madman's been buying drinks all night. He's got a century!

Will: Come on, let me get you home.

Borel: Soon as I finish this drink.

Henry: Hey! You! You! More everything!

Will: Excuse me. You need to get out of here. Somebody's gonna clean that clock.

Henry: Yes!

Will: I mean, they aren't going to rob you. They are going to kill you. They can't take that much time and let you live to tell about it.

Henry: Yes.

Will: I don't think you understand. You should not be here!

Borel: Will! Will! Minutemen! Minutemen! Walk away, Will. Those gangsters aren't playing around.

Will: Wait, wait.

Borel: He's asking for it. Let's go. He's not one of us. You think he'd help us?

Will: Don't worry. I won't do anything stupid. Go.

Fortis: The name's Fortis. And that, sir, is a very nice watch. Do you mind if I try it on? I think it would suit me.

Will: Let's get you out of here.

Fortis: Get him!

Henry: Stop. What are you doing? I can take care of myself.

Will: Yeah, it looked like it.

Henry: I know what I'm doing.

Will: Run. Run!

New Words

genetically 从遗传学角度

currency 货币，通货

overtime 超时地

loan 贷款，借款

garment 衣服

decent 得体的，相当不错的

reminisce 缅怀往事，叙旧，回忆

shift 轮班

quota 配额，份额

gamble 赌博

gangster （结成团伙的）匪徒

Phrases and Expressions

make a fortune 发财，赚大钱

play around 胡闹，轻率对待

Notes

Greenwich 格林尼治，英国伦敦的一个区，位于伦敦东南部、泰晤士河南岸。1675—1948 年设皇家格林尼治天文台。1884 年在华盛顿召开的国际经度会议决定以经过格林尼治的经线为本初子午线，也是世界计算时间和地理经度的起点。在电影中，"格林尼治"是所谓的"富人区"，这里的人们拥有无穷的"时间"，因此他们是永生的。

Minutemen "一分钟人"，美国独立战争时期马萨诸塞殖民州的特殊民兵组织，成员从美国各地民兵中挑选，以具有高机动性、快速部署的能力而著称。在电影中，"一分钟人"则是指掠夺他人"时间"的恶棍。

IV. Exercises for understanding

1. Decide whether the following statements are true or false according to the video clip you have just watched. Write "T" for true or "F" for false.

_____ (1) Will worked overnight yesterday to buy her mother a birthday present.

_____ (2) Will's mother would work for two days in the clothes factory.

_____ (3) Borel got only one shift today.

_____ (4) The "madman" in the bar had over a decade in his clock.

_____ (5) Henry thanked Will for saving his life.

2. Put the following sentences in the right order according to the video clip you have just watched.

_____ (1) Will had a conversation with Borel about a fight and making money.

_____ (2) Will encountered a person named Mya who needed his help with bills.

_____ (3) Will promised to meet his mother at the bus stop after she paid off the loan.

_____ (4) Will warned Henry about the dangers of being in that place.

_____ (5) Will's mother mentioned Bela's daughter asking about him.

3. Explore interculturally.

(1) Do you want to live in a world where everyone stops aging at 25? Why or why not?

(2) If the story happened in the real world, what would Chinese and American people do with the century's time they have, taking into consideration their different understanding of time?

 **Reading**

微课

Time & Chronemics

Time is the manifestation of motion, the continuity of variation and the succession of events and existences. People usually use time as a parameter to describe the process of material motion or event occurrence. Chronemics, the study of time, not only focuses on the study of people's understanding and use of time, but also covers contents within the study of human tempo as it relates to interdependent and integrated levels of time-experiencing. Different cultures perceive time differently, some considering it monochronic whereas some others regarding it polychronic.

Monochronic Time & Polychronic Time

In the monochronic time system, people usually have a long-term plan but only make short-term arrangements. The low-involving monochronic people will only do one thing at a time and they barely tolerate any change in their time schedules. Besides, they put special emphasis on efficiency and personal privacy. A typical example of this time system existed in the United States during the Industrial Revolution, when time was considered to be so precious a resource that a minute or even a second was not allowed to be wasted. People at that time, basically working in factories, always lived a scheduled life, in which everything would start and end at certain times, not only when they were working but also when they were doing daily routines such as watching TV shows. Under such time system, the accomplishment of missions or tasks can be guaranteed, but those things, which need some extra time or efforts, are very possibly going to fail on the verge of success.

Different from the monochronic people, polychronic people are so involved with each other that they prefer to keep several operations going at once. People with this kind of culture usually treasure human relationship and feelings more than results. They tend to believe that success will come when conditions are ripe. Flexibility is the character of their way of doing things. This leads to the comparatively lower-efficiency in everything but on the other hand, a person will feel respected and cared when working or living in the country with such a culture. Taking the dining experience as an example, when having a dinner in a restaurant of the polychronic countries, it is possible for you to be served first even if you are the last to enter as long as you are really running out of time. Moreover, polychronic people often understand time as a fluid and adjustable concept, which is why cultures that use the polychronic time system often schedule multiple appointments simultaneously and for them, keeping on schedule is an impossibility.

According to Edward Hall, the Industrial Revolution caused many Western cultures to grow more dependent on schedules and promptness. He cited the US, Great Britain, and countries in Northern Europe as cultures who are predominantly monochronic. This reliance is pervasive in business environments today. People in the monochronic mode (or M-people as Hall called them) see time as a resource to be carefully managed.

In general, M-people:

- Value promptness and deadlines;
- Tend to do things one at a time;
- Do not get distracted;
- Commit to work and adhere to plans;
- Relate punctuality to reputation;
- Value and respect privacy.

On the other end of the spectrum, polychronic people (or P-people) developed out of the Mediterranean and Colonial-Iberian-Indian cultures. Polychronic time prioritizes context over process, and makes it difficult for people to abruptly end conversations when the clock strikes the hour. As opposed to M-people who focus on one task at a time, P-people thrive when faced with multiple tasks at once.

In general, P-people:

- Juggle multiple assignments;
- Value interpersonal relationships heavily;
- Put less value into schedules and dates;
- Change plans often and easily;
- Forge lifetime relationships easier than M-people.

For managers, understanding the monochronic/polychronic dichotomy can help prepare team assignments, schedules, and productivity goals. M-people take things step-by-step. They need details, direction, and feedback. P-people are the opposite. They thrive off of freedom and interaction with others to produce. Aligning these personality types, either by grouping them similarly or balancing them together, is a key component of success.

Scheduling software can be a helpful tool to promote this alignment. For the monchronic types, it provides solidarity. Deadlines can be easily set and viewed. Tasks can be laid out step by step, just the way monochrons like. And it can also promote accountability, which would appeal to their sense of work commitment.

For polychrons, scheduling software is a great way to manage their multiple tasks without micro-managing them. Plus, it gives them an ability to set their own pace by changing their schedule when it suits them.

Time Orientations

Time orientation refers to the sense of time held by the members of a particular culture. How people value and attach significance to time varies in cultures with different time orientations. Basically speaking, there are mainly three types of time orientations, namely, past-oriented, present-oriented and future-oriented.

Past-Oriented Cultures

Past-oriented cultures are more likely to revere the success and glory in the past and respect previous experiences, which are thought to have important reference value to present and future activities. A typical example of this kind of culture is China. Filial piety, which means the elderly are to be respected and maintained properly, is considered one of the most essential virtues in Chinese culture. Countless time-honored brands, some of which may have enjoyed a history of over hundreds of years, still own great popularity in the modern society. In such cultures, history and former experiences play a vital role in the measuring of the value of both people and things.

Present-Oriented Cultures

Present-oriented cultures are mainly rooted in the Central and South American countries, such as Brazil, Argentina and Mexico. Various carnivals and celebrations are one of the most outstanding features of these cultures. Present-oriented people won't get themselves entangled in the existing troublesome facts or unpredictable potential annoyances. Instead, all they care about is the present living experiences. Brazil owns the world's largest carnival, the Brazil Carnival, which is held 47 days before Easter. During the three-day celebration, the passionate Brazilians, both man and women, rich and poor, will join into the parading procession, venting whatever kind of feelings they have at the moment. With the lissome Samba steps, you might find yourself totally lost and immersed in the festive atmosphere. The Latin word "carpe diem" best displays the spirit of present-oriented culture, namely enjoying the pleasures of the moment, without concern for the upcoming future.

Future-Oriented Cultures

People in a future-oriented culture always put their focus on the possible outcomes in the future, while barely caring about the happened or ongoing events. They will set an achievable and realistic goal before taking actions and take advantage of all the available resources to reach this goal. They observe the world in a broad picture, in which former experience may not definitely be a valuable reference and the current gains and losses are never in their concern. Immigrant countries like the US, Australia and New Zealand well present the characteristics of future-oriented culture. Compared with the four cradles of civilization, the history of the US is neither long nor consecutive, but full of struggles on the way to get itself independent and prosperous. The American people are thus a little indifferent to what took place in the past. Nevertheless, their concern lies in the development trend of the country, which in their opinion should be a place of freedom and democracy. This is also why the famous notion "American Dream" would have been so inspiring for the youngsters in that particular era.

📝 Exercises for Understanding

1. Answer the following questions according to the passage you have just read.

(1) How do monochronic people typically approach their tasks and responsibilities?

(2) How do polychronic people handle multiple tasks?

(3) How do past-oriented cultures view the importance of history?

(4) What is the focus of present-oriented cultures?

(5) How do future-oriented cultures approach goal-setting?

2. Choose the most appropriate answers to the following questions.

(1) According to the passage, which culture is more likely to consider being late as disrespectful and damaging to one's reputation?

A. Monochronic culture

B. Polychronic culture

C. Past-oriented culture

D. Present-oriented culture

(2) The passage mentions that in polychronic cultures, it is common to engage in _____ during meetings or gatherings.

A. multiple tasks simultaneously

B. strict adherence to schedules

C. focused discussions on a single topic

D. detailed planning and organization

(3) Which culture referenced in the passage values traditions and historical experiences as important factors in decision-making?

A. Monochronic culture

B. Polychronic culture

C. Past-oriented culture

D. Present-oriented culture

(4) From the passage, we can infer that individuals from present-oriented cultures prioritize _____.

A. long-term planning

B. nostalgic experiences

C. immediate gratification

D. reflecting on past achievements

(5) According to the passage, future-oriented cultures emphasize _____.

A. maintaining strong interpersonal relationships

B. balancing work and personal life

C. learning from past mistakes

D. setting goals and utilizing resources efficiently

3. Decide whether the following statements are true or false according to the passage you have just read. Write "T" for true or "F" for false.

_____ (1) Monochronic cultures tend to have a more flexible concept of time.

_____ (2) According to the passage, individualistic cultures prioritize personal achievement and independence over group goals.

_____ (3) Collectivistic cultures emphasize interdependence and harmony within the group.

_____ (4) High-context cultures rely more on nonverbal cues and implicit communication.

_____ (5) According to the passage, low-context cultures place a greater emphasis on indirect communication.

4. Case study.

Watch the video clip of *The Glorious Course of the Centennial Struggle of the CPC* and discuss your understanding of China as a past-oriented culture.

5. Small group task: How to use time concept tactfully for project completion?

An American engineer was once entrusted by the local government to carry out a soil and water conservation project in the Navajo settlement area in northern New Mexico. He attempted to convey to the locals that they needed to temporarily stop herding, make efforts to repair the earthen dams, and retain more water resources in the settlement area so that the herds and the tribe members could live better. However, what gave him a headache was that persuading the Navajo people to work hard for future benefits using existing resources was extremely challenging because, in the traditional Navajo perspective, only the present moment is considered real, and the future holds no concrete meaning. The engineer realized that it was futile to convince the Navajo people to exert effort in exchange for intangible future benefits. Linear logic and reasoning were not applicable to their perception of time. Therefore, he adopted a different approach, informing the workers that the government would pay off their debts, provide job opportunities for their families, and supply water to the herds, but in return, they needed to work eight hours a day. This time, the Navajo people immediately agreed.

Scan and Listen

Section C Case

The Scenario

An "Urgent" Call

Tim, a 45-year-old American, had been working in the fashion industry for over 20 years and was the supervisor of a clothing factory on an island somewhere in the Caribbean Sea. He was in charge of the recruitment affairs, thus trying his best to find low-cost labors for his factory. With more and more workers coming by to apply for positions in the factory, things seemed to go in the right direction. However, something unexpected and tough was just around the corner.

The problem lay in the number of people who were hired. In fact, the natives of the island had long been living under a certain status system, which helped to keep the existing balance of power. To get more job opportunities, some of the natives lowered their expected salary. Their successful recruitment broke the balance, arousing great dissatisfactions among the natives of all parts, so the leaders of each party decided to meet each other and have a discussion on the current situation, looking for a proper solution.

The discussion lasted for quite a long time and when they finally reached an agreement about the reallocation of jobs, it was already 2 o'clock in the morning. They were so excited about their decision that an immediate phone call was made to Tim, who they thought might feel as pleased as their supporters to hear about the reached agreement. Whereas it turned out that after picking up the phone Tim got very anxious as he did not understand the local language and, what's worse, this phone call was made at a time which shows a sign of extreme urgency, so he turned to the US Marines for help. Due to the huge language gap, it took hours before the locals finally managed to make the Americans believe that they were not meant to cause any trouble.

On the second day, with the help of an interpreter, the natives finally were able to have a discussion with Tim about their concern and the solution on the recruitment problem. Tim was very confused about the reason why the natives cared about the recruiting so much that they couldn't wait until the next morning, because he believed that such recruitment bias seemed meaningless compared to the overall picture. While on the other hand, the natives insisted that they could only fully devote to their work when the current situation was properly dealt with. A mutual consensus was eventually built, but the production was far behind schedule.

✎ Exercise

Listen to the case above and answer the following questions.

(1) What did Tim do on the island?

(2) What was the "unexpected and tough" thing mentioned in Paragraph 1?

(3) What did the natives think of the recruitment of Tim's factory?

(4) Why did the leaders decide to call Tim immediately?

(5) Why did Tim call the US Marines for help?

Unit 10 Space

- **Knowledge Objective:**

  Guide students to master the definition of proxemics, the characteristics of four spatial distances as well as different spatial distances in different cultures.

- **知识目标：**

  指导学生掌握跨文化交际中空间学的定义、人际交往中四类空间距离的特点以及不同文化中人际交往空间距离的差异。

- **Ability Objective:**

  Guide students to abide by different cultural norms regarding spatial distance and engage in effective intercultural communication.

- **能力目标：**

  指导学生遵守不同文化对空间距离的约定，进行有效的日常沟通和商务沟通。

- **Educative Objective:**

  Guide students to analyze the spatial design of "social distance" in some countries during the pandemic and be aware of the functional significance of space in safeguarding social health and redefining urban space. Guide students to understand that "No one should underestimate the resolve, the will, and the ability of the Chinese people to defend their national sovereignty and territorial integrity".

- **素质目标：**

  通过分析疫情期间一些国家有关"社交距离"的空间设计，引导学生感受空间在社会健康层面和城市未来空间定义层面的功能意义，引导学生了解"任何人都不要低估中国人民捍卫国家主权和领土完整的坚强决心、坚定意志、强大能力"。

Section A Video Clip Appreciation

I. Introduction to the Movie *Wonder*

Auggie is a 10-year-old boy born with rare facial deformity. He has been home-schooled but it does not conceal his cleverness and fondness for astronomy. At his fifth grade, his parents decide to enroll him into a local school. He is initially isolated by many classmates because of his different appearance. Supported by his family, teachers and some friends, Auggie struggles to fit into the larger community. Inspired by this extraordinary boy, people around Auggie also learn to discover their compassions and respect.

II. Introduction to the Video Clip

Before Auggie starts school, the principal arranges a tour for him with three other students: Jack, Julian, and Charlotte. When school starts, Auggie is teased by Julian and some unfriendly classmates. He sits alone in the classroom and eats alone. He feels upset and his family helps to comfort and encourage him. Then Auggie starts to show his smartness in science class and develops a close relationship with Jack.

III. Script of the Video Clip

Photographer: Guys, can you please... [*Chattering*] Okay. You... you guys, skooch. Sit. Just be closer.

Mr. Browne: Ladies and Gentlemen.

Photographer: Stay. Stay, good. Hey, hey. What's your name?

Mr. Browne: Auggie. Nice boots.

Photographer: Great. Thanks. Okay, everybody, here we go. We're skooching and say "Cheese".

Video Clip

All: Cheese!

Auggie: School became... Well, I got used to it. Except for dodgeball. What evil man invented dodgeball? But my least favorite zone at school is courtyard. Because the whole school's there. No one does anything mean. Or says anything. Or laughs. They all just look, then look away, then look back. They're just being normal kids. I kinda wanna tell them, "Hey, I know I look weird, but it's okay." I mean, if Chewbacca started going to school here one day, I'd probably stare at him a bit, too.

[*Chewbacca grunting*]

Auggie: I'm sorry if my staring made you feel weird.

[*Grunting*]

Ms. Petosa: In order for any of us to see, we need light. So right now, light is bouncing off this card traveling through the air, through the glass, to your eye. But what if we added water?

All: Whoa!

[*Chuckles*]

Ms. Petosa: Whoa, indeed. Any time light passes from one material or medium to another, it bends. This bending of light is also known as...

Auggie: Refraction.

Ms. Petosa: Very good, Auggie. Jack, you okay?

Jack: Yeah, yeah, refraction.

Ms. Petosa: Good. Clear your desks. Pop quiz.

[*All groaning*]

Auggie: [*Whispers*] Hurry.

[*Kids chattering*]

Julian: Hey, Jack, come sit here.

Jack: In a sec.

Miles: Where's he going?

Jack: Hey. Thanks for your help today.

Auggie: No problem.

Jack: And don't worry, I got a couple wrong so Ms. Petosa wouldn't know.

Auggie: I'm not worried. The worst they can do is kick me out.

Jack: Not loving school either, huh?

Auggie: Oh, it's great.

Jack: [*Chuckles*] I wanted to go to Wayne Middle. The one with the great sports teams.

Auggie: Then why'd you come here?

Jack: They gave me the scholarship.

Auggie: Well, if you need help in science, you can come to my house after school. You know,
if you want.

Jack: Great. Thanks! What's wrong?

Auggie: I just don't like eating in front of people.

Jack: What do you mean?

Auggie: It's a long story, but when I eat, I think I chew like some prehistoric swamp turtle.

Jack: No joke? Me too!

[*Both laughing*]

Auggie: Now there's tuna on your face.

Jack: Yeah! Tuna, man!

Auggie: No, no, no, let me show you how it's done.

[*Chuckles*]

[*Mimics chomping*]

[*Both chuckling*]

Jack: Dude, that's even more gross.

Auggie: I'm going as Boba Fett this year.

Jack: I like Halloween, but Christmas is still the best holiday.

Auggie: No way. Halloween is the best.

Jack: A pillowcase of candy versus two weeks off school. You're nuts.

[*Barks*]

Jack: You see? Even your dog agrees.

Auggie: Hey, Mom, is it okay if Jack comes over? Yes!

Jack: Thanks, Mrs. P. I mean, you get snow on Christmas.

Auggie: But you can get snow on Halloween.

Jack: How?

Auggie: If you live in Alaska or there's a blizzard.

Isabel: [*Exhales*] I've got to be cool.

[*Both grunting*]

Jack: You ever thought about having plastic surgery?

Auggie: No, I've never thought about it. Why?

[*Chuckles*]

Auggie: Dude, this is after plastic surgery! It takes a lotta work to look this good.

[*Both laughing*]

Auggie & Jack: Oh my God! Oh my God. 1, 2, 3, 4, I declare a thumb war. Bow, kiss, begin.

Isabel: Nate. Fire.

[*Inaudible*]

New Words

deformity 畸形

skooch 挪位子

dodgeball 躲避球游戏

refraction 折射

swamp 沼泽

blizzard 暴风雪

Notes

Chewbacca 楚巴卡，《星球大战》系列电影中的人物

Boba Fett 波巴·费特，《星球大战》系列电影中的人物

IV. Exercises for understanding

1. Decide whether the following statements are true or false according to the video clip you have just watched. Write "T" for true or "F" for false.

_____ (1) Auggie liked to play with friends in the courtyard at school.

_____ (2) The words on the paper changed from *now* to *won* because of reflection.

_____ (3) Jack asked Auggie to help him with the quiz because he had difficulties.

_____ (4) Jack was the first student to eat with Auggie.

_____ (5) Isabel called Nate because the house was on fire.

2. Put the following sentences in the right order according to the video clip you have just watched.

_____ (1) Auggie answered a question correctly in the science class.

_____ (2) Auggie's mom was glad to see that Auggie had invited his friend to come over.

_____ (3) Auggie faced both curiosity and avoidance from the people he met at school.

_____ (4) Auggie helped Jack with the quiz.

_____ (5) Jack expressed kindness and started to eat with Auggie.

3. Explore interculturally.

(1) During the group photo shoot, Auggie stepped aside when the photographer asked everyone to get closer. Why did Auggie want to keep a distance from everyone?

(2) Jack managed to make friends with Auggie after the science class. What do you think Auggie and Jack had done respectively to establish this friendship? What communication techniques can you conclude from it?

Section B Reading

微课

When you are having lunch by yourself in the school cafeteria, would you mind someone coming over and asking to sit with you? Or would you mind asking to sit with someone you do not know? How you answer this request largely depends on your concept of comfortable space between you and strangers. We have around ourselves a certain boundary that encompasses a personal territory, analogized as a "bubble" of space. Compared with general national boundaries, this invisible boundary between people is more complex and largely dependent on the living environment.

Personal Space

Edward T. Hall coined the study of personal space and its effect on human communication as proxemics. Within this concept, interpersonal distance is divided into four zones. The closest is the intimate distance (0–50 cm) reserved for close friends, family members and lovers in embracing, touching and whispering. The second is the personal distance (> 50–120 cm) among ordinary friends and relatives in daily conversations. The third is the social distance (> 120– 270 cm) for newly formed groups and new acquaintances. The farthest is the public distance (> 270 cm) for public speeches and lectures which involve a larger group of audience.

People are usually sensitive about the space within their intimate and personal distance. Allowing other people to enter personal space indicates the recognition of mutual relationship. If unfamiliar people enter the personal "bubble", for example, touching or talking within the distance of close friends, people may feel violated, discomforted or anxious. By contrast, if close friends suddenly keep a distance, it may also reveal something unpleasant.

Most people implicitly agree to the rule of protecting their own bubbles while preventing themselves from invading other bubbles. However, this does not seem like an easy job as the size of the "bubble" is highly variable. What appears to be natural for us may be offensive for others, due to different cultural backgrounds or individual preferences. People living in the overcrowding capital, for example, may discover their spatial attitudes different from those in other parts of the region.

What Happens When Our Space Is Violated?

Individuals vary in terms of their reactions to people entering certain zones, and determining what constitutes a "violation" of space is subjective and contextual. For example, another person's presence in our social or public zones doesn't typically arouse suspicion or negative physical or communicative reactions, but it could in some situations or with certain people. However, many situations lead to our personal and intimate space being breached by others against our will, and these breaches are more likely to be upsetting, even when they are expected. We've all had to get into a crowded elevator or wait in a long line. In such situations, we may rely on some verbal communication to reduce immediacy and indicate that we are not interested in closeness and are aware that a breach has occurred. People make comments about the crowd, saying, "We're really packed in here like sardines," or use humor to indicate that they are pleasant and well-adjusted and uncomfortable with the breach like any "normal" person would be.

Different Spatial Attitudes around the World

Northern Europeans, Scandinavians for example, have quite large space bubbles where people tend to guard their privacy. Finnish, for instance, perform a distinctive queuing habit. Instead of standing closely one after another, they tend to keep a long distance from the person in front of them. In Germany, it is common to maintain an arm's length during conversations. Any further approaching may be considered as an encroachment of personal space. The German dwellings are organized accordingly. Fences and hedges separate houses and gardens. Gate and room doors are often locked. During conversations, Scandinavians or British people traditionally do not touch or hug whereas they reserve such intimate actions to closer friends or family members.

However, the case is much different in Southern Europe, such as France, Italy, Greece and Spain. Usually, the newcomers will find the natives extremely amiable when they are greeted with a kiss or a hug. Daily conversations take place in closer distance. Many places in these countries also face the problem of overcrowding. If a Northern European comes to the south, he or she may find the pushing or shoving in crowded train stations very awkward or anxious, which in the eyes of the Southern European is quite common.

Japan is another example of land scarcity. Small houses and narrow roads create a cramped living environment. Nonetheless, Japanese pay large attention to the protection of their personal bubble. They set up strict borderline between personal space and public space. Family members love to cling together in private. Yet in the public, they keep a certain distance. Unlike some broader countries, it is hard for the Japanese to guarantee their personal distance physically. They think of other ways to make up for it. For instance, in the urban area such as Tokyo, many people like to wear hygiene masks. Except for sickness precaution, masks are used to create anonymity and a mental interpersonal distance.

Middle Eastern cultures also distinguish personal and public space rigidly. Houses have few or no windows facing towards the streets. Families separate themselves from each other as a unit. Inside the house, however, individual space is limited. Family members emphasize close relationship together. Gender is also an important factor especially in many Islamic backgrounds. Men and women keep a longer distance than the same sex. Physical touching between two women such as walking hand in hand is acceptable, yet the opposite sex is not.

Cultures over the world have their own spatial customs and interpretation. These concepts and behaviors are changeable due to socioeconomic development. Before visiting a country or meeting with foreigners, it is always important to familiarize ourselves with the appropriate space in that culture in order to make sure we do not come across as too aggressive or too remote.

⚡ Exercises for Understanding

1. Answer the following questions according to the passage you have just read.

(1) What are the four zones of interpersonal distance identified by Edward T. Hall, and how do they differ in terms of relationships and contexts?

(2) Apart from the example in the passage, describe a situation in which breaches of personal space might occur. How will people respond to such breaches?

(3) Explain how cultural background can influence one's perception of personal space violations. Provide examples of cultural factors that may contribute to these differences.

(4) Reflect on the personal space preferences and behaviors in Chinese culture. How is personal space valued in China? Can you provide examples based on your daily interactions?

(5) Imagine a situation where you find yourself in a culture with different space perceptions from your own. How would you adapt your behavior and communication style to respect the local norms while maintaining your own comfort level?

2. Choose the most appropriate answers to the following questions.

(1) According to the article, what is the term used to describe the study of personal space and its effect on human communication?

    A. Social dynamics

    B. Anthropometrics

    C. Proxemics

    D. Psychometrics

(2) Which of the following distances is associated with close friends, family members, and lovers in embracing, touching, and whispering?

    A. Intimate distance

    B. Personal distance

    C. Social distance

    D. Public distance

(3) How do people tactically react when their personal space is violated in crowded situations like elevators or long lines?

    A. They confront the person violating their space.

    B. They use humor to diffuse the situation.

    C. They become aggressive and push back.

    D. They immediately leave the crowded area.

(4) In which of the following regions is it common to maintain an arm's length during conversations to avoid encroaching on personal space?

    A. Northern Europe

    B. Southern Europe

    C. Middle East

    D. Japan

(5) What is the way in which Japanese people make up for the lack of physical personal distance in crowded urban areas?

    A. Using simple greetings

    B. Wearing hygiene masks

    C. Avoiding eye contact

    D. Speaking loudly on the phone

3. Decide whether the following statements are true or false according to the passage you have just read. Write "T" for true or "F" for false.

_____ (1) Personal space boundaries are consistent across cultures and are not affected by socioeconomic development.

_____ (2) People living in an overcrowded capital may have different spatial attitudes compared to those in other regions.

_____ (3) Northern Europeans tend to have smaller personal space bubbles compared to Southern Europeans.

_____ (4) Japanese people tend to maintain a larger personal distance in public spaces compared to private settings.

_____ (5) In Middle Eastern cultures, it is common for men and women to maintain the same personal space boundaries in both public and private settings.

4. Case study.

Study the following pictures of spacial design of social distance during the pandemic and discuss the functional significance of space in safeguarding social health and redefining urban space.

(1) Beach belt kit（沙滩带套件）

(2) Personal square（个人广场）

(3) Painted circles（喷漆圆圈）

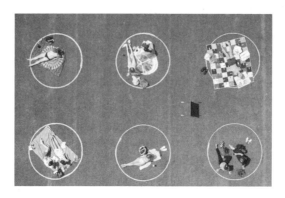

(4) Petticoat dress（连衣裙）

(5)Wave-distanciation line（波浪线道路）

(6) Mi casa, your casa（我们的公共房子）

(7) Capsule by casala（太空舱胶囊）

Section C Case

The Scenario

Scan and Listen

Too Close for Comfort

Bill had just arrived from the United States to study engineering at a Chinese university. He studied Chinese back at his home university and was confident that doing his graduate study at a Chinese university would give him an edge in taking advantage of future opportunities in the growing economy.

In the first few days, he met and moved in with his roommate Zemin and met several of the students who lived in nearby dormitory rooms. Most of them were also studying engineering but had little experience with Americans. He usually went to the student cafeteria with them and they were very helpful in showing him around and in gently correcting his classroom Chinese.

One evening, he settled in for his study session in his room. After some time, Zemin left to visit another room where his friends were listening to a radio broadcast. Bill said he would join later. When Bill decided to take a break and see what the "guys" were up to, he found Zemin and two other boys huddled over the radio. Bill found it quite odd, however, that Zemin was draped over the back of the boy seated in front of the radio. Moreover, that boy had his feet propped up on his roommate who was seated nearby. It seemed to Bill that he had startled them, since they jumped up and welcomed him and even offered him tea. After Bill had a cup of tea and a chair to sit in, the group returned to the radio.

Bill shrugged the incident off, but over the next few days he noticed that female students on campus frequently walked arm-in-arm or even holding hands. He noticed, too, that students of both sexes, but especially the boys would huddle around newspaper displays in a fashion of close contact similar to Zemin and others around the radio. Bill felt rather uncomfortable and wondered how he would respond if one of his classmates were to put his arms around him.

🄴 Exercise

Listen to the case above and answer the following questions.

(1) Why did Bill come to China to study engineering?

(2) Did Bill get along well with his Chinese roommates?

(3) What did Bill do one evening before he joined his roommates for a radio broadcast?

(4) How did the Chinese guys behave one evening when they listened to a radio?

(5) How did Bill feel about Chinese' close body contact with each other?

Module 5

Barriers and Bridges

Unit 11 Ethnocentrism and Stereotypes

INTRODUCTION

● **Knowledge Objective:**

Guide students to master the definitions of ethnocentrism and stereotypes, their impact on intercultural communication, and the ways to overcome ethnocentrism and stereotypes.

● **知识目标：**

指导学生掌握民族中心主义和刻板印象的定义、它们对跨文化交际的影响以及克服民族中心主义和刻板印象的路径。

● **Ability Objective:**

Guide students to understand the irreproducibility and value characteristics of each culture, overcome traps of ethnocentrism and stereotypes behaviorally and cognitively, cultivate empathy, and engage in intercultural communication on the basis of respect and equality.

● **能力目标：**

指导学生了解每种文化的不可复制性和价值特性，从行为和认知上摆脱民族中心主义和刻板印象的陷阱，培养共情能力，在尊重和平等的基础上进行跨文化交际。

● **Educative Objective:**

Guide students to analyze why Dolce & Gabbana's short video *Eating with Chopsticks* met its Waterloo in China. Guide students to understand that dialogue and game-play will be a state of interaction between China and Western cultures for a considerable period of time in the future. Guide students to learn to eliminate foreign prejudices and stereotypes against China, enhance national pride, promote mutual learning with other civilizations and present China as "a country worthy of friendship, trust and respect".

● **素质目标:**

通过对杜嘉班纳《赶筷吃饭》短视频在中国遭遇负面评价的案例分析，引导学生了解对话与博弈将是未来相当长时间内中国与西方文化相处的状态。引导学生在跨文化交际中学会消除外国人对中国的偏见和刻板印象，提高民族自豪感，促进文明互鉴，展示"可信、可爱、可敬的中国"。

Section A Video Clip Appreciation

I. Introduction to the Movie *Crash*

Over a thirty-six-hour period in Los Angeles, a handful of disparate people's lives intertwine as they deal with the tense race relations that belie life in the city. Among the players are: the Caucasian district attorney, who uses race as a political card; his Caucasian wife, who has recently been carjacked by two black men and believes that her stereotypical views of non-whites is justified and cannot be considered racism; the two black carjackers who use their race to their advantage and as an excuse; partnered Caucasian police constables—one who is a racist and uses his authority to harass non-whites, and the other who hates his partner because of his racist views, but may have the same

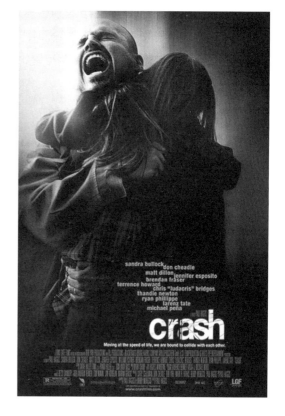

underlying values; a black film director and his black wife, who believes her husband doesn't support their black background enough, especially in light of an incident with the racist white cop; partnered police detectives and sometimes lovers—one Hispanic female and the other black male, among whom the latter is dealing with a drugged-out mother that feels he isn't concerned enough about taking care of the family; an East Asian man who is run over but is hiding some valuable cargo in the back of his van; a Persian store owner, who feels he isn't getting satisfaction from American society after his store has been robbed time and time again; and a Hispanic locksmith, who just wants to keep his family, especially his young daughter, safe in a seemingly unsafe world.

II. Introduction to the Video Clip

A black man, Detective Graham Waters, speaks dazedly about the nature of Los Angeles and the need for people to crash into each other. A Latino woman in the driver's seat of the car, Ria, mentions they were hit from behind and spun around. She gets out of the car and goes to the cop and the other driver, an Asian woman. The two women blame each other for the mishap and make racial jibes. The Latina identifies herself as a detective.

Waters gets out and walks toward more police cars and a crime scene. Another cop mentions they have a body. An intense stare crosses Waters' face as he looks at something.

The scene flashes back to "Yesterday".

At a gun shop a Persian man Farhad and his daughter Dorri are buying a handgun. The shop owner gets upset with the Persians speaking Farsi and the two men quickly begin exchanging angry insults. Farhad leaves fuming and Dorri tells the shop owner that she'll either take the gun or take their money back, stating that she hopes she gets the money back. She also selects a red box of free bullets as she takes the gun, despite the owner making a cryptic remark about the type of bullets she's chosen.

Two young black men, Anthony and Peter, leave a restaurant. Anthony claims they were victims of racism and poor service, and Peter laughs it off. Jean and Rick Cabot, a white couple, walk down the sidewalk. Jean notices the two black men, averts her gaze and clutches Rick's arm. Anthony takes it as a racial slight, but then the two young men suddenly draw handguns and carjack the Cabots' black Lincoln Navigator. Peter places a St. Christopher statue on the dashboard over Anthony's objections.

Detective Waters and his partner Ria arrive at a crime scene. A uniformed cop tells them there was shooting between two drivers. The surviving white man is identified as an undercover cop named Conklin. The dead driver in a Mercedes is also a cop, a black man named Lewis. The investigators are unsure who started the shooting in the road rage incident.

At the Cabots' house, Jean is still upset, and a locksmith is changing the door locks. Seeing that the smith has several tattoos and is Latino, she angrily tells her husband she wants the job done again the next day. Jean loudly claims the locksmith will sell the keys and they will be robbed again. The locksmith, Daniel, overhears and leaves two sets of keys on the kitchen counter as he leaves. Rick is running for District Attorney re-election and wonders how to use the carjacking to an electoral advantage while talking to his assistants.

III. Script of the Video Clip

Detective Graham Waters: It's the sense of touch.

Ria: What?

Detective Graham Waters: Any real city, you walk, you know? You brush past people. People bump into you. In L.A., nobody touches you. We're always behind this metal and glass. I think we miss that touch so much... that we crash into each other just so we can feel something.

Video Clip

Lt. Dixon: You guys okay?

Ria: I think he hit his head.

Detective Graham Waters: You don't think that's true?

Lt. Dixon: Stay in your car.

Ria: Graham, I think we got rear-ended. I think we spun around twice. And somewhere in there, one of us lost our frame of reference. And I'm gonna go look for it.

Lt. Dixon: Calm down, ma'am.

Kim Lee: I am calm!

Lt. Dixon: I need to see your registration and insurance.

Kim Lee: Why? It's not my fault! It's her fault! She do this!

Ria: My fault?

Lt. Dixon: Ma'am, you really need to wait in your vehicle.

Ria: My fault?

Kim Lee: Stop in middle of street! Mexicans no know how to drive. She "blake" too fast.

Ria: I "blake" too fast? I "blake" too fast. I'm sorry you no see my "blake" lights.

Lt. Dixon: Ma'am.

Ria: See, I stop when I see a long line of cars stopped in front of me. Maybe you see over steering wheel, you "blake" too!

Lt. Dixon: Ma'am!

Kim Lee: I call immigration. Look what you do my car.

Ria: Officer, can you please write in your report how shocked I am to be hit by an Asian driver!

Lt. Dixon: Ma'am!

Ria: Ma'am, no. See, Detective...

Lt. Dixon: All right. You've got to calm down.

Police Officer: Hey, Detective! Nice entrance.

Detective Graham Waters: Fuck you.

Police Detective: Hey, you okay?

Detective Graham Waters: I'm freezin'.

Police Detective: Shit. I heard it might snow.

Detective Graham Waters: Get outta here.

Police Detective: That's what I heard.

Detective Graham Waters: You got a smoke?

Police Detective: Nah. I quit.

Detective Graham Waters: Yeah, me too. What do you got?

Police Detective: Dead kid.

Detective Graham Waters: Hey, Bob.

****

[*Yesterday*]

Gun Store Owner: You get one free box of ammunition. What kind do you want?

[*Farhad and Dorri talking in Spanish*]

Gun Store Owner: Yo, Osama! Plan a jihad on your own time. What do you want?

Farhad: Are you making insult at me?

Gun Store Owner: Am I making insult "at" you? Is that the closest you can come to English?

Farhad: Yes, I speak English! I am American citizen.

Gun Store Owner: Oh, God, here we go.

Farhad: I have right like you. I have right to buy gun.

Gun Store Owner: Not in my store, you don't! Andy, get him outta here now!

Dorri: Go wait in the car.

Gun Store Owner: Now. Get out!

Farhad: You're an ignorant man!

Gun Store Owner: I'm ignorant? You're liberating my country and I'm flying 747s into your mud huts and incinerating your friends? Get the fuck out!

Farhad: No, you get the fuck out! No, don't touch me! He cheat me!

Gun Store Owner: Andy, now!

Security Guard: Let's go.

Dorri: Okay. You can give me the gun or give me back the money. And I am really hoping for the money.

Gun Store Owner: What kind of ammunition do you want?

Dorri: Whatever fits.

Gun Store Owner: We got a lot of kinds. We got long colts, short colts, bull heads, flat noses, hollowpoints, wide cutters, and a dozen more that'll fit any size hole. Just depends upon how much bang you can handle.

Dorri: I'll take the ones in the red box.

Gun Store Owner: You know what those are?

Dorri: Can I have them?

****

Anthony: Did you see any white people waiting... an hour and 32 minutes for a plate of spaghetti? And how many cups of coffee did we get?

Peter Waters: You don't drink coffee! And I didn't want any.

Anthony: Man, that woman poured cup after cup to every single white person around us. But did she even ask you if you wanted any?

Peter Waters: We didn't get any coffee that you didn't want and I didn't order, and that's evidence of racial discrimination? Did you notice that our waitress was black?

Anthony: And black women don't think in stereotypes? You tell me. When was the last time you met one… who didn't think she knew everything about your lazy ass… before you even opened your mouth, huh? That waitress sized us up in two seconds. We're black, and black people don't tip. So she wasn't gonna waste her time. Somebody like that? Nothing you can do to change their mind.

Peter Waters: How much did you leave?

Anthony: You expect me to pay for that kind of service? What? What the fuck is you laughin' at, man?

D. A. Rick Cabot: I'm seriously starting to think that you're jealous of Karen.

Jean Cabot: Hardly. I'd just like to see you get through a meal without calling her or anyone else.

D. A. Rick Cabot: Okay, no more phone calls. As a matter of fact, you can hold the battery. Okay?

Jean Cabot: Ten bucks says she calls you in the car.

Anthony: Wait, wait, wait. See what that woman just did? You see that?

Peter Waters: She's cold.

Anthony: She got colder as soon as she saw us.

Peter Waters: Ah, come on, don't start.

Anthony: Man, look around you, man. You couldn't find a whiter, safer or better-lit part of this city right now. But yet this white woman sees two black guys... who look like UCLA students strolling down the sidewalk, and her reaction is blind fear? I mean look at us, dog. Are we dressed like gangbangers? Huh? No. Do we look threatening? No. Fact. If anybody should be scared around here, it's us! We're the only two black faces surrounded by a sea of over-caffeinated white people... patrolled by the trigger-happy L. A. P. D. So you tell me. Why aren't we scared?

Peter Waters: 'Cause we got guns?

Anthony: You could be right.

Peter Waters: Get the fuck outta the car!

Anthony: Gimme the keys!

Peter Waters: Hurry up! Get down!

Jean Cabot: Okay, okay, okay, okay.

D.A. Rick Cabot: No, no! Please!

Peter Waters: Don't look at me! Turn around!

D.A. Rick Cabot: Come on! Go! We're fine! Just keep moving!

Anthony: No, no, no! Take that voodoo-assed thing off of there right now.

Peter Waters: I know you just didn't call Saint Christopher voodoo. Man's the patron saint of travelers, dog.

Anthony: You had a conversation with God, huh? What did God say? "Go forth, my son, and leave big slobbery suction rings on every dashboard you find?" Why the hell do you do that?

Peter Waters: Look at the way your crazy ass drive, then ask me again.

Officer Johnson: Chevy pickup and Mercedes driving north on Balboa. Pickup cuts in front. Driver of the Mercedes gets pissed, pulls a gun. Doesn't realize the guy in the pickup is a cop coming off shift.

Detective Graham Waters: This Barry Gibb dude is a cop?

Officer Johnson: Yeah. Name's Conklin. He's a narc out of Wilshire.

Ria: I got the Mercedes.

Officer Johnson: Mercedes takes a shot at him. Detective Conklin returns fire. One shot. Mercedes rolls to a stop. Driver opens the door, falls out dead.

Detective Graham Waters: He looks very relaxed for just having shot somebody.

Officer Johnson: He says he kept tryin' to drive away. The Mercedes kept pulling up next to him, screaming, waving a gun. Shot back in self-defense.

Detective Graham Waters: Anybody actually see who shot first?

Officer Johnson: They just heard two bangs.

Detective Graham Waters: Find me a witness. That is a nice gun.

Ria: The car's registered to a Cindy Bradley. And that's not Cindy. That is a William Lewis. Found under the front seat. Hollywood Division.

Detective Graham Waters: Looks like Detective Conklin shot himself the wrong nigger.

****

Jean Cabot: How much longer are you gonna be?

Daniel Ruiz: This is the last one.

Jean Cabot: Thank you.

D. A. Rick Cabot: You don't think reporters listen to police calls?

Jean Cabot: I need to talk to you for a second.

D. A. Rick Cabot: You just give me a minute, all right? Find Flanagan, will you? Now.

Bruce: Yes, sir.

D. A. Rick Cabot: Yes, honey?

Jean Cabot: I want the locks changed again in the morning.

D. A. Rick Cabot: You want... Why don't you just go lie down? Have you checked on James?

Jean Cabot: Of course. I've checked on him every five minutes since we've been home. Do not patronize me. I want the locks changed again in the morning.

D. A. Rick Cabot: It's okay. Just go to bed.

Jean Cabot: You know, didn't I just ask you not to treat me like a child?

Maria: I'm sorry, Miss Jean. It's okay I go home now?

D. A. Rick Cabot: It's fine. Thank you very much for staying.

Maria: You're welcome, no problem. Good night.

Jean Cabot: Good night.

D. A. Rick Cabot: We'll see you tomorrow.

Jean Cabot: I would like the locks changed again in the morning. And you might mention that we'd appreciate it if next time they didn't send a gang member.

D. A. Rick Cabot: A gang member? You mean that kid in there?

Jean Cabot: Yes. The guy with the shaved head, the pants around his ass, the prison tattoo.

D. A. Rick Cabot: Those are not prison tattoos.

Jean Cabot: Oh, really? And he's not gonna sell our key... to one of his gangbanger friends the moment he is out our door?

D. A. Rick Cabot: We've had a tough night. It'd be best if you went...

Jean Cabot: And wait for them to break in? I just had a gun pointed in my face.

D. A. Rick Cabot: You lower your voice!

Jean Cabot: And it was my fault because I knew it was gonna happen. But if a white person sees two black men walking towards her, and she turns and walks in the other direction, she's a racist, right? Well, I got scared and I didn't say anything. And ten seconds later I had a gun in my face! I am telling you. Your amigo in there is gonna sell our key to one of his homies. And this time it'd be really fucking great if you acted like you actually gave a shit!

New Words

ammunition 弹药

insult 侮辱，辱骂，冒犯

incinerate 把……烧成灰烬

racial 种族的

discrimination 歧视

pickup 小卡车

patrol 在……巡逻

gimme 给我（等于 give me）

voodoo 伏都教（一种西非原始宗教），伏都教徒

slobbery 潮湿的，流口水的，过于伤感的，懒散的

suction 抽吸（液体、汽体等）

dashboard （机动车辆的）仪表板

narc 缉查毒品的刑警

nigger 黑人（对黑人的一种极具侮辱性的称呼）

patronize 以高人一等的态度对待

amigo 朋友（源于西班牙语 amigo）

Phrases and Expressions

brush past 擦肩而过

rear-ended 追尾的

steering wheel 驾驶盘

flat nose 平头弹

size up 估计

stroll down 漫步，闲逛

patron saint 守护神

cut in front of 突然插到……前

off shift 下班

Notes

UCLA 加州大学洛杉矶分校，位于美国洛杉矶市，是世界著名的公立研究型大学。

L. A. P. D. 洛杉矶警察局

Chevy 雪佛兰，美国通用汽车公司旗下的一个汽车品牌，1918 年被通用汽车收购，现为通用汽车旗下最为国际化和大众化的品牌之一。

Mercedes 梅赛德斯－奔驰，世界闻名的豪华汽车品牌，以高质量、高性能的汽车产品著称。

IV. Exercises for understanding

1. Decide whether the following statements are true or false according to the video clip you have just watched. Write "T" for true or "F" for false.

_____ (1) Ria was sarcastic at a Korean woman on the latter's confusion between "black" and "brake".

_____ (2) Peter Waters and Anthony tipped the waitress when they had spaghetti in a restaurant.

_____ (3) The gun shop owner got upset with the two Persians speaking Farsi and didn't want to sell ammunition to them in the beginning.

_____ (4) Jean Cabbot felt unsafe when she noticed the locksmith had tattoos.

_____ (5) Detective Graham inferred that detective Conklin shot a wrong black.

2. Put the following sentences in the right order according to the video clip you have just watched.

_____ (1) Two black UCLA students Peter Waters and Anthony robbed the car of a white couple at one night.

_____ (2) Peter Waters insisted that the patron saint be put on the dashboard of the robbed car.

_____ (3) Two women quarreled about whose fault it was for the car crash.

_____ (4) Jean Cabbot bet with Rick Cabbot that Karen would call Rick again.

_____ (5) Jean Cabbot demanded that the locks be changed again the next day.

3. Explore interculturally.

(1) Why does Detective Graham Waters say in the very beginning "we crash into each other just so we can feel something"?

(2) What does Jean Cabot complain to Rick Cabot? Do you think it is a stereotype?

Section B Reading

Ethnocentrism

微课

"Ethnocentrism" is the tendency to think of one's own culture as being at the center of the world and assume that your own culture's way of thinking and acting is more natural, normal, and correct than the way people from other cultures think and act.

People are almost always ethnocentric to some degree. In fact, it is almost impossible not to be ethnocentric. As we grow up and learn what is right and wrong, true and false, normal and abnormal, and so forth, we naturally learn to view the world as our culture views it. For example, children who grow up in cultures where men usually greet each other by kissing naturally assume that this is the normal way for men to greet. In contrast, children who grow up in cultures where men never kiss each other will probably find it strange and even offensive if they see men greet each other by kissing. The process of learning about our world and the process of learning our own culture are so thoroughly mixed together that most people grow up without being able to clearly distinguish one from the other.

Because our ideas about the world are formed in childhood, they are so deeply rooted in our minds and hearts that often we are not even aware of them. We also tend to feel quite strongly about many of them, and it is not easy for us to change them. For example, even if Chinese men go to live in a country where men greet each other by kissing, they will probably always feel at least a little uncomfortable kissing other men, no matter how hard they try to adapt to local customs, and they may not be willing to adapt to such a custom at all.

How Does Ethnocentrism Impede Intercultural Communication?

While ethnocentrism is very natural, it is also the root of many problems in intercultural communication. Because we naturally feel that the ways and ideas of our culture are more natural and correct than those of other cultures, we tend to use the norms of our own culture—our ideas of what is good/bad, right/wrong, normal/abnormal—as standards when we judge the behavior of people from other cultures. Chinese tend to judge Westerners according to the standards of Chinese culture, and Westerners tend to judge Chinese according to Western standards, and so on. So when we encounter foreigners who behave or think in ways that differ from our cultural norms, we too quickly tend to judge these other ways as strange, wrong, or bad.

Few of us believe that our own culture is perfect, but deep in our hearts most of us feel that our own culture is generally superior to other cultures, especially with regard to the issue of right and wrong. Ethnocentrism is one major reason why people are prone to judge the behavior of foreigners negatively.

Effective intercultural communicators must learn to be careful about using their own cultural norms to judge people from other cultures. One of the best ways to learn this is to cultivate the habit of learning about other cultural perspectives, and of trying to understand the world from other cultural perspectives. The norms of our own culture are not necessarily wrong—often they are very good—but we should learn not to judge other cultures' ways of acting and thinking as bad only because they differ from our own.

Stereotype

Another obstacle in the process of effective intercultural communication is stereotype. The term of stereotype is derived from two Greek terms: stereos, which means firm and solid; typoes, which means impression. In other words, it shows how ideas make an impression. Stereotypes are at their most basic level a set of assumed characteristics about a certain group of people whose actual beliefs, habits and realities more often than not disagree with the imposed assumptions.

How Does Stereotype Impede Intercultural Communication?

Stereotypes are usually based on factors such as exaggeration, distortion, ignorance, racism, cultural factors or even historical experiences. Stereotyping is therefore rightly seen as a negative way of seeing people. This is even true of what is called "positive stereotype". A positive stereotype is where we use a blanket expression for a whole people. For example, all the Chinese are great at math, all Germans are well organized or all English people are well mannered. Although the intent behind the statement is positive, it does not reflect the truth.

Stereotypes don't just appear out of nowhere—they are based on ideas and experiences with certain groups and then extended to apply to an entire group. The problem is that people don't function solely as members of a group. We know this to be true about ourselves and our close friends. Most of us fit into different categories and have a variety of interests. We might like watching sports but are non-athletic. We might like rock and roll as well as classical music. But when we think about other people, particularly people who are a different race from us, we often have a harder time understanding that complexity. So we put people into categories and thus—stereotypes are formed.

Many stereotypes are negative, such as assuming that certain people are lazy, criminal or poor. Some are seemingly positive, such as assuming that people are athletic, religious or musically inclined. Others are just neutral, such as assuming that people eat certain foods or share similar hobbies. But all of them are harmful.

The purpose of stereotypes is to help us know how to interact with others. Each classification has associations, scripts and so on that we use to interpret what they are saying, decide if they are good or bad, and choose how to respond to them.

Three Ways to Change Stereotypes

We change our stereotypes infrequently. Even in the face of disconfirming evidence, we often cling to our obviously-wrong beliefs. When we do change the stereotypes, we do so in one of three ways.

Bookkeeping model: As we learn new contradictory information, we incrementally adjust the stereotype to adapt to the new information. We usually need quite a lot of repeated information for each incremental change. Individual evidence is taken as the exception that proves the rule.

Conversion model: We throw away the old stereotype and start again. This is often used when there is significant disconfirming evidence.

Subtyping model: We create a new stereotype that is a sub-classification of the existing stereotype, particularly when we can draw a boundary around the sub-class. Thus if we have a stereotype for Americans, a visit to New York may result in us having a "New Yorkers are different" sub-type.

We often store stereotypes in two parts. First there are generalized descriptions and attributes. To this we may add exemplars to prove the case, such as "the policeman next door". We may also store them hierarchically, such as "black people" "Africans" "Ugandans" and "Ugandan military", with each lower order inheriting the characteristics of the higher order, with additional characteristics added.

Stereotyping can go around in circles. Men stereotype women and women stereotype men. In certain societies this is intensified as the stereotyping of women pushes them together more and they create men as more of an out-group. The same thing happens with different racial groups, such as "white/black".

Stereotyping can be subconscious, where it subtly biases our decisions and actions, even in people who consciously do not want to be biased.

Stereotyping often happens not so much because of aggressive or unkind thoughts. It is more often a simplification to speed conversation on what is not considered to be an important topic. To change a person's view of stereotype, be consistently different from it. Beware of your own stereotyping blinding you to the true nature of other individuals. Stereotyping can be reduced by bringing people together. When they discover the other people are not as the stereotype, the immediate evidence creates dissonance that leads to improved thoughts about the other group.

Cultural competency is a term used to describe the ability to work, communicate and live across cultures and cultural boundaries. One achieves this through an instilled understanding of cultures on a general level as well as an informed one about specific cultures on a more detailed level. It has to work in tandem with behavioral and attitudinal changes. We, as citizens of the planet earth, are no longer confined to our national and cultural borders. We mix with people from different cultures, ethnicities, religions and colors on a daily basis. In order to make this intercultural experience work on all levels from education to business to government, people have to develop basic skills in intercultural communication and understanding.

📝 Exercises for Understanding

1. Answer the following questions according to the passage you have just read.

(1) What is "ethnocentrism"? Why are people ethnocentric?

(2) Why does ethnocentrism cause difficulties in intercultural communication?

(3) How to deal with ethnocentrism?

(4) What does the term "stereotype" mean? What kind of impact can stereotypes have on individuals?

(5) In what ways can we reduce stereotyping?

2. Choose the most appropriate answers to the following questions.

(1) Which of the following is NOT the feature of ethnocentrism?

A. Ethnocentrism is to assume that one's own culture has a more natural, normal, and correct way of thinking and acting.

B. Ethnocentrism tends to use the norms of one's own culture as standards to judge the behaviors of people from other cultures.

C. Ethnocentrism may cause people to judge the behaviors of foreigners negatively.

D. Ethnocentrism is a lubricant in intercultural communication.

(2) The term of stereotype is derived from _____.

 A. Greek

 B. Latin

 C. German

 D. Spanish

(3) Bookkeeping model, as one of the ways to change stereotypes, is to _____.

 A. throw away old stereotype and start again

 B. create a new stereotype that is a sub-classification of the existing stereotype

 C. gather much repeated information for incremental changes

 D. cling to stereotyped beliefs despite disconfirming evidence

(4) Which of the following is NOT the feature of stereotyping?

 A. Stereotypes are divided into positive, negative and neutral ones.

 B. Stereotypes are caused by exaggeration, distortion, ignorance, racism, cultural factors or historical experiences.

 C. Stereotypes, once formed, are easy to change.

 D. Stereotypes can be reduced by bringing people together.

(5) People develop cultural competency by the following ways EXCEPT _____.

 A. having an instilled understanding of cultures on a general level

 B. becoming an informed one about specific cultures

 C. having behavioral and attitudinal changes

 D. getting rid of ethnocentrism and stereotypes

3. Decide whether the following statements are true or false according to the passage you have just read. Write "T" for true or "F" for false.

_____ (1) People are always ethnocentric to some degree.

_____ (2) As ethnocentric ideas are usually formed in childhood, they are easy to change when we grow up.

_____ (3) Cultivating the habit of learning about other cultural perspectives is a way to reduce ethnocentrism.

_____ (4) A negative stereotype is where people use a blanket expression for a whole people.

_____ (5) Stereotypes lie hidden and do not bias people's decisions and actions.

4. Case study.

What stereotypes against China did Dolce & Gabbana demonstrate in its short video entitled *Eating with Chopsticks*? Why did the short video meet its Waterloo in China?

5. Small group task.

(1) Read the following old joke about national stereotypes and discuss the reasons implied.

Heaven is where the police are English, the cooks are French, the mechanics are German, the lovers are Italian and everything is organized by the Swiss. Hell is where the police are German, the cooks are English, the mechanics are French, the lovers are Swiss, and everything is organized by the Italians.

(2) Read the following poem "We and They" and then discuss how to overcome ethnocentrism and stereotypes properly.

We and They

Father and Mother, and Me,

Sister and Auntie say

All the people like us are We,

And every one else is They.

And They live over the sea,

While We live over the way,

But—would you believe it?—

They look upon We as only a sort of They!

We eat pork and beef

With cow-horn-handled knives.

They who gobble Their rice off a leaf,

Are horrified out of Their lives;

While they who live up a tree,

And feast on grubs and clay,

(Isn't it scandalous?) Look upon We

As a simply disgusting They!

We shoot birds with a gun.

They stick lions with spears.

Their full-dress is un-.

We dress up to Our ears.

They like Their friends for tea.

We like Our friends to stay;

And, after all that, They look upon We

As an utterly ignorant They!

We eat kitcheny food.

We have doors that latch.

They drink milk or blood,

Under an open thatch.

We have Doctors to fee.

They have Wizards to pay.

And (impudent heathen!) They look upon We

As a quite impossible They!

All good people agree,

And all good people say,

All nice people, like Us, are We,

And every one else is They:

But if you cross over the sea,

Instead of over the way,

You may end by (think of it!)

looking on We

As only a sort of They!

Section C Case

The Scenario

Scan and Listen

Sharing the Wealth

Anna Bilow has been working for a Chinese-owned and operated company in Nanjing for about six months. The division she is working in has a small collection of Chinese-English dictionaries, English language reference books, and some videos in English including a couple of training films and several feature films that Anna brought at her new employer's request when she came from Europe. Anna knows that some of the other sections have similar collections. She has sometimes used her friendship with one of the women in another department, Gu Ming, to borrow English novels and reference books and in return has let Gu Ming borrow books from her section's collection. On other occasions, she has seen friendly, noisy exchanges, where one of the other workers in her division has lent a book or video to a colleague from another section.

Anna thought it was a great idea when a memo was circulated saying that the company's leaders had decided to collect all the English language materials together into a single collection. The plan was to put them in a small room that was currently being used for storage so that all employees could have equal access to them. Now she would no longer have to go from department to department trying to find the materials she needed.

Anna was surprised to hear her co-workers complaining about the new policy. When the young man in charge came to the department to collect their English language materials, she was astounded to see them hiding most of the books and all but one of the videos in their desks. When she checked out the new so-called collection, she found that the few items were all outdated or somehow damaged. She also noticed that none of the materials she had borrowed from Gu Ming were in the collection. She asked her friend why the Chinese were unwilling to share their English language materials with all their co-workers, when they seemed willing to share them within their departments.

📝 Exercise

Listen to the case above and answer the following questions.

(1) What materials did the Anna's division have?

(2) How did Anna manage to find other English language materials apart from her own division?

(3) What was Anna's plan for people to have equal access to English materials?

(4) What was Anna astounded at?

(5) What did Anna find when she checked out on the new collection of English materials?

Unit 12 Culture Shock and Adaptation

◉ INTRODUCTION

● **Knowledge Objective:**

Guide students to master the definition, causes and impacts of cultural shock as well as the four stages of intercultural adaptation.

● **知识目标：**

指导学生掌握文化休克的定义、缘由、影响以及跨文化休克的四个阶段和跨文化调适路径。

● **Ability Objective:**

Guide students to recognize that cultural shock is a new cultural experience and psychological feeling. Guide students to understand the other party as much as possible in handling affairs in order to seek better cooperation. Guide students to overcome cultural prejudices and psychological biases, and treat different cultures equally so as to feel "strange" instead of "surprised" at alien cultures.

● **能力目标：**

指导学生认识到文化休克是一种新的文化体验和心理感受，在交际中尽量理解对方，在认识问题和处理事务方面尽可能达成一致，以寻求与对方更好的合作。引导学生克服文化偏见与心理偏差，以平视的眼光来看待异质文化，做到对异质文化"奇"而不"惊"。

● **Educative Objective:**

Guide students to analyze the report "The Rise of Asian Americans" released by the Pew Research Center in 2013 and think about how to enhance cultural confidence and identity of young overseas Chinese towards fine traditional Chinese culture. Guide students to know that "We should build an open and inclusive world through exchanges and mutual learning. There is no such thing as a superior or inferior civilization, and civilizations are different only in identity and location.

Diversity of civilizations should not be a source of global conflict; rather, it should be an engine driving the advance of human civilizations".

素质目标：

通过分析美国皮尤研究中心 2013 年发布的报告《美国亚裔的崛起》引导学生思考如何提升海外年轻华裔对中国优秀传统文化的文化自信和文化认同，引导学生理解"坚持交流互鉴，建设一个开放包容的世界。文明没有高下、优劣之分，只有特色、地域之别。文明差异不应该成为世界冲突的根源，而应该成为人类文明进步的动力"。

Section A Video Clip Appreciation

I. Introduction to the Movie *English Vinglish*

Shashi Godbole is a homemaker, who makes and sells laddoos as a home-run business. Her husband Satish and daughter Sapna take her for granted, mock her poor English skills, and generally treat her with disrespect, making Shashi feel negative and insecure.

Shashi's older sister Manu, who lives in New York, invites Shashi's family to her daughter Meera's wedding to Kevin. It is decided that Shashi will go to New York alone five weeks before the wedding to help Manu organize. Her husband and children will join her as the wedding approaches. During her flight to New York, Shashi is given inspirational advice by a fellow passenger. While Shashi is in New York, she has a traumatic experience at a cafe due to her inability to communicate in English. She is comforted by a French chef Laurent, who happened to be queuing up behind her at the cafe.

Using the money she made from selling laddoos, Shashi secretly enrolls in a conversational English class that offers to teach the language in four weeks, showing her resourcefulness at navigating an unfamiliar city alone. The class comprises David Fischer, the instructor; Eva, a Mexican nanny; Salman Khan, a Pakistani cab driver; Yu Son, a Chinese hairstylist; Ramamurthy, a Tamil software engineer; Udumbke, a closeted African-Caribbean man; and Laurent. Shashi quickly becomes a promising and committed student, earns everyone's respect with her charming behavior and her cuisine, and gains self-confidence.

Laurent becomes attracted to Shashi. When he tries to kiss her at the rooftop of a building, Shashi rejects him and runs off, but fails to explain that she is married.

Meanwhile, Shashi's niece Radha, who is Meera's younger sister, finds out about her secret English classes and is supportive of her pursuit. Shashi starts watching English films at night and does her homework assiduously. To complete the English-speaking course and get a certificate, each student must write and deliver a five-minute speech. Shashi's family joins her in New York earlier than planned, to surprise her. Shashi tries to continue attending class but decides to quit because of scheduling conflicts. She asks Radha to inform Fischer. The test date coincides with that of the wedding, forcing Shashi to miss the test.

Radha invites Fischer and the entire class to the wedding, where Satish is taken aback at being introduced to a diverse group of people by his wife. Shashi gives a touching and enlightening toast to the married couple in English, surprising everyone who knew her as a typical, conservative, Indian homemaker. In her speech, Shashi extols the virtues of being married and having a family, describing the family as a safe space of love and respect where weaknesses are not mocked. Satish and Sapna regret treating her with disrespect. Fischer declares that she has passed the course with distinction and issues her the certificate. Shashi thanks Laurent for making her feel better about herself. Shashi's family returns to India. During their flight home, Shashi asks the flight attendant in fluent English whether she has any Hindi newspapers.

II. Introduction to the Video Clips

Clip 1

We are learning about the experiences of an Indian woman in New York. Some of these experiences might be similar to what some of you have had, or will have when traveling overseas. The main character, Shashi, is in New York to help with a family wedding. Nevertheless, she comes across an embarrassing situation at a coffee shop simply because she was not able to communicate clearly in English. In other words, she felt humiliated because her English was not understood. The clerk at that coffee shop quickly became quite impatient with her, and as a result, Shashi became very upset. She dropped someone's meal and ran out of the shop as fast as she could while crying desperately. Soon after, a kind Frenchman cheered her up and gave her a coffee from that same coffee shop while letting her know that the clerk over there isn't a nice person. From now on, let's see what Shashi decides to do to overcome her linguistic handicap and make better use of her time in New York. Will she withdraw into a shell by only speaking with others who speak Hindi or will she take the bull by the horn and try to improve her English?

Clip 2

The end of the movie *English Vinglish* leaves a lump in your throat. Every word and every expression of Shashi's speech in the last scene is so balanced. Her transformation from a conscious housewife to a confident entrepreneur becomes clearly evident. Her husband and children have arrived for the occasion, not knowing her secret English lessons. In front of all the guests, Shashi is asked to make a speech to the newlyweds. Shashi stands up and uses her new-found voice to urge the bride and groom to value equality and treat each other with respect. This is one of the most moving and heartfelt wedding speeches in films that brings tears of remorse to her daughter.

III. Script of the Video Clips

Clip 1

[*Lyrics of the song*]

Manhattan.

Touching heaven, oh my god!

Manhattan.

New avenues of joy.

Shops full of dreams.

A new surprise, at every stop.

To your left is Prada.

To your right is Zara.

Giorgio Armani.

Thank God it's Friday!

Gucci and Versace.

Jimmy Choo, Givenchy.

Diesel, Dior, Hokey Pokey, Gap and Bloomingdale's.

Louis Vuitton.

Moschino.

Valentino...

So much to say yet speechless.

All together, still alone.

Video Clip 1

What a city! Touch wood.

5, 6, 7, 8 avenues.

Million billion legs and shoes.

Lots of colors, dollars dollars.

Sense of pidlee poo.

Breakfast is for all day.

Straight and gay they all sway.

Lexington, and Madison, it's all so ooh!

Frappuccino.

Mochaccino.

Cappuccino...

****

Meera: You gotto say balle balle while you do that...

Kevin: Balle balle balle balle!

Meera: Aunty, you're not eating food's not good?

Shashi: This parantha is really good.

Line: It's Mexican food, Quesadilla.

Shashi: Whatever it is. It's good!

Kevin: What's that? What did she say?

Line: She just abused you.

Kevin: So tell me about the dowry. What are you giving me?

Line: What am I giving you? We are not buying you. That's not how it works.

Crowd: The boy gives the girl's family the dowry. And lots and lots of gifts.

Kevin: So I'm going to go broke?

Shashi: I don't know why but I'm really sleepy.

Manu: Go sleep, my dear.

Shashi: Is that alright?

Manu: Yes of course.

Background: I feel so bad... she must be so tired. Must be the jet lag.

Shashi: Hello Satish... how are the kids? Have they gone to school? Have they taken their lunch boxes? Please do try to get home early... I'm feeling a bit strange here... without all of you...

Satish: Shashi... just enjoy yourself... I'm getting into an elevator... will talk later.

Manu: Slept well? Sorry... got to go to office for a bit. I'll try to be back as soon as possible... we'll start on the wedding plans.

Shashi: Drive carefully.

Manu: Bye darling, see you!

Meera: Good morning Aunty!

Shashi: Good morning. Should I make you some breakfast?

Meera: No. I have cereal. What are you going to do by yourself? We do have Zee TV Hindi but... I have an idea, why don't you come with me to college!

Shashi: What will I do there?

Meera: I have class for 2 hours... and you can hang out at a cafe... and I'll come join you.

Meera: You got cash... change?

Shashi: Yes.

Meera: And don't worry. In case you get lost... if you do get lost just call me.

Shashi: Don't worry, go now. The parks here are so beautiful.

Meera: Washington Square Park.

Shashi: Washington... Square... Park...

Meera: Good!

Passenger: Wow... that's a beautiful dress you're wearing!

****

Customer 1: Can I get a regular coffee and a blueberry muffin.

Waitress: Here's your receipt... please pick up your food over there.

Customer 1: Okay... have a nice day.

Waitress: Next! How are you doing today ma'am?

Shashi: I want...

Waitress: I asked how you were doing today.

Shashi: Doing... I'm doing... I'm doing...

Waitress: You can't take all that time. I got a long line here.

Shashi: Sorry... what to eat?

Waitress: Are you kidding me right now? Please hurry up, lady.

Shashi: Vegetarian.

Waitress: Vegetarian is fine. What do you want to eat?

Shashi: Only vegetarian.

Waitress: A bagel, a wrap, a sandwich?

Shashi: Sandwich.

Waitress: Okay. And what kind of filling do you want inside? Do you want cheese, tomatoes, lettuce?

Shashi: Ah?

Waitress: Lady, you're holding up my line. This is not rocket science. Cheese?

Shashi: Yes. Cheese.

Waitress: Yes to cheese! Anything to drink? Water, still or sparkling?

Shashi: Only water.

Waitress: Still or sparkling?

Shashi: Coffee... ?

Waitress: Americano? Cappuccino? Latte?

Customer 2: Lady, I ain't got all day.

Waitress: Americano? Cappuccino? Latte?

Shashi: Nescoffee.

Waitress: What?

Shashi: Nescoffee.

Waitress: Yes we have nice coffee. We have the best coffee in Manhattan. You know... I'll just give you an Americano. Small or medium?

Shashi: Small.

Waitress: Small. Is that it? $10.20.

Shashi: 10 dollars. Sorry. Thank you.

Waitress: Hello. The least you could do is say thank you!

Shashi: Sorry. Thank you.

Customer 3: Stupid idiot!

Shashi: Sorry...

Waitress: I am not cleaning that up!

Customer 4: Don't bother.

Customer 5: What a stupid woman.

Laurent: Madam. Your coffee, from the coffee shop. Cafe not good. Woman... not nice! Okay.

Shashi: Thank you.

Laurent: Bye.

Clip 2

Video Clip 2

Manu: Shashi, it's time for the ceremony.

Manu: To my darling daughter Meera and my dear son Kevin. How I wish Anil was here. When Meera was going through her troubled teens, she was 14. She was only 14 years old when she came in fuming and asked us: Why did you give birth to me? She was so angry with life that she was furious that we gave birth to her without asking for her permission! I will answer that today Meera. You were born so your dad and I could share complete happiness. You were born so you could bring happiness into our lives. I am so sorry I didn't take your permission. Love you both sweethearts! God bless both of you always.

Kevins's Father: Son, you just got lucky! But fortune smiles on those who embrace its offerings. So love each other. And son, leave me and your mother alone! It's time for us to focus on each other.

Meera: Shashi Aunty, your turn.

Crowd: Yes. Come on.

Satish: Sorry, my wife's English is not very good so…

Shashi: May I? Meera, Kevin. This marriage is a… Oops sorry… I started in Hindi. This marriage is a beautiful thing. It is the most special friendship… friendship of two people who are equal. Life is a long journey. Meera, sometimes you will feel you are less. Kevin, sometimes you will also feel you are less than Meera. Try to help each other to feel equal. It will be nice. Sometimes married couple don't even know how the other is feeling. So how they will help the other? It means marriage is finished? No. That is the time you have to help yourself. Nobody can help you better than you if you do that. You will return back feeling equal. Your friendship will return back. Your life will be beautiful. Meera, Kevin, maybe you'll very busy, but have family, son, daughter in this big world, your small little world. It will make you feel so good. Family, family can never be… never be judgemental! Family will never put you down, will never make you feel small. Family is the only one who will never laugh at your weaknesses. Family is the only place where you will always get love and respect. That's all. Meera and Kevin, I wish you all the best. Thank you.

[*Applause*]

David: Well Shashi. You don't "return back," you just return, and you missed a few "a"s and "the"s. else you passed with distinction!

Meera: Shashi Aunty you were amazing! Yes. I'm so proud of you. Do you want me to help?

Shashi: Bring the other tray.

Shashi's Son: Next time you speak in English in front of mama, please think she can talk better than you!

Shashi: David Sir... ladoo!

David: Thank you. I have something for you!

Laurent: Shashi...

Shashi: When you don't like yourself, you tend to dislike everything connected to you. When you learn to love yourself, then the same old life starts looking new, starts looking nice. Thank you for teaching me how to love myself! Thank you for making me feel good about myself. Thank you so much! Ladoo.

Meera: Broke the French heart, didn't you?

Satish: Shashi. Do you still love me?

Shashi: If I didn't, why would I give you two ladoos? And, good choice!

[*Music and dance*]

****

Flight Attendant: What newspaper would you like sir?

Satish: *New York Times* please.

Flight Attendant: And you, ma'am?

Shashi: *The New York*. Sorry, do you have any Hindi newspaper?

Flight Attendant: No, sorry.

Shashi: It's OK. Thank you.

New Words

avenue 林荫大道

dowry 嫁妆

cereal 麦片

blueberry 蓝莓

muffin 小松饼

vegetarian 素食主义者

bagel 百吉饼

lettuce 生菜

still 不起泡的

sparkling（饮料）起泡的

furious 狂怒的

tease 取笑

sneak 溜进

blushing 脸红的

kohl 眼影粉

cappuccino 卡布奇诺咖啡

latte 拿铁咖啡

Phrases and Expressions

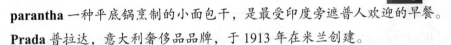

go broke 破产

jet lag 飞行时差反应

hang out 闲逛

Notes

parantha 一种平底锅烹制的小面包干，是最受印度旁遮普人欢迎的早餐。

Prada 普拉达，意大利奢侈品品牌，于 1913 年在米兰创建。

Zara 西班牙服装零售连锁品牌，创建于 1975 年，隶属于印地纺集团（Inditex Group）。该品牌在 87 个国家和地区设有超过两千家连锁店。

Armani 阿玛尼，世界知名奢侈品品牌，1975 年由时尚设计大师乔治·阿玛尼（Giorgio Armani）创立于意大利米兰。该品牌以使用新型面料及制作精良而闻名。

Gucci 古驰，意大利时装品牌，由古驰奥·古驰在 1921 年创办于意大利佛罗伦萨。古驰的产品包括时装、皮具、手表、领带、丝巾、香水、家居用品及宠物用品等。

Versace 范思哲，意大利奢侈品品牌，创立于 1978 年，品牌标志是希腊神话中的蛇发女妖美杜莎（Medusa），代表着致命的吸引力。该品牌产品以鲜明的设计风格、独特的美感和极强的先锋艺术表征风靡全球。

Givenchy 纪梵希，法国的时装品牌，以优美、简洁、典雅的风格著称。最初以香水为其主要产品，后开始涉足护肤及彩妆事业。

Dior 迪奥，法国著名时尚品牌，总部设在巴黎。主要经营服装、首饰、香水、化妆品等高档消费品。

Bloomingdale's 布鲁明戴尔百货店，美国著名的百货商店，成立于 1861 年，是美国梅西百货（Macy's）旗下的连锁商店。该商店气氛与品牌既有年轻化和摩登的一面，也有务实的一面。

Louis Vuitton 路易威登，法国奢侈品牌。自 1854 年以来，路易威登以卓越品质、杰出创意和精湛工艺成为时尚旅行艺术的象征。其产品包括手提包、旅行用品、小型皮具、配饰、鞋履、成衣、腕表、高级珠宝及个性化订制服务等。

IV. Exercises for understanding

1. Decide whether the following statements are true or false according to the video clips you have just watched. Write "T" for true or "F" for false.

_____ (1) In Indian culture, it is usually the men who prepare dowry for weddings.

_____ (2) Shashi could not make her well understood by the waitress in the cafeteria because of her poor English.

_____ (3) From the clip, it could be inferred that Anil was the father of Meera.

_____ (4) Shashi thought that men were superior to women in an Indian family.

_____ (5) Shashi didn't love her husband any more.

2. Put the following sentences in the right order according to the video clips you have just watched.

_____ (1) Shashi felt homesick and phoned her husband for consolation.

_____ (2) A French man comforted Shashi who was reproved by a cafeteria waitress.

_____ (3) Shashi was dazzled by the luxuries, richness and wonder of Manhattan.

_____ (4) Teacher Davie made positive comments on Shashi's English speech about family.

_____ (5) On the plane back to India, Shashi asked the stewardess for a newspaper in Indian language but in vain.

3. Explore interculturally.

(1) What is the first impression of Shashi about Manhattan?

(2) In the eyes of Shashi, what is the real meaning of family?

Section B Reading

Culture Shock

微课

Culture shock is troublesome feelings such as depression, loneliness, confusion, inadequacy, hostility, frustration and tension caused by the loss of familiar cues from the home culture. It is a common experience of people who have been suddenly transplanted abroad.

Reasons for Culture Shock

Then why do people suffer from culture shock? Many reasons bring about culture shock. Some factors including the characteristics of the communicating participants and others are related to the situation to which the participants are trying to adapt. The traditional explanation for the onset of culture shock is somewhat lined with the sorrow people feel after losing their beloved ones. Today, culture shock is mainly due to three reasons: the theory of negative events, the theory of decrease in social support and the theory of different values.

Culture shock results from the anxiety of losing all our familiar signs and symbols of social contact. Those cues or signs include various ways in which we adapt ourselves to the situation of daily life: when to shake hands and what to say when we meet people, when and how to give tips, how to buy things, when to accept and when to refuse invitations, when to take statements seriously and when not. These cues, which may be words, gestures, facial expressions, or customs, are acquired by all of us in the course of growing up and are as much a part of our culture as the languages we speak or the beliefs we accept. All of us defend for peace of mind and our efficiency on hundreds of cues, most of which we do not carry on the level of conscious awareness.

Symptoms of Culture Shock

People experiencing culture shock may undergo a series of uncomfortable changes both physically and mentally. When you have culture shock, you may first have mental discomfort: loneliness, helplessness, anxiety, unease and withdrawal. Then physical discomforts like insomnia, inattentiveness, loss of appetite and headaches may occur. Finally, people may have social stress such as disruption, fragility, indulgence in smoking and drinking, loss of self-confidence, and even overindulgence on others. It is like a fish out of water.

Realize that what you are going through is normal. Remember that the unpleasant feelings are temporary, natural and common to any transition that a person makes during their life. Be patient and give yourself time to work through the process. Keep in touch with your home country. Read newspaper from home, international magazines, etc. Watch international television channels or surf the Internet. Call home regularly. Have familiar things around you that have personal meaning, such as photographs or ornaments. Find a supplier of familiar foods or visit restaurants that are similar to your home cuisine. Take care of yourself. Eat well, exercise, and get enough sleep. Talk to someone. Find friends who are going through a similar process. Call your family back home, or see a counselor. Have fun and relax! Join student groups. Get out and volunteer to help others. Take up a sport. Participate in activities, clubs and student organizations of interest to you. Make a point to join activities that give you the opportunity to share in conversation and express your identity.

Intercultural Adaptation

Culture shock is not that scaring because most people can go through the process of intercultural adaptation. Adaptation is a process with identifiable stages. Learning about the process will not prevent culture shock, but it will help you understand what is happening to you.

Stage One: Honeymoon Phase

There are four stages in the process of intercultural adaptation. In Stage one, which is called honeymoon phase, you have excitement about the new situation. You have a sense of pleasure and self-satisfaction. Except for refugees and others who are being pushed to leave home against their will, most people who go abroad to live temporarily or permanently in a new culture do so willingly. They have some specific purpose in mind such as furthering their education, pursuing economic or professional opportunities, or simply experiencing something new. During this period, nearly everything appears wonderful. The food is exciting; the people seem friendly. Although you may experience some of the symptoms mentioned earlier, such as sleeplessness and mild anxiety, your enthusiasm and curiosity quickly overcome these minor discomforts. The sense of euphoria is so great that some writers call this stage the honeymoon stage.

Stage Two: Crisis/Culture Shock Phase

In Stage two, the crisis/culture shock phase, honeymoon is over. Things have gone sour. After a while, you begin to feel anxious, restless, impatient, and disappointed. You are meeting more people who do not speak your language, and yet your foreign language knowledge has not improved dramatically. You are confused when faced with the hidden aspects of culture. You suffer from frustration when old ways of dealing with situations fail to work. This period of adaptation is marked by a loss of social cues and a time of inconvenience that you had not experienced earlier. The confusion heightens with the unfamiliar smells, sounds, food, and cultural customs. You are angry and homesick. Instead of blaming or doubting yourself, you start to put the blame for the difficulties on the new culture and its people.

Stage Three: Adjustment Phase

Now things begin to get better, and you enter the period of initial adjustment. After several months in the new culture, you may find that you view both the negative and positive in a balanced manner. You finally have learned a lot more about the culture and while you still do not like some things, you now like more than a few months ago. Now everyone is a crook, you think to yourself, and in fact, there are some good folks along with some bad. By now, you have become more accustomed to the food, sights, sounds, smells, and nonverbal behaviors of the new culture. Also, you have few headaches and upset stomach problems and less confusion, uncertainty and loneliness. Your physical health and mental health have improved. Normal contacts with host nationals are increasing, and you do not feel that you must defend yourself. You can accept yourself and others around you. Congratulations! You have just made it through the worst of culture shock.

Stage Four: Adaptation Phase

The fourth stage is the period of acceptance and integration. You pick up a sense of effectiveness as new skills are acquired and are fully ready to have more challenging intercultural experiences. Your efforts pay off. You may improve your language skills and equally important you have growing ability to communicate nonverbally. You know what facial expressions and body movements are called for in most situations. You know what you can say or should say. You are able to make more accurate assessments about what the behavior of the host country people means and you can choose your responses deliberately rather than being overwhelmed by feelings of doubt or anger. Further, you can move beyond effectiveness in the new culture to an attitude of appreciation. You are able to live a full life, experiencing the full range of human feelings in the new culture. You can love, trust, laugh and solve problems, just about everything you can do at home. You are becoming more creative, expressive and able to take initiative and responsibility. A more positive way of moving through this state is to become a culture interpreter who helps others bridge the gap between cultures.

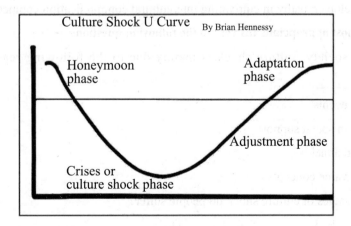

People who have spent considerable time outside their home cultures may experience a similar process when they return to their native countries, although the stages are often shorter and less intense. No one wants to admit that he or she is having difficulty readjusting to the home culture, so the reentry process has often involved people suffering quietly with stress.

In order to adapt to a new culture successfully, we need to develop competence in intercultural communication. The competence of intercultural communication is often evaluated from the cognitive, affective and behavioral perspectives. Related to these three dimensions, knowledge, a willing motivation and a mastery of skills are required to better understand a new culture and effectively adapt to it. Developing empathy is also important. That is being able to see things from the point of view of others so that we can better know and adjust to other people. Doing this, you are suggested that you resist the tendency to judge others' verbal and nonverbal actions from our culture's orientation. Learn to suspend, or at least keep in check, the cultural perspectives that are unique to your experience. Knowing how the frame of reference of other cultures differs from your own will assist you in accurately reading what meaning lies behind words and actions.

📝 Exercises for Understanding

1. Answer the following questions according to the passage you have just read.

(1) What are the reasons for culture shock in today's society?

(2) What are the physical and mental symptoms of culture shock?

(3) According to the passage, how to deal with culture shock properly?

(4) How do people feel in the second period of intercultural adaptation?

(5) How to develop empathy in cultivating intercultural communication competence?

2. Choose the most appropriate answers to the following questions.

(1) In today's society, culture shock is mainly due to the following reasons EXCEPT

_____.

    A. negative events

    B. decrease in social support

    C. emotional attack

    D. different value concepts

(2) How many stages of culture shock do people suffer?

    A. 2   B. 3   C. 4   D. 5

(3) Which stage of intercultural adaptation is a most sour one?

    A. Honeymoon period

    B. Culture shock period

    C. Adjustment period

    D. Adaptation and integration period

(4) Intercultural communication competency is evaluated from the following perspectives EXCEPT _____.

    A. behavioral

    B. affective

    C. physical

    D. cognitive

(5) It is suggested that people develop intercultural communication competency from the following ways EXCEPT _____.

    A. stock up knowledge

    B. enhance physical strength

    C. master relevant skills

    D. develop empathy

3. Decide whether the following statements are true or false according to the passage you have just read. Write "T" for true or "F" for false.

_____ (1) People who are suddenly transplanted abroad are likely to suffer from cultural shock.

_____ (2) People usually tend to defend their familiar cues and seek peace of mind on the level of unconscious awareness.

_____ (3) People endure physical discomfort such as insomnia, loss of appetite, headaches and so on before they suffer from mental uneasiness.

_____ (4) In the third stage of intercultural adaptation, you improve both your verbal and nonverbal communication skills to solve problems.

_____ (5) When returning back to home country after a long time in a foreign culture, people may suffer from reentry shock, although the stages are shorter and less intense.

4. Case study.

    Study the following case and discuss how to arouse and enhance young American Chinese' devotion to China's fine traditional culture.

    The Pew Research Center's 2013 report "The Rise of Asian Americans" pointed out that due to the opening up of the United States to skilled workers and wealthy investors, Asian Americans ranked first among immigrant groups and made significant contributions to the political and economic development of the United States. However, mainstream white people still have prejudice and discrimination against Asian Americans, and cultural clashes still exist. 28% of people say they rarely interact with Asian Americans, leading to the problem of cultural shock among Asian Americans. Therefore, most Asian Americans have begun to reposition their values and social status, gradually giving up their submission to mainstream American culture and establishing their own status, reflecting the awakening of Asian pan-ethnic consciousness.

5. Small group task.

Imagine that you are going to a large urban American university for study. To evaluate your adaptation potential, rate yourself on the Adaptation Checklist below. Give yourself a score for each item according to the following scale.

1—Poor

2—Not as good as most people

3—Average

4—Better than most people

5—Excellent

Adaptation Checklist	
Score	**Adaptation Factors**
	Background and preparation
	Age—youth is an advantage
	Education—the higher the better
	Urban background—city dwellers do better than rural residents
	High level of professional skills
	General knowledge of the new culture: its history, customs, arts, etc.
	Special knowledge of the new situation: company, city, university, etc.
	Oral and written fluency in the language of the new culture
	Previous out-of-culture experiences
	Similarities of home culture to the new culture
	Personality Factors
	Tends to be accepting of different ways of doing things
	Likes to meet new people and do new things

	Stays calm in difficult situations
	Pays attention to people and not just tasks
	Can tolerate ambiguous or uncertain situations
	Has a sense of humor
	Strong but flexible in character
	Willing to take risks; not too concerned about social and psychological security
	Attitudes and Motivation
	Voluntarily chooses to be in contact with the new culture
	Attracted to the new situation rather than escaping problems at home
	Has admission and respect for the new culture
	Does not think that one culture is superior or inferior to another
	Has few stereotypes (inaccurate broad generalizations) about the new culture
	Health
	Has robust good health
	Has good health habits
	Has high energy level
	Total Score

After you have completed the checklist, discuss it with your classmates.

(1) What are your advantages and disadvantages in adapting to a new culture?

(2) What can you do to increase your adaptation potential?

6. Knowledge application.

Talk with a foreigner living in your country about his or her adaptation, the greatest difficulties he or she has met and the strategies he or she uses to overcome difficulties. The following is a chart about Strategies for Coping with Adaptation Stress for your reference.

Strategies for Coping with Adaptation Stress
(1) Do what you can to increase your score on the above cultural adaptation checklist.
• You can't change your age, but you can learn more about your company or city and you can adjust your thinking.
(2) Be alert for signs of adaptation stress.
• Health problems
• Loss of self-confidence

• Loneliness, sense of loss, severe homesickness
• Withdrawal from social contacts
• Negative feelings
• Behaving more aggressively than usual
(3) Tell people at home what kind of support you really need from them.
• You may need freedom to make new decisions and their understanding of the difficulties you face more than their advice.
(4) Use your "retreats" from the new culture constructively.
• Find home culture time and friends to refresh yourself and restore your positive feelings (speak your language, eat familiar food, etc.).
• Look for people from your home country with positive attitudes.
• Don't spend time with people from home who reinforce negative feelings.
(5) Pay attention to differences within the new culture.
• Avoid making broad generalizations about everybody in the host culture.
• Notice differences in background, motivation, personality; some people will be more like you than others.
• Just as you are not like anyone from your culture, so not anyone from the new culture is alike.
• People from the host culture may also be experiencing adaptation stress. When you are sensitive to their adaptation stress, you won't take their responses to you too personally.
(6) Try to find two mentors (experienced helpers).
• Look for someone from your home culture who has more experience in the new culture than you do.
• Look for someone from the new culture with much experience with your culture.
• Consult your mentors to check your interpretations of intercultural events.
• Use your mentors to learn about hidden aspects of the new culture.
(7) Seek out positive experiences within the new culture.
• If you like to watch football, watch football with the people from the new culture.
• If you enjoy music, enjoy it with people from the new culture.
• That is, take your pleasures and relaxing activities into the new culture.
(8) Be tolerant of yourself and others.
• Keep your sense of humor; misunderstandings can turn into funny stories.
• Assume that new culture associates have reasons for their actions even if you don't understand them.
• Recognize that you are leaning cultures as you go through difficult experiences.
• If necessary, adjust your goals and time frame to make them more realistic.
(9) Use your intercultural experiences to increase your skills.
• Notice and imitate the communication styles of the people from the new culture.
• Use concepts from intercultural communication study to interpret your experience and adjust your behavior.

7. Eastern and Western cultures comparing.

The following are observations of the differences in emphasis between Eastern and Western cultures made by an Asian Christian cleric. Do you agree with them? Why or why not?

Eastern Cultures	Western Cultures
Live in "time"	Live in "space"
Value rest and relaxation	Value activity
Passive, accepting	Assertive, confronting
Contemplative	Diligent
Accept what it is	Seek change
Live in nature (part of nature itself)	Live with nature (co-existing with nature)
Want to know meaning	Want to know how it works
Freedom of silence	Freedom of speech
Lapse into meditation	Strive for articulation
Marry first, then love	Love first, then marry
Love is silent	Love is vocal
Focus on considerations of others' feelings	Focus on self-assuredness and own needs
Learn to do with less material assets	Attempt to get more of everything
Ideal: love of life	Ideal: being successful
Honor austerity	Honor achievement
Wealth or poverty: results of fortune	Wealth or poverty: results of enterprise
Cherish wisdom of years	Cherish vitality of youth
Retire to enjoy the gift of one's family	Retire to the rewards of one's work

Section C Case

The Scenario   Scan and Listen

A Peruvian in the United States

Soon after arriving in the United States from Peru, I cried almost every day. I was so tense that I heard without hearing, and this made me feel foolish. I also escaped into sleeping more than twelve hours at a time and dreamed of my life, family, and friends in Lima. After three months of isolating myself in the house and speaking to no one, I ventured out. I then began to have severe headaches. Finally, I consulted a doctor, but she only gave me a lot of drugs to relieve the pain. Neither my doctor nor my teachers ever mentioned the two magic words that could have changed my life: culture shock! When I learned about this, I began to see things from a new point of view and was better able to accept myself and my feelings.

I now realize most of the Americans I met in Lima before I came to the US were also in one of the stages of culture shock. They demonstrated a somewhat hostile attitude toward Peru, which the Peruvians sensed and usually moved from an initally friendly attitude to a defensive, aggressive attitude or to avoidance. The Americans mostly stayed within the safe cultural familiarity of the embassy compound. Many seemed to feel that the difficulties they were experiencing in Peru were specially created by Peruvians to creat discomfort for foreigners. In other words, they displaced their problem of adjustment and blamed everything on Peru.

📝 Exercise

Listen to the case above and answer the following questions.

(1) What's the state of the Peruvian when he first arrived in the United States?

(2) Why did the Peruvian consult a doctor?

(3) How did he change his attitude after learning about culture shock?

(4) Why did Americans choose to stay in the embassy compound when they were in Peru?

(5) Whom did the Americans blame for their discomfort in Peru?

Unit 13 Acculturation and Cultural Identity

● **Knowledge Objective:**

Guide students to master the concepts, strategies, contributing factors, and implementation ways of cultural adaptation and cultural identity.

● **知识目标：**

指导学生掌握文化适应和文化认同的概念、策略、影响因子和实现路径。

● **Ability Objective:**

Guide students to use English as a medium to tell stories of Chinese treasures that feature Chinese spirit, Chinese aesthetics and Chinese values, making it easier for the audience both at home and abroad to understand Chinese culture.

● **能力目标：**

指导学生以英语为载体，介绍国宝背后的中国精神、中国审美和中国价值观，带领中外观众读懂中华文化。

● **Educative Objective:**

Guide students to analyze the third season of *Every Treasure Tells a Story*, which has become a hit and enjoys a reading volume of 600 million on Weibo. Guide students to enhance cultural identity, strengthen cultural confidence and improve global competence and international understanding. Guide students to understand that "Cultural identity is the key link to lifting cultural confidence".

● **素质目标：**

通过分析成为"爆款"的、微博相关话题阅读量高达六亿的《如果国宝会说话》第三季，引导学生增强文化认同，坚定文化自信，提升全球胜任力，增强国际理解和跨文化交际能力。引导学生理解"文化认同是提升文化自信的关键环节"。

Section A Acculturation and Cultural Identity

I. Introduction to the Video *Tenet*

Christopher Nolan's sci-fi spy movie *Tenet* exploded into cinemas in 2020, which is rich, complicated, packed to the rafters with twists, mind-blowing action. A co-production between the United Kingdom and the United States, it stars John David Washington, Robert Pattinson, Elizabeth Debicki, Dimple Kapadia, Michael Caine, and Kenneth Branagh. The plot follows a secret agent as he manipulates the flow of time to prevent World War III.

A CIA agent, the "Protagonist", participates in an undercover operation at a Kyiv opera house. His life is saved by a masked soldier with a red trinket, who "un-fires" a bullet through a hostile gunman. After seizing an artifact, the Protagonist is captured by mercenaries. He endures torture before consuming cyanide. He awakens to learn that the cyanide was a test of his loyalty. His team has been killed, and the artifact lost.

The Protagonist joins a secret organization called Tenet. A scientist shows him bullets with "inverted" entropy, which allows them to move backwards through time. She believes that they are manufactured in the future, and a weapon exists that can wipe out the past. Aided by a local contact Neil, the Protagonist traces the bullets to arms dealer Priya Singh. He discovers that she is a member of Tenet, whose cartridges were purchased and inverted by Russian oligarch Andrei Sator.

The Protagonist approaches Sator's estranged wife Kat, an art appraiser, who authenticated a Goya drawing forged by a man named "Arepo", which Sator thereafter purchased for $9 million from Arepo. Sator uses the drawing to blackmail her and keep her under his control. The Protagonist plots to steal the drawing with Neil from a free port facility in Oslo Airport. There they find a machine, a "turnstile", and fend off two masked men. Priya explains that the turnstile can invert the entropy of objects and people, and the masked men were the same person.

In the Amalfi Coast, Kat introduces the Protagonist to Sator, but learns that the drawing is intact. The three go boating, and Kat attempts to drown Sator, but the Protagonist saves him. The Protagonist offers to help Sator retrieve a case, which, he says, contains Plutonium-241. In Tallinn, the Protagonist and Neil ambush an armored convoy and steal the case, which contains the artifact lost in Kyiv. They are ambushed by an inverted Sator, who holds Kat hostage. The Protagonist gives Sator an empty case, and he retreats. The Protagonist saves Kat but is captured and taken to Sator's warehouse.

The inverted Sator shoots Kat with an inverted round, while the normal Sator demands the location of the artifact. The Protagonist gives him false information. Tenet operatives led by Ives rescue the Protagonist while Sator escapes. The group takes Kat through Sator's turnstile to invert her, reversing the effect of the round. The Protagonist returns to the ambush site and chases Sator. His vehicle is overturned, and Sator sets it on fire. The Protagonist is saved by Ives' team again. Neil reveals that he is a member of Tenet.

The Protagonist and Neil travel back in time to the free port in Oslo. There the Protagonist fights his past self and enters the turnstile to revert himself, followed by Neil and Kat. Priya explains that the artifacts are parts of an "algorithm", which Sator is assembling, capable of catastrophically inverting entropy.

Kat reveals that Sator is dying from pancreatic cancer. He will trigger the algorithm with a dead man's switch, believing that the world should die with him. Kat believes that Sator will kill himself during their vacation, when they were last happy together. The Protagonist, Neil, Kat, and the Tenet forces invert back to that day, so Kat can delay Sator's death, while Tenet secures the algorithm.

Tenet tracks the algorithm to Sator's hometown of Stalsk-12 in Northern Siberia. In a "temporal pincer movement", red team troops move forward in time, while the blue team troops move backward. The Protagonist and Ives are aided by a masked corpse of a blue-team trooper with a red trinket on his backpack after seeing him dying in reverse. In Vietnam, Kat boards Sator's yacht and kills him, as the Protagonist and Ives secure the algorithm.

The Protagonist, Neil, and Ives break up the algorithm and part ways. The Protagonist notices the trinket on Neil's rucksack. Neil reveals that he was recruited by the Protagonist years in the future and that this mission is the end of a long friendship. Priya attempts to have Kat assassinated, but is killed by the Protagonist, who has realized that he is the future mastermind behind Tenet.

II. Introduction to the Video Clip

Once again in Oslo, the Protagonist meets Priya. Priya reveals that in the future, an "Oppenheimer"-like scientist has devised a method to invert half of the earth. The half that is inverted can dominate the world. This scientist divided this technology, known as the "Algorithm", into nine parts. One piece of this "Algorithm" is Plutonium-241.

Aboard a boat that seems to move backward through time, the Protagonist, Neil, and Kat discuss their next move. Neil mentions that Sator has a "dead man's switch". This means that if Sator dies before hiding the Algorithm, its GPS location would be exposed. They believe this "switch" is the sports wristband Sator constantly wears.

At that moment, the Protagonist, Kat, Neil, and Sator are all inverting their way back to a point in the "past". Kat deduces that Sator plans to return to a point 10 days before the present, on Valentine's Day, when he was holidaying with her in Vietnam. Diagnosed with inoperable pancreatic cancer, Sator intends to end his life, taking the whole world down with him.

The trio devises a plan to "return" to February 14th and secure the Algorithm, which is under guard by Sator's men. Sator's intention is to use a bomb to bury the Algorithm at the center of a Soviet city. Kat's mission is to delay Sator in Vietnam, ensuring he doesn't commit suicide before the Protagonist and his team retrieve the Algorithm.

Bidding Kat goodbye, the Protagonist hands her a phone, advising her to call him if she ever feels in danger.

Two teams, one inverted (the blue team) and one moving forward in time (the red team), are airlifted to the Soviet city, encased in blue and red shipping containers respectively. They're set for a large-scale temporal pincer movement, clashing with Sator's forces.

As this ensues, Mahir takes Kat aboard a yacht in Vietnam. Over the radio, Sator confesses to the Protagonist that his only regret is bringing his son into a doomed world. In a fit of rage, Kat kills Sator with a silenced gun and throws his body overboard, preempting the Protagonist's plans.

Underground in the Soviet city, the Protagonist takes down Sator's henchmen. Above ground, Neil drives a Hummer to the Protagonist and Ives' underground location, rescuing them with a winch and securing the Algorithm. Despite Kat's premature assassination of Sator, the bomb safely detonates.

Ives suggests to Neil and the Protagonist that they each take a piece of the Algorithm and hide it anywhere in the world.

In London, the Protagonist intercepts Priya, who is attempting to assassinate Kat. Freed from Sator's clutches, Kat and her son stroll peacefully down a street.

III. Script of the Video Clip

Video Clip

Protagonist: Hello, Priya.

Priya: What's going on? Where is Neil?

Protagonist: Nersing Katherine Barton, who almost died because of you.

Priya: What did I do?

Protagonist: It's what you're going to do. In two days, you're gonna have me dangle plutonium-241 in front of the world's most dangerous arms dealer. Now, I wanna know why.

Priya: You let Sator get hold of 241?

Protagonist: No, I let him get ahold of the algorithm. So tell me about it, Priya.

Priya: It's... It's unique. The scientist to build it took her own life, so she couldn't be forced to make another.

Protagonist: A science in the future?

Priya: Generations from now.

Protagonist: Why does she have to kill herself?

Priya: You're familiar with the Manhattan Project? As they approached the first atomic test, Oppenheimer became concerned that the detonation might produce a chain reaction, engulfing the world.

Protagonist: They went ahead anyway and got lucky.

Priya: Think of our scientist as her generation's Oppenheimer. She devises a method for inverting the world, but becomes convinced that by destroying us, they're destroying themselves.

Protagonist: The grandfather paradox.

Priya: But unlike Oppenheimer, she rebels, splitting the algorithm into nine sections and hiding them the best place she can think of.

Protagonist: The past. Here, now.

Priya: There are nine nuclear powers. Nine bombs. Nine sets of the most closely guarded materials in the history of the world. The best hiding place possible.

Protagonist: Nuclear containment facilities.

Priya: Sator's lifelong mission, financed and guided by the future, has been to find and reassemble the algorithm.

Protagonist: Why do they choose them?

Priya: Because he was at the right place at the right time.

Protagonist: The collapse of the Soviet Union.

Priya: The most insecure moment in the history of nuclear weapons.

Protagonist: How many sections does he have?

Priya: After the 241, all nine.

Protagonist: Jesus Christ. And that's why you're going to do things differently this time.

Priya: To change things? So Katherine won't get hurt?

Protagonist: So Sator won't get the algorithm.

Priya: If that universe can exist... we don't live in it.

Protagonist: Well, let's try. You're going to warn me.

Priya: No, I'm not. Ignorance is our ammunition.

Protagonist: Come on.

Priya: If you had known what the algorithm was, would you have let it fall into Sator's hands?

Protagonist: You want Sator to get the last section.

Priya: That is the only way he'll bring together the other eight.

Protagonist: I was supposed to steal it and then lose it?

Priya: Mission accomplished.

Protagonist: You used me.

Priya: As you used Katherine. Standard operating procedure. You've done your part.

Protagonist: My part? I'm the protagonist of this operation.

Priya: You... are a protagonist. Did you think you were the only one capable of saving the world?

Protagonist: No. But I am. Because I haven't told you where he's assembling the algorithm or when.

Priya: You're about to.

Protagonist: No, I'm not. So deal us in.

Priya: "Us"? Why would you want to involve her again?

Protagonist: Because she can get close to him.

Priya: Does he still trust her?

Protagonist: He thinks she's dead. But he used to.

Priya: You have started looking at the world in a new way.

Protagonist: And now it's your turn. Assuming she makes it out alive, whether or not you feel she knows too much.

Priya: I can't.

Protagonist: If you don't have the authority, then talk to whoever in charge of loose ends. I need your word that she and her son will be safe, Priya.

Priya: What good is someone's word in our line of business? They'll be safe. There's a rally point offshore at Trondheim. Get yourselves up there. Ives has a team ready to invert.

Protagonist: You have a turnstile? The exact technology that we're trying to suppress.

Priya: Fighting fire with fire's a treacherous business. But there are some people, in the future, who want to continue the algorithm's journey into the past. You see... Tenet wasn't founded in the past. It will be founded in the future.

****

Kat: Can't get over the birds.

Protagonist: How're you feeling?

Kat: Tell me you're gonna kill him.

Protagonist: I can't.

Kat: Why not? Bet you've probably killed a lot of people.

Neil: Not with a dead man's switch.

Protagonist: The fitness tracker he wears.

Kat: He's obsessive about his health.

Neil: It'll be linked to a switch, probably a simple e-mail burst that reveals the location of the dead drop. Set to fire if his heart stops.

Protagonist: His death activates the algorithm. He dies, the world ends. No one dares kill him.

Kat: No, you've missed the point. He is intending to end his life.

Protagonist: Why?

Kat: He's dying. Inoperable pancreatic cancer.

Protagonist: And he's taking the world with him.

Kat: If he can't have her, no one can.

Neil: He gets to choose the time and place for the end of the world. What moment? What does he choose?

Protagonist: You told me about a holiday where you let him feel loved.

Kat: Vietnam.

Protagonist: You said he vanished. What day?

Kat: I went ashore with Max, and he flew off, but I don't know what day it was.

Neil: It was the 14th. Ten days ago. He was in Ukraine.

Protagonist: At the Kiev opera siege. How do you know about that?

Neil: The point is, he wasn't on his yacht, so that's his window.

Kat: To go back to that golden moment and have it be his last.

Protagonist: Everyone's last. We have to lift the algorithm from the dead drop without Sator knowing. If he believes it's there, he kills himself.

Neil: And not the rest of us. Where's the dead drop?

Protagonist: Knowledge divided, my friend.

Neil: You're not gonna tell me?

Protagonist: Ignorance is our ammunition. But I need you back on that yacht, Kat.

Kat: Why?

Protagonist: You have to stop him killing himself until we know the algorithm is out of the dead drop.

Kat: But if I'm caught there, my son sees. I don't want those moments to be full of anguish if they're gonna be his last.

Protagonist: They are not.

Ives: It's time. We're working our way back to the 14th, but without knowing where the dead drop is. There's so much I can do to prepare.

Protagonist: You know what a hypocenter is? It's ground zero for an underground nuclear test. Sir Michael Crosby told me about a detonation in Stalsk-12 on the 14th. The dead drop is at the bottom of the hypocenter. That explosion seals up the algorithm.

Ives: Well, then we better pull it out of that hole before the bomb goes off, eh?

A male's voice: Line it up. Move forward. Next. Line it up.

Kat: Where's Neil?

Protagonist: He must've gone through already.

Kat: I didn't get to say goodbye. This is goodbye, isn't it?

Protagonist: I'd like to say... that you don't have to do this, Kat.

Kat: Worst thing Andrei ever did to me was that offer he made me. Let me go if I agreed never to see my son again. I shouted and ... swore. But he'd seen it on my face, just for an instant. I considered it. I don't know if I hate him more for what he's done, or because he knows that about me. A chance to help save my child. You can't know what that means to a mother.

Protagonist: No.

Kat: You've killed people you've hated before.

Protagonist: It's not usually personal.

Kat: Well, he's dying anyway. Maybe it doesn't even count.

Protagonist: It always counts, Kat. You're not there to kill him, you're the backstop. If we don't lift that algorithm and he kills himself, he takes us all with him.

Kat: You just keep up your end, okay?

Protagonist: Today is the 14th. Offshore of Siberia. Time for us to go. You keep going back another day; give you some time to get back into Vietnam.

Kat: And who gets me on the yacht?

Protagonist: I've got somebody good lined up. When it's over, when you're raising your boy, carry this. There may be a time and place you feel threatened. Hit "talk", state your location, hang up.

Kat: Who gets the message?

Protagonist: Posterity.

****

Ives: Stalsk-12, hidden from the world, is a city where anything can happen. And today, ladies and gents, for ten minutes, it most assuredly does. You've been divided into two teams for temporal pincer movement. We're Red Team, moving forward. In order to distinguish the teams, you'll wear these. Our friends over there, Blue Team, led by Command Wheeler, are inverted.

Soldier A: Why don't they let us see them?

Soldier B: Maybe we won't like what happened.

Ives: One hour from now, they had this briefing. Then we drop down on the ridge above the hypocenter, as close in time to the detonation as possible. Their objectives were clearance and clarification. This briefing has the benefit of their experience. Both teams have countdown watches. Ours count down from ten, from landing to zero to the explosion. Blue Team is reversed.

Wheeler: Everybody look to your left. If you are not at the LZ at zero, you are not leaving. Do you understand?

Ives: We drop in. Clear LZs for Blue Team evacuation. We make our way into the city proper. These buildings are abandoned, but we learned there is a turnstile. Expect a bitemporal response.

Red Soldier 1: They'll have inverse ordinance?

Ives: Inverse, conventional, forward antagonist, inverted antagonists, they have it all. On the other side of the city, the ground rises to the ridge above the hypocenter. A splinter unit will take this tunnel from the city to the floor of the hypocenter. Blue Team located an entrance here. The bomb is in this rock, high above, to trigger a collapse, sailing the cavern.

Blue Soldier 1: How do we defuse the bomb up there?

Ives: We don't. The explosion takes place as planned. Now, our job is to fail to defuse that bomb while splinter unit achieves its task on undetected.

Soldier X: Which is?

Ives: Need-to-know, and you don't. Any other stupid questions? Good. Well, let's go. Let's get ready.

Protagonist: I wanted to be on the first wave.

Ives: There is no first wave. Red Team and Blue Team operate simultaneously. Look, don't get on the chopper if you can't stop thinking in linear terms. Now, you wanna be on the team that lifts the contents of the capsule?

Protagonist: Absolutely.

Ives: Yeah, that's us. We're splinter unit.

Protagonist: Just us?

Ives: No one knows the contents of that capsule can leave the field. I thought we'd manage ourselves.

Mahir: It's 40 feet from the private deck to the water. Can you jump in?

Kat: I can dive it.

Mahir: Until you see my signal, you don't let him die.

Ives: Thirty seconds! Go! Go! Go!

Wheeler: We're coming in on a shockwave. Hang on, people. On your feet.

Someone in Blue Team: There.

Steward: Ma'am. We thought you'd gone ashore.

Kat: Well, I snuck back to surprise Andrei.

Steward: Oh, the boss left.

Kat: Well, have Mr. Sator find me here. And don't tell the others. I'll get the mess.

Someone in the Team: Mines! Mines!

Andrei Sator: They told me you'd gone ashore.

Kat: They told me you'd flown off.

Andrei Sator: I came back to see you and Max.

Kat: Max is on shore with Anna. We need time, just you and me, after what happened.

Andrei Sator: I was joking. It was a stupid joke

Kat: You think I'm a terrible mother.

Andrei Sator: We both know my opinion of you is higher than yours of me.

Kat: I want things to be better, Andrei.

[*Voices from the Battleground*]

Take cover!

Get me a goddam AT4!

Take him out, now!

Provide some cover!

Move, move, move! Let's go!

Move, move, move!

Wheeler! Get out here!

Wheeler: Come on!

Ives!

Splinter unit. Here.

Andrei Sator: You know, it's going to be a beautiful sunset. I'll get Max brought back. We should share the moment with him.

Kat: I'll make you a drink.

Andrei Sator: Bring my son back to the boat.

Ives: We're running out of time. Let's go!

Protagonist: If they see us, it's all for nothing. We need a distraction.

Protagonist: Don't worry about that.

Wheeler: On my mark! PRG, hit the base! That building on my mark!

Protagonist: Three! Two!

Wheeler: One! Fire! Fire! Move, move. We're committed now. Come on.

Kat: What's that?

Andrei Sator: I borrowed it from the CIA.

Kat: What is it?

Andrei Sator: The way the world ends. Not with a bang, but a whimper.

Kat: I don't understand.

Andrei Sator: When I take this, it's all over.

Kat: Then don't take it yet.

Andrei Sator: Why not?

Kat: Because we have the sunset coming. And a little Vodka left.

Andrei Sator: And Max will be here soon. They said they thought it was you, not Anna, ashore with Max.

Kat: So as long as you can tell the difference.

Andrei Sator: A moment's business, my love.

Protagonist: Machir, do you copy? Not clear, I repeat, not clear!

Machir: Copy that.

Protagonist: I repeat, not clear!

Wheeler: Neil! Neil! Go!

Protagonist: We don't have anything big enough to blow this. Try him. See if he's got a grenade. Anything? Nah, nothing. Here, you try having a look. Can you pick it?

Andrei Sator: I hope not. I paid a lot for that lock. How do you like where my journey began and yours ends?

Protagonist: Little radioactive for my taste.

Andrei Sator: My fate was always bound up with radiation. We'd work where no one else would. I made a bargain with the devil. Money for time. We sold our futures.

Protagonist: And now you're about to make the same mistake for the entire world.

Andrei Sator: It wasn't the mistake. I made the bargain I could. What was yours? You fight for a cause you barely understand with people you trust so little; you've told them nothing. When I died, the world dies with me. And your knowledge dies with you, buried in a tomb like an anonymous Egyptian builder, sealed in a pyramid to keep you secret. Your faith is blind. You're a fanatic.

Protagonist: What's more fanatical than trying to destroy the world?

Andrei Sator: I'm not. I'm creating a new one. Somewhere, sometime, a man in a crystalline tower throws a switch. And Armageddon is both triggered and avoided. Now time itself switches direction. The same sunshine we basked in will warm the faces of our descendants generations to come.

Protagonist: How could they wanna kill us?

Andrei Sator: Because their oceans rose and their rivers ran dry. Don't you see? They have no choice but to turn back. We're responsible. Knowing this, do you still want me to stop?

Protagonist: Yes. Each generation looks out for its own survival.

Andrei Sator: That's exactly what they're doing.

Protagonist: But not you. You are a traitor, bringing death to all, because you have no life.

Andrei Sator: When I'm done life continues.

Protagonist: Not your son's.

Andrei Sator: My greatest sin was to bring a son into a world I knew was ending. You think God will forgive me?

[*Voices from the Battleground*]

Wait!

God...

Cover me!

Go! Go! Go!

Protagonist: You don't believe in God, or a future, or anything outside, of your own experience.

Andrei Sator: The rest is belief. And I don't have it.

Protagonist: Without it, you're not human. You're just a madman.

Andrei Sator: Or a God.

Protagonist: Don't. Jesus.

Andrei Sator: Our time is up. I'll give your love to my wife.

Protagonist: You're forgetting I haven't met her yet.

Andrei Sator: That's right. After you meet her, she dies. I'll just give her my love instead.

Volkov… shoot him in the head.

Kat: Enough business, my love.

Andrei Sator: You have no idea what I'm talking about, do you?

Kat: But it sounds terribly important.

Andrei Sator: Where are you going?

Kat: Aren't you hot?

Andrei Sator: What are you doing now?

Kat: I spilled sunscreen.

Andrei Sator: So what?

Kat: Slippery.

Andrei Sator: Just come here.

Kat: Turn over. You will like it.

Kat: I can't do this. I can't let you think you've won.

Andrei Sator: Don't spoil this moment, Kat.

Kat: I'm not letting you go to your grave thinking we're coming with you. You're dying alone, Andrei.

Protagonist: Come on, Come on, Come on.

Protagonist: Tunnel's sealed, gate's closed. Mahir, do you copy?

Mahir: Yeah.

Protagonist: Hold, I repeat, hold!

Kat: Look in my eyes. What do you see? Despair or anger? I'm not the woman who could find love for you even though you scarred on the inside. I'm the eventual bitch you scarred on the outside.

Andrei Sator: No!

Mahir: Shit!

Mahir: Ives, she's killed him. lves, do you copy? She's killed him.

lves: She jumped the gun. She killed him.

Come on, Come on. Do you think they made it?

Neil: Ah, screw it.

Neil: Kat! You jumped the gun!

Kat: I couldn't do it. I couldn't let him die thinking he'd won. I knew you'd find a way. Wait, you found a way, we're okay, right?

Neil: Yeah, found a way. Be safe.

****

Protagonist: Thought you were inverted.

Neil: Changed gears halfway. Looked like you needed help here.

Ives: Here? We needed help down there. How'd you get that lock open?

Protagonist: Wasn't me. Didn't your team need you?

Neil: I'll get'em on the next pass. All right, Ives?

Ives: Once I've caught my breath.

Protagonist: No one who's seen this leaves the field.

Ives: All right. We hide it. We end our lives. That's the only way to be sure. As to when, maybe that's every man's decision to make for himself.

Neil: You're not gonna kill us?

Ives: If I ever find you, I will.

Neil: But you won't look too hard.

Ives: Yes, I will.

Neil: You're not going back to London to check on Kat, are you?

Protagonist: No, it's far too dangerous.

Neil: Even from afar?

Protagonist: Even from afar.

Neil: Ives! Wait!

Protagonist: Are you really going back in?

Neil: I'm the only one who could've got that door open in time, right, Ives?

Ives: Well, I don't know any locksmiths as good as you.

Neil: See? It's me in there again, weaving another past in the fabric of this mission.

Protagonist: Neil, wait!

Neil: Just save the world. Can't leave anything to chance.

Protagonist: But can we change things if we do it differently?

Neil: What's happened's happened, which is an expression of faith in the mechanics of the world. It's not an excuse to do nothing.

Protagonist: Fate?

Neil: Call it what you want.

Protagonist: What do you call it?

Neil: Reality. Now let me go.

Protagonist: Hey, you never did tell me who recruited you, Neil.

Neil: Haven't you guessed by now? You did. Only not when you thought. You have a future in the past. Years ago for me. Years from now for you.

Protagonist: You've known me for years?

Neil: For me, I think it's the end of a beautiful friendship.

Protagonist: But for me, it's just the beginning.

Neil: We get up to some stuff. You're gonna love it. You'll see. This whole operation's a temporal pincer.

Protagonist: Whose?

Neil: Yours! You're any halfway there. I'll see you at the beginning, friend.

Protagonist: We're the people saving the world from what might have been. World will never know what could have happened. And even if they did, they wouldn't care. 'Cause no one cares about the bomb that didn't go off. Only the one that did.

****

Priya: Do it before the boy comes out.

Protagonist: That's your idea of mercy? You gave me your word.

Priya: And I told you then what it would be worth. Here, today, how did you know?

Kat: Cannon Place 3: 00. Probably nothing，I'm…

Kat: Posterity, Cannon Place 3: 00. Probably nothing, I'm…

Protagonist: I told you you'd have to start looking differently at the world.

Priya: I have to tie up to loose ends.

Protagonist: That was never your job.

Priya: Then whose was it?

Protagonist: Mine. I realized I wasn't working for you. We've both been working for me. I'm the Protagonist.

Priya: Then you'd better tie up those loose ends.

Protagonist: Mission accomplished.

It's the bomb that didn't go off. The danger no one knew was real. That's the bomb with the real power to change the world.

New Words

dangle 诱惑某人

plutonium 钚（放射性元素）

algorithm 演算机

detonation 爆炸

engulf 吞噬

devise 发明

invert 逆转，反转

paradox 悖论

containment 控制，遏制

reassemble 重新组装

ammunition 弹药

rally 集合

turnstile 逆转门

treacherous 危险的

inoperable 无法治愈的

pancreatic 胰脏的

siege 包围，围攻

anguish 痛苦

hypocenter 震源

backstop 逆止器

posterity 后代，子孙

pincer 钳子，钳形

briefing 简报

bitemporal 双颞的

antagonist 对手

splinter 碎片

defuse 拆除（炸弹）引信

capsule 容器

whimper 呜咽，悄然一声

cause 使命

seal 封存

fanatic 极端分子，疯子

crystalline 水晶的

Armageddon 世界末日

scar 留下疤痕

Phrases and Expressions

get hold of 获得

Notes

Ukraine 乌克兰

Kiev 基辅，乌克兰首都

Oppenheimer 奥本海默，美籍犹太裔物理学家

Siberia 西伯利亚，北亚地区的一片广阔地带

IV. Exercises for understanding

1. Decide whether the following statements are true or false according to the video clip you have just watched. Write "T" for true or "F" for false.

_____ (1) Sator didn't know that he had pancreatic cancer.

_____ (2) Mahir took Kat aboard a yacht in Vietnam where she and Sator enjoyed the Valentine holiday.

_____ (3) Kat killed Sator in time as arranged by the trio.

_____ (4) Ives saved Neil and the Protagonist by driving a Hummer which dragged them out of the underground with the winch.

_____ (5) Priya kept her promise not to kill Kat.

2. Put the following sentences in the right order according to the video clip you have just watched.

_____ (1) Two teams launched a temporal pincer movement against Sator's forces.

_____ (2) The Protagonist talked with Priya about the grandfather paradox.

_____ (3) Priya went to London and tried to have Kat assassinated.

_____ (4) The Protagonist, Ives and Neil finally secured the Algorithm.

_____ (5) The Protagonist told Kat to give him a phone call if she ever felt danger.

3. Explore interculturally.

(1) Why doesn't the Protagonist have a real-name identity?

(2) How do you understand Neil's pet phrase "What's happened is happened"?

Section B Reading

What Is Acculturation?

Acculturation refers to the process that occurs when groups of individuals of different cultures come into continuous first-hand contact, which changes the original culture patterns of either or both groups. The encounter causes cultural diffusion of varying degrees and may have one of three possible outcomes: (1) acceptance, when there is assimilation of one group into the other; (2) adaptation, when there is a merger of the two cultures; and (3) reaction, which results in antagonistic contra-acculturative movements.

Acculturation is a concept that applies to individuals' living in communities other than where they were born, such as immigrants, refugees, and asylum seekers. It does not apply to groups whose ancestors were subjected to involuntary subjugation in their own land, such as Native Americans, or to individuals whose ancestors were brought to the United States by force and subjugation, such as African Americans. Today more than ever before acculturation has become a relevant concept as a result of the phenomenon of globalization, which defines the sociocultural climate of the 21th century.

Globalization occurs when there is an acceleration of movement of people, products, and ideas between nations. It is characterized by an increase in fluidity between the financial and political borders between countries, which in turn increases the complexity of everyday problems that are faced by inhabitants of countries. Another important aspect of globalization is the increase of migration in the last decades, predominantly from poor countries to more developed ones.

As a result of migration, many societies become culturally plural. People of many cultural backgrounds come to live together in a diverse society. In many cases they form cultural groups that are not equal in power and the variety is primarily due to voluntariness, mobility, and permanence.

Four Typical Acculturation Strategies

How to acculturate? A conceptual framework is generated which posits four acculturation strategies. The best known model was developed by John W. Berry, and is composed of four acculturation strategies. From the view of non-dominant groups, when individuals do not wish to maintain their cultural identity and seek daily interaction with other cultures, the **assimilation** strategy is defined. When individuals place a value on holding on to their original culture, and at the same time wish to avoid interaction with others, then the **separation** alternative is defined. When there is an interest in both maintaining one's original culture, while in daily interactions with other groups, **integration** is the option. Finally, when there is little possibility or interest in cultural maintenance, and little interest in having relations with others, then **marginalization** is defined.

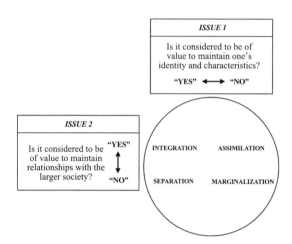

Berry's research with various immigrant groups shows that integration is the preferred mode of acculturation, followed either by assimilation or separation, while marginalization is the least preferred mode. However, it is obvious that individuals and groups do not have complete freedom to choose their particular strategy for acculturation, since the "choice" of strategy largely depends on how the dominant society responds to the acculturation group. For example, integration can only be freely chosen and successfully pursued by acculturating individuals or groups when the dominant society is open and inclusive in its orientation towards cultural diversity. Thus, a mutual accommodation is required for integration to be attained. This is why acculturation, unlike adaptation, results in changes in the host culture as well.

What Is Identity?

In childhood, from the age of 3 to 4 years old, children are already capable of detecting differences in language use, and between 4 and 8 years of age children develop a sense of ethnic identity. They identify as members of a particular ethnic group, consolidate a sense of group identity, and develop curiosity about other groups that are different from their own.

Identity formation has been historically viewed as one of the principal tasks of the passage into adulthood. Identity is a synthesis of personal, social, and cultural self-conceptions, which has been divided into: (1) personal identity, which refers to the goals, values, and beliefs that the individual adopts and holds; (2) social identity, which refers to the interaction between the personal identity and the group with which one identifies; and (3) cultural identity, which refers to the sense of solidarity with the ideas, attitudes, beliefs, and behaviors of the members of a particular cultural group.

How about Cultural Identity?

Cultural identity is a rich tapestry of an individual's life experiences, race, nationality, heritage, beliefs, language, customs and worldview. Understanding and celebrating cultural identity can boost pride and self-esteem. In an increasingly diverse society and interconnected global world, awareness of cultural identity is essential to effective intercultural communication. Cultural identity is at the forefront of discussions in education, politics, medicine, social policy, businesses and international relations.

Cultural identity is not just defined by an ethnic group or culture with which you identify. It also consists of racial, religious, class, gender, sexuality, socioeconomic status, familial identities, to name a few. Additionally, national, social and personal identities also contribute to one's cultural identity. Each person has multiple identities that intersect and shape their view of the world.

Throughout history, cultural identity differences spark tensions. For example, in early America, Caucasians and Africans co-existed in owner-slave relationships where Africans were viewed as uncivilized. The World War II involved the holocaust where Nazi troops killed over 6 million Jewish people because the Germans felt they were "racially superior". Even today there are conflicts between Catholics and Protestants in Ireland and in France the fight to prevent females who follow Islamic beliefs from wearing burkas continues.

Cultural identity development can help people withstand oppression and be motivated to support social transformation. One way to work toward understanding cultural identity is to ask and answer questions instead of shying away from issues. Diversity education is being offered in schools, workplaces and communities to teach tolerance and acceptance around the world.

What Can Be Done?

In order to reduce identity conflict, it is helpful to try to negotiate some compromises among different cultural identities. It is often recognized that travelers and immigrants may not only be influenced by the host culture, but also largely retain their cultural values or, alternatively, develop an entirely new, expanded identity that transcends either the original cultural identity or the identity of the host culture.

The term "intercultural identity" refers to the perfect negotiation of cultural identities. Intercultural identity assumes an open-ended, adaptive, and transformative "self-other" orientation. The term involves two key elements—individuation and universalization in self-other orientation. Individuation involves both a clear self-definition and the definition of "other" as a singular individual rather than a member of a conventional social category. In this capacity, one is better able to see oneself and others in terms of unique individual qualities rather than group stereotypes. This element of individuation is significant, given the fact that the greatest error potential in intercultural communication lies in the overgeneralization about cultural individuals or groups.

The other element, universalization, focuses on the universal aspect of human nature, which will enable people to see the common humanity that exists across different cultures and to observe their common features, even among the points of difference. As people advance in the process of identity transformation, they are able to adopt vital outlook that rises above the provincial interests of one's own group membership. Instead, the individual sees himself or herself to be a part of a larger whole that includes other groups, as well. In fact, this element of intercultural identity helps us be more tolerant of all kinds of cultures and ethnicities.

In conclusion, intercultural identity assumes a more open, flexible and inclusive mindset towards both ourselves and others. Changing cultural identities is not an act of "surrendering" one's personal and cultural integrity, but an act of cultural respect for differences. This process will lead us to function more appropriately and effectively as we engage in intercultural communication in our rapidly globalizing world.

A Case in Point

Ives, a 17-year-old Haitian adolescent, was sent away by his family to a prestigious boarding school in the Midwest United States, to protect him from violence and the possibility of being kidnapped in Haiti. His father occupied an important government position on the island and the family belonged to the mulatto aristocratic class. Ives was unable to adapt or fit in at the school. He complained that his peers "were not used to dealing with an educated black person and didn't know what to do with me," and that they talked down to him and treated him with fear and contempt. He added that he could not find anything in common with the American blacks who attended the school, most of whom came from poor families, had come from the adjacent urban ghettos, and were studying on scholarship. Ives became depressed and suicidal at the school and eventually moved to Miami, where he began residing with extended family and attending day school. At this time, Ives was also seen in weekly psychotherapy. Immediately, he began to question his Hispanic male therapist about the perceptions his therapist had of him, given that both were of a different culture and race, and together they were able to explore his emotional pain, his sense of alienation, and his fears of rejection. Ives slowly became aware that sometimes he presented with a hostile attitude toward others, which was a defense against the anticipation of being rejected, and realized that this attitude kept people away from him. Slowly, Ives became less defensive and together with his therapist began discussing Haitian culture and history. Ives also developed an interest in the short stories of Haitian folk author Edwidge Danticat, which he described and discussed during the therapy sessions. One day, after several months in psychotherapy, he told his therapist, "I had never given much thought to the fact that I'm black until I came to the United States. I have now discovered that I am 'Black and Haitian'. I feel proud of my heritage, because Haiti was the first free Black Republic in the world. Now I feel more Haitian than ever, and in Miami I have found enough people that are like me. Yet, I am also beginning to feel like an 'American'. I consider that the United States is my home and I have no interest in ever going back to live in Haiti." In the therapy, and with the help of the supportive community of compatriots in Miami, Ives was able to discover new aspects of his ethnicity and culture of origin; these identity fragments became integrated into a new, richer, and more cohesive sense of self. In turn, this allowed him to successfully integrate to his new peer group, which included adolescents of various ethnic origins and nationalities.

📝 Exercises for Understanding

1. Answer the following questions according to the passage you have just read.

(1) What is acculturation, and how does it occur when different cultural groups come into contact?

(2) Explain the three possible outcomes of acculturation and provide examples of each.

(3) How does globalization contribute to the relevance of the concept of acculturation in the 21st century?

(4) What are the four acculturation strategies proposed by John W. Berry, and what factors influence the choice of these strategies?

(5) Define cultural identity and its components. How does understanding cultural identity contribute to effective intercultural communication?

2. Choose the most appropriate answers to the following questions.

(1) How does migration contribute to cultural diversity in societies?

A. Migration primarily leads to the dominance of a single culture.

B. Migration does not significantly impact cultural diversity.

C. Cultural groups of various backgrounds come together due to migration.

D. Migration only occurs between countries with similar cultural backgrounds.

(2) Which of the following acculturation strategies involves individuals' maintaining their original culture while engaging in daily interactions with other cultural groups?

A. Assimilation

B. Separation

C. Integration

D. Marginalization

(3) At what age do children typically develop a sense of ethnic identity?

A. Around 3 to 4 years old

B. Between 4 and 8 years old

C. During adolescence

D. In early adulthood

(4) What is the main concept of "intercultural identity"?

A. It emphasizes the superiority of one's own culture.

B. It promotes the rejection of cultural diversity.

C. It focuses on maintaining traditional cultural boundaries.

D. It involves skillful negotiation of cultural identities and an adaptive approach.

(5) How did Ives' experience with psychotherapy and exploration of his cultural identity affect him?

A. He became more defensive and isolated.

B. He felt disconnected from his heritage.

C. He developed a negative attitude toward his therapist.

D. He integrated various aspects of his identity for a richer sense of self.

3. Decide whether the following statements are true or false according to the passage you have just read. Write a "T" for true or an "F" for false.

_____ (1) Acculturation is the process that occurs when individuals of the same culture come into contact.

_____ (2) Cultural pluralism is a result of migration and leads to a diverse society.

_____ (3) Marginalization is the preferred mode of acculturation according to Berry's research.

_____ (4) "Intercultural identity" involves open-ended, adaptive, and transformative orientation.

_____ (5) Ives felt a connection with American blacks who came from ghettos and poor families.

4. Case study.

Study the third season of *Every Treasure Tells a Story*, which has become a hit and enjoys a reading volume of 600 million on Weibo and discuss how to enhance cultural identity and strengthen cultural confidence.

Section C   Case

Scan and Listen

The Scenario

Goodnight Kiss

Xiaohong is a graduate student in China and over the last few weeks, she has become friends with Mark, a Western student who is studying Chinese at her university. They have a number of friends in common, so they often see each other at various social gatherings. They enjoy talking to each other and have gotten to know each other fairly well.

Last weekend Mark asked Xiaohong if she would like to see a movie with him. Xiaohong said yes, so they had dinner and saw a movie together. After the movie, they talked for a long time as they walked home. When it was time to say goodnight, Mark first took Xiaohong's hand and then he kissed Xiaohong. Xiaohong was a little surprised when he kissed her, but she was not unhappy because she likes him quite a bit.

Now Xiaohong has started to tell people that Mark is her boyfriend. However, when

Xiaohong told one of her Chinese girlfriends about all of this, the girlfriend said that Westerners are very casual about relationships between men and women. The goodnight kiss can mean that Mark has fallen in love with Xiaohong and wants to have a more serious relationship. Or Mark was moved more by the romance of the moment than by any deeper feelings, and he doesn't know for sure himself how he feels about Xiaohong. It is also possible that Mark's interest in Xiaohong is more superficial. Perhaps he just finds Xiaohong physically attractive or he is lonely in China and enjoys Xiaohong's company. In order to sort things out, Xiaohong can consider talking to Mark about their relationship. Talking about a romantic relationship in this way may seem somewhat awkward and difficult—even for Westerners—but it will help Xiaohong get a better understanding of what Mark thinks about the relationship.

Exercise

Listen to the case above and answer the following questions.

(1) How did Xiaohong and Mark get along with each other in the beginning?

(2) What happened to Xiaohong and Mark last week?

(3) How did Xiaohong interpret the goodnight kiss?

(4) According to Xiaohong's girlfriend, what are the possible implications of Westerners' goodnight kiss?

(5) What can Xiaohong do to figure out the genuine meaning of Mark's goodnight kiss?

Module 6

Contexts of Intercultural Communication

Unit 14 Intercultural Communication in Business Context

● **Knowledge Objective:**

Guide students to master intercultural communication strategies in business context.

● **知识目标：**

指导学生掌握商务语境中的跨文化交际策略。

● **Ability Objective:**

Guide students to use different business strategies for effective communication in different business contexts.

● **能力目标：**

指导学生在不同的商务语境下使用不同的商务策略进行有效交际。

● **Educative Objective:**

Guide students to analyze why Shanghai Disneyland is known as the "Disney of China" and how China has overcome cultural differences and successfully built the Mombasa-Nairobi Railway in Kenya. Guide students to realize that in addition to language barriers, intercultural communication conflicts along "the Belt and Road" construction also stem from cultural conflicts, interest deviations, political misunderstandings and so on. Guide students to learn to respect local culture, convey positive Chinese image, and expand China's influence. Guide students to understand "We need to build an inclusive world economy to strengthen the foundation for win-win outcomes".

● **素质目标：**

　　通过分析为什么上海迪士尼乐园被称为"中国的迪士尼"以及中国是如何克服文化差异，成功在肯尼亚建设蒙内铁路的，引导学生认识到在"一带一路"建设中，跨文化交际的矛盾除了语言障碍外，还源自文化冲突、利益偏差、政治误解等多种因素，要尊重当地文化，传递中国国家形象，提高中国影响力。引导学生理解"我们要努力建设包容型世界经济，夯实共赢基础"。

Section A   Video Clip Appreciation

I. Introduction to the Movie *Shanghai Calling*

Imagine a steady stream of emigrants, traveling across a vast ocean to a foreign country, searching for new jobs and better lives. But the emigrants are Americans, and the country they are moving to is China. *Shanghai Calling* is a romantic comedy about modern-day American emigrants on an unfamiliar land.

When ambitious New York attorney Sam is sent to Shanghai on assignment, he immediately stumbles into a legal mess that could end his career. With the help of a beautiful relocation specialist, a well-connected old-timer, a clever journalist, and a street-smart legal assistant, Sam might just save his job, find romance, and learn to appreciate the beauty and wonders of Shanghai.

II. Introduction to the Video Clip

Got-getting New York lawyer Sam Chao who's proud that he's "never been above 79th Avenue" and describes himself as only "technically" Chinese, is transferred to Shanghai for a three-month stint. Bracing himself for a hardship posting, he is almost peeved to be proven wrong by "relocation specialist" and eventual love-interest Amanda Wilson, who not only furnishes him with a six-star luxury apartment complete with a tiger mother housekeeper, but shows him Shanghai's glittering surfaces and can-do spirit, with a dash of shrewd insight into the current Sino-American relations.

III. Script of the Video Clip

Video Clip

Voice Over: We have a saying here in China. Shanghai… is like a beautiful woman. Seductive. Mysterious. And these days, very attractive to foreign businessmen. Executives, bankers, engineers, salesmen. Hundreds of thousands of Americans now live and work in Shanghai. This is a story of an American named Sam. A good man. Easy to get along with. Never arrogant or crocky. And because of this, he was loved by everyone he met in Shanghai. Or maybe not.

[*New York City, a short time ago*]

Voice Over: Sam just won the most important court case in his life. Sam Chao… is on his way to the top.

Powell & Davis: … and after poaching the client from a senior associate no less. Ballsy.

Sam: Thank you, sir. Thank you.

Powell & Davis: The reason we asked you here? Sam, we've got exciting news for you.

Imagined Crowd: Yeah, Sam! Way to go!

Powell & Davis: We are sending you to China.

Sam: I'm sorry?

Powell & Davis: Groff Technologies just moved its headquarters to Shanghai. Word is they're onto sth big. A game changer. And if our top client goes to Shanghai, that means we go, too. We've been in touch with Donald Cafferty from AmCham, the American Chamber of Commerce out there. He's found us an office and hired us a local staff. Now we need someone to head it up. You're the obvious choice. You're single, you're a go-getter. And you're even Chinese.

Sam: Technically, yes, I'm Chinese. Isn't there something else you guys wanted to say to me?

Powell & Davis: We're aware of the rumors. We're just not ready to name a new partner just yet. But we are ready to send you to China. This is a huge opportunity, Sam.

Sam: Well, it's an incredibly attempting offer, but I just feel I'm more of an asset here… in New York. I know the ins and outs, I know everything. And my thirtieth birthday is coming. I've rented Thomas Keller's restaurant, I've got a DJ coming, I've got a lot of stuff going on.

Powell & Davis: You know what we like around here, Sam? A team player. Three months, that's all we ask. What do you say?

****

Sam: That's me.

Amanda: Welcome to China. Amanda Wilson, relocation specialist. It's my job to help you get adjusted.

Sam: Hi.

Amanda: I thought I missed you. I was running late. My Ayi was sick, and I have to find a babysitter and so… Everything OK?

Sam: Yeah… I was just expecting someone with… slightly darker hair.

Amanda: Here's your survival pack. Some Chinese yuan, money, in other words. A map of Shanghai, your business card, and your mobile phone. Your number is right on the back. Before going to your apartment, I want you to meet Donald from AmCham. He's kind of the "mayor of Americatown".

Sam: "Americatown"?

Amanda: Yeah, it's what we call our expat community over here. It's kind of like Chinatown in the US, but the other way around.

Sam: Ah.

Amanda: Here you go. (转身对出租车司机) 我们去浦西，淮海路。

Taxi driver 1: 好。

Sam: You speak Chinese?

Amanda: Of course, don't you?

Sam: …

Sam: What's going on here?

Amanda: Restaurant opening.

Sam: Oh yeah? I love a good restaurant. What kind of food do you have?

Amanda: Donald!

Donald: Amanda! Good morning! Well this must be Sam. Donald Cafferty, president of JFC China.

Sam: Sam Chao. Nice to meet you. Never see so much fanfare at a fast-food place before.

Donald: Our eight thousandth store opening called for a little celebration. The Chinese are crazy about fried chicken. Here, have a coupon for a free spicy chicken sandwich. Welcome to Shanghai. What are you doing Thursday night?

Sam: Um…

Donald: Great. Meet me for drinks out on the Bund. I'll introduce you to all of the top business execs in town. Microsoft, P&G, Ford... I'm gonna drive a lot of business your way. Ever been to China before?

Sam: I have never been above 79th street before. New York. It's a street. Joke.

Donald: He's gonna be a homesick one, I can tell. Lucky for you, I own an American bar out in Hongqiao. You ever get lonely, come on by.

Sam: OK. Sounds great.

Donald: Good man. Now if you'll excuse me, I'm late for my photo shoot.

Amanda: Modeling career finally taking off?

Donald: No, AmCham election's coming up.

Amanda: Hmn...

Donald: See you Thursday, Sam.

Sam: Yeah, Thursday.

Amanda: So, ready to see your new apartment?

Sam: As ready as I'll ever be.

Amanda: Sorry?

Sam: Look, I had a nice life back in New York, so whatever you found me... better not be too much of a letdown.

Amanda: OK. Here we are. Two bed, two bath, hardwood floor, recycled glass windows, hi-def TV, solar panels on the roof, and the entire building is brand new. What do you think?

Sam: That's awesome. I'll take it.

Amanda: OK, I'll get the papers ready. You've got to be kidding me.

Sam: What the hell was that?

Amanda: Construction. But they're supposed to be finished by now.

Sam: Are you telling me this building is still being built?

Amanda: Shanghai and construction go hand in hand. Sometimes these greener buildings take a little bit longer to get... OK, I have to get you out of here. I have a backup apartment down the street. It's not as nice as this one, but at least it's finished.

Sam: Is it a dump?

Amanda: No... I mean, umm... it's a tad smaller, and the amenities are less new. But it's a really nice place, in a good neighborhood.

Sam: It's a dump. I'm staying here, forget about it.

Amanda: Sam, I cannot let you stay here with all that noise going on upstairs.

Sam: I completely agree. So here is what you do: just tell them the future partner of a huge US law firm just moved in. They need to shut it down for three months, or I'll sue them. Here's my card.

Amanda: This may not work.

Sam: Amy?

Amanda: Amanda.

Sam: Your job was to find me a nice quiet place to live, and you failed. Are you going to resolve this issue, or do I need to replace you?

[*Phone rings*]

Amanda: It's you.

Sam: This is Sam.

Fang Fang: Hello, Mr Chao. This is Fang Fang, your new assistant. I hope you had a good flight. Are you planning to attend the Marcus Groff meeting today?

Sam: Today? No. I thought the meeting was tomorrow, the 17th.

Fang Fang: Yes. But today is the 17th.

Sam: That's impossible. I left New York on the 15th. I lost one day crossing the date line. That makes today the 16th.

Fang Fang: Actually, you lost two days. It became the 16th in the US while you were in the air. When you crossed the date line, it became the 17th. And Mr. Groff will be here in 30 minutes.

Sam: I'll be right there. Problem…

Amanda: I heard… you know what, you get to your office, and I will go upstairs and see what I can do about the constructions.

Sam: When did I do this… Oh jeez! Who the hell are you?

Nanny: 我都替你挂好了。你应该好好保管你的东西，它放在箱子里都弄皱了。

Sam: I got nothing. I don't speak Chinese. Who are you?

Nanny: 哦，你不会说中文，你是老外是不是啊？我是你的阿姨，阿姨。

Sam: "Ayi"?

Nanny: 阿姨。

Sam: Amanda said that word. Are you my nanny? You're like a housekeeper? You clean? Housekeeper?

Nanny: 哎哎，嗯。

Sam: Sleep? What? You live here, you live with me, you're my housekeeper, and you don't speak English. ¿Hablas español? That was really offensive on many, many levels. I am sorry about that, but I have to go. See you later.

Sam: OK… This is Yincheng Road. So that's gotta be… I have no idea. Which means…Screw it. Taxi! Can you take me to this address, please?

Taxi driver 2: 你要到的那个地方，就在那儿。

Sam: Just take me to the address.

Taxi driver 2: 你不需要坐出租车，走过去就行啦。

Sam: Why are we arguing?

Taxi driver 2: 看见了吗？前面的大楼就是你要去的地方。

Sam: Hohoho, all right. I get it. I'm from New York City. So don't think just because I'm from out of town, you can pad the fare by going the long way, or whatever it is you are trying to do. Just take me there!

Taxi driver 2: 到了。

Sam: Thank you.

New Words

seductive 诱人的

arrogant 傲慢的

crocky 老朽的，体弱的

poach （通过不正当的手段或秘密）挖走（其他组织的成员或顾客）

ballsy 有胆量的

fanfare （特别仪式上的）嘹亮短曲

backup 后备（设备、物资或人力）

dump 垃圾场

sue 诉讼，控告

Phrases and Expressions

go-getter 干将，非常积极能干的人

hi-def 高清的

DJ 流行音乐播音员，流行音乐节目主持人

Notes

Microsoft 美国微软公司，由比尔·盖茨与保罗·艾伦始创于 1975 年，是一家美国

跨国科技公司，也是世界个人电脑软件开发的先驱。公司总部设立在华盛顿州的雷德蒙德市，以研发、制造、授权和提供多种电脑软件为主要业务。

P&G 宝洁公司，总部位于美国俄亥俄州的辛辛那提市。宝洁在日化品市场上知名度相当高，其产品包括洗护发用品、护肤用品、化妆品、婴儿护理用品、家居用品、个人清洁用品等。

Ford 福特，世界著名的汽车品牌，为美国福特汽车公司旗下的众多品牌之一，公司及品牌名来源于创始人亨利·福特（Henry Ford）。福特汽车公司是世界上最大的汽车生产商之一，旗下拥有福特（Ford）和林肯（Lincoln）等汽车品牌，总部位于美国密歇根州的迪尔伯恩市。

IV. Exercises for understanding

1. Decide whether the following statements are true or false according to the video clip you have just watched. Write "T" for true or "F" for false.

_____ (1) Sam was eager to go to work in China because he is a Chinese.

_____ (2) Sam could speak Chinese fluently while Amanda was unable to understand Chinese at all.

_____ (3) Sam was very satisfied with the apartment Amanda had chosen for him.

_____ (4) Sam was confused about his arrival date in China.

_____ (5) Sam insisted that he be taken to the company building by taxi.

3. Put the following sentences in the right order according to the video clip you have just watched.

_____ (1) Sam complained about the noise in his apartment.

_____ (2) Sam learned that he was going to be sent to China.

_____ (3) Sam warned the taxi driver not to go a long way.

_____ (4) Sam was arranged to meet Donald, nicknamed as the "mayor of America town" in China.

_____ (5) Sam was told by his assistant Fangfang to go to a conference in 30 minutes.

3. Explore interculturally.

(1) Why didn't Sam want to be sent to China?

(2) What kind of culture shock did Sam encounter after he arrived in China?

Section B Reading

Fundamental Changes in Modern Business Community

As a professional in the modern business community, you need to be aware that the very concept of community is undergoing a fundamental transformation. A merchant supplied salt and sugar, and people made what they needed. The products the merchant sold were often produced locally because the cost of transportation was significant. A transcontinental railroad brought telegraph lines, shipping routes, and ports together from coast to coast. Shipping that once took months and years was now measured in days. A modern highway system and cheap oil products allowed for that measurement unit to be reduced to days and minutes. Just-in-time product delivery reduced storage costs from renting a warehouse at the port to spoilage in transit. Bar code and RDIF (radio frequency identification) tagged items instantly updated inventories and initiated orders at factories all over the world.

Communication, both oral and written, linked communities in ways that we failed to recognize. A system of trade and the circulation of capital and goods that once flowed relatively seamlessly have been challenged by change, misunderstanding, and conflict. Integrated markets and global networks bind us together in ways we are just now learning to appreciate, anticipate, and understand. Intercultural and international communication is critical areas of study with readily apparent, real-world consequences.

Agrarian, industrial, and information ages gave way to global business and brought the importance of communication across cultures to the forefront. The Pulitzer Prize-winning journalist Thomas Friedman calls this new world "flat", noting how the integration of markets and community had penetrated the daily lives of nearly everyone on the planet, regardless of language or culture. While the increasing ease of telecommunications and travel have transformed the nature of doing business, Friedman argues that "the dawning 'flat world' is a jungle pitting 'lions' and 'gazelles', where 'economic stability is not going to be a feature' and 'the weak will fall farther behind'. "Half of the world's population that earn less than $2 (USD) a day felt the impact of a reduction in trade and fluctuations in commodity prices even though they may not have known any of the details. Rice, for example, became an even more valuable commodity than ever. To the individuals who could not find it, grow it, or earn enough to buy it, the hunger felt was personal and global. International trade took on a new level of importance.

New Role of Intercultural Communication in Business

Intercultural and international business communication has taken on a new role for students as well as career professionals. Knowing when the European and Asian markets open has become mandatory, so has the awareness of multiple time zones and their importance in relation to trade, shipping and the production cycle. Managing production in China from an office in Chicago has become common. Receiving technical assistance for your computer often means connecting with a well-educated English speaker in New Delhi. We compete with each other via Elance.com or Desk.com for contracts and projects, selecting the currency of choice for each bid as we can be located anywhere on the planet. Communities are no longer linked as simply "brother" and "sister" cities in symbolic partnerships. They are linked in the daily trade of goods and services.

We explore this dynamic aspect of communication. If the foundation of communication is important, its application in this context is critical. Just as Europe once formed intercontinental alliances for the trade of metals, leading to the development of a common currency, trade zone, and new concept of nation-state, now North and South America are following with increased integration. Major corporations are no longer affiliated with only one country or one country's interests but instead perceive the integrated market as team members across global trade."Made in X", more of a relative statement as products from cars to appliances to garments now comes with a list of where components were made and assembled and what percentage corresponds to each nation.

Global business is more than trade between companies located in distinct countries; indeed, that concept is already outdated. Intercultural and international business focuses less on the borders that separate people and more on the communication that brings them together. Business communication values clear, concise interaction that promotes efficiency and effectiveness. You may perceive your role as a business communicator within a specific city, business, or organization, but you need to be aware that your role crosses cultures, languages, value and legal systems, and borders.

We are not created absolutely equal. We are born light- or dark-skinned, to parents of education or parents without access to education, and we grow up short or tall, slender or stocky. Our life chances or options are in many ways determined by our birth. The Victorian *Rags to Riches* novels that Horatio Alger wrote promoted the ideal that individuals can overcome all obstacles, raising themselves up by their bootstraps. Some people do have amazing stories, but even if you are quick to point out that Microsoft founder Bill Gates became fabulously successful despite his lack of a college education, you must know that his example is exception, not the rule. We all may use the advantages of our circumstances to improve our lives, but the type and extent of those advantages vary greatly across the planet.

Cultures reflect this inequality, this diversity, and the divergent range of values, symbols, and meanings across communities. Can you tie a knot? Perhaps you can tie your shoes, but can you tie a knot to secure a line to a boat, to secure a heavy load on a cart or truck, or to bundle a bale of hay? You may not be able to. But if you were raised in a culture that place a high value on knot-tying for specific purposes, you would learn that which your community values.

People and their relationships to dominant and subordinate roles are a reflection of culture and cultural viewpoint. They are communicated through experience and create expectations for how and when managers interact with employees. The three most commonly discussed management theories are often called X, Y, and Z.

Business Management Theories of X Y Z

In an influential book titled *The Human Side of Enterprise*, MIT management professor Douglas McGregor, described two contrasting perceptions on how and why people work, formulating Theory X and Theory Y, which are both based on Maslow's hierarchy of needs. According to this Maslow, people are concerned first with physical needs (e.g. food, shelter) and second with safety. At the third level, people seek love, acceptance, and intimacy. Self-esteem, achievement, and respect are the fourth level. Finally, the fifth level embodies self-actualization. William Ouchi's Theory Z combines elements of both Theory X and Y.

Theory X

McGregor's Theory X asserts that workers are motivated by their basic (low-level) needs and have a general disposition against labor. In this viewpoint, workers are considered lazy and predicted to avoid work if they can, giving rise to the perceived need for constant, direct supervision. A Theory X manager may be described as authoritarian or autocratic who does not seek input or feedback from employees. The view further holds that workers are motivated by personal interest. The Theory X manager uses control and incentive programs to provide punishment and rewards. Responsibility is the domain of the manager. Lack of training, inferior machines, or failure to provide the necessary tools are all reasons to stop working, and it is up to the manager to ffx these issues.

Theory Y

In contrast to Theory X, Theory Y views employees as ambitious, self-directed, and capable of self-motivation. Employees have a choice, and they prefer to do a good job as a representation of self-actualization. The pursuit of pleasure and avoidance of pain are part of being human, but work is also a reward in itself and employees take pride in their efforts. Employees want to reach their fullest potential and deffne themselves by their profession. A job well done is reward in and of itself, and the employee may be a valuable source of feedback. Collaboration is viewed as normal, and the worker may need little supervision.

Theory Z

Theory X and Y may seem like two extremes across the range of management styles, but in fact they are often combined in actual work settings. William Ouchi's Theory Z combines elements of both and draws from American and Japanese management style. It promotes worker participation and emphasizes job rotation, skills development, and loyalty to the company. Workers are seen as having a high need for reinforcement, and belonging is emphasized. Theory Z workers are trusted to do their jobs with excellence and management is trusted to support them, looking out for their well-being.

Each of these theories of management features a viewpoint with assumptions about people and why they do what they do. While each has been the subject of debate, and variations on each have been introduced across organizational communication and business, they serve as a foundation for understanding management in an intercultural context.

📝 Exercises for Understanding

1. Answer the following questions according to the passage you have just read.

(1) Why is intercultural communication of significance to the integrated markets today?

(2) How do you understand Thomas Friedman's interpretation of the world as "flat"?

(3) What does intercultural business communication value most?

(4) What does the author imply by the metaphor of "tying a knot"?

(5) How does Theory X differ from Theory Y in terms of employees' self-motivation in a company?

2. Choose the most appropriate answers to the following questions.

(1) The following statements are features of a "flat world" EXCEPT _____.

A. the integration of markets penetrates into people's daily life

B. the ease of telecommunications has changed the nature of doing business

C. the strong help the weak to move forward together

D. economic stability is broken

(2) Which of the following is NOT included in "Made in X" list of a car?

A. Name of the nation for product's components

B. Name of the nation for product's assemble

C. Name of the nation for product's percentage

D. Name of the nation for product's after-sale

(3) The highest level in Maslow's hierarchy of needs is _____ .

A. self-esteem

B. self-actualization

C. safety

D. love and intimacy

(4) According to theory X, managers tend to apply control and incentive programs to provide punishment and reward due to the following reasons EXCEPT _____ .

A. workers are predicted to be lazy

B. workers seldom give feedback

C. workers complain about inferior machines

D. workers are self-directed and self-motivated

(5) Which of the following is NOT one of the features of theory Z?

A. Workers are motivated by personal interest.

B. Job rotation is emphasized.

C. Workers' participation is promoted.

D. Workers' loyalty to the company is encouraged.

3. Decide whether the following statements are true or false according to the passage you have just read. Write "T" for true or "F" for false.

_____ (1) In the context of global business, proper communication is of utmost importance.

_____ (2) In the flat world brought about by network, business communities are more linked by sister and brother cities than by daily trade of goods and services.

_____ (3) Intercontinental alliance is commonly seen in todays' world for increased integration of business and trade.

_____ (4) For efficiency and effectiveness, international business focuses more on the borders that separate business communicators than on the communication that brings them together.

_____ (5) Theories X, Y and Z are oriented toward the cultural values about people and their relations to supervisers and subordinates.

4. Case study.

What cultural differences did China encounter in the construction and operation of Mombasa-Nairobi Standard-Gauge Railway in Kenya? How did China overcome these difficulties?

5. Small group task.

Imagine that you are a manager in charge of approximately a dozen workers. Would you prefer to rely primarily on Theory X, Y, or Z as your management style? Why? Write a short essay defending your preference, giving some concrete examples of management decisions you would make. Discuss your essay with your classmates.

 **Section C   Case**

Scan and Listen

The Scenario

Cocktail Party

The cocktail party is perhaps a typical US symbol of entertainment, but an unfamiliar social phenomenon to many other cultures. Thus it may cause problems in intercultural communication.

A US manager may invite employees, clients, and customers so that they get to know one another. The goal at a cocktail party is to meet as many people as possible. Nobody expects to get into deep discussions. In fact, it would be rude to monopolize any one person. One makes small talk and walks the room, exchanging business cards and phone numbers so that one can get into contact later and establish future business relationships.

To Europeans, the cocktail party is a curious phenomenon. In Germany, for example, one invites only as many people as one has chairs for. To invite crowds and expect them to stand would not be polite and thus not acceptable. The art of small talk is not a forte of most Europeans either. They tend to view the US style of entertaining as superficial and lacking sincerity.

A US firm that hosts a cocktail party in Japan creates all sorts of problems because the cocktail party is based on the premise that one can walk up to anyone in the room and introduce oneself. In Japan, with its hierarchy and protocol for how to address others, it is almost impossible to introduce oneself without knowing the age and status of the other person. What it intends to do as a friendly gesture by the manager from the United States may cause discomfort and embarrassment for the Japanese guests.

People of different cultures may have different interpretations to the length of the cocktail party. For example, invitations in the United States may announce: "Cocktail party 5:00–7:00 p.m." Americans find this arrangement very considerate and efficient. The guests know that they don't have to reserve the entire evening for the event; they can make other plans for the rest of the evening. But it's unthinkable in cultures where hospitability is supposed to be unlimited, because to invite someone for a set time period is rude.

🖉 Exercise

Listen to the case above and answer the following questions.

(1) What's the goal of a cocktail party in the United States?

(2) Do people discuss deeply at a cocktail party in the United States?

(3) How do Europeans usually comment on the cocktail parties in the United States?

(4) What problems will a US firm face when it holds a cocktail party in Japan?

(5) What do cultures where hospitality is thought to be unlimited think of Americans' set time length of cocktail party?

Unit 15　Intercultural Communication in Tourism Context

● **Knowledge Objective:**

Guide students to master intercultural communication strategies in tourism context.

● **知识目标：**

指导学生掌握旅游语境中的跨文化交际策略。

● **Ability Objective:**

Guide students to use different strategies for effective communication in different tourism contexts.

● **能力目标：**

指导学生在不同的旅游语境下使用不同的策略进行有效交际。

● **Educative Objective:**

Guide students to analyze the story of Zhang Yang, a foreign language tour guide from China Youth Travel Service, who is known as a "civilian diplomat" and leads nearly 10,000 foreign tourists to explore the land of China and showcases the charm of Chinese culture, as reported by *People's Daily* (Overseas Edition) in March 2023. Guide students to understand the professional requirements of tourism industry and get prepared in professional knowledge, service skills, and psychological construction in order to respond to new challenges of tourism industry and become excellent cultural ambassadors. Guide students to understand "Tourism is a bridge for communicating civilization, exchanging cultures, and enhancing friendship. It is an important indicator of improving people's living standards".

● **素质目标:**

通过分析《人民日报》（海外版）在 2023 年 3 月报道的被称为"民间外交官"的中青旅国际公司外语导游张洋带领近万名外国游客畅游华夏大地、展现中华文化魅力的"中国故事"，引导学生充分了解导游行业的从业要求，并做好业务知识、服务技能和心理建设等多方面的准备工作，从容应对未来导游行业的新需求和新挑战，做一名优秀的文化传播大使。引导学生理解"旅游是传播文明、交流文化、增进友谊的桥梁，是人民生活水平提高的重要指标"。

Section A Video Clip Appreciation

I. Introduction to the Movie *Little Miss Sunshine*

Sheryl Hoover is an overworked mother of two living in Albuquerque, New Mexico. Her brother, Frank, an unemployed scholar of Proust, is temporarily living at home with the family after having attempted suicide. Sheryl's husband Richard is a Type A personality striving to build a career as a motivational speaker and life coach. Dwayne, Sheryl's son from a previous marriage, is a Nietzsche-reading teenager who has taken a vow of silence until he can accomplish his dream of becoming a test pilot. Richard's foul-mouthed father, Edwin, recently evicted from a retirement home for snorting heroin, lives with the family. Olive, the daughter of Richard and Sheryl and the youngest of the Hoover family, is an aspiring beauty queen who is coached by Edwin.

Olive learns she is qualified for the "Little Miss Sunshine" beauty pageant that is being held in Redondo Beach, California in two days. Her parents and Edwin, who has been coaching her, want to support her, and Frank and Dwayne cannot be left alone, so the whole family goes. Because they have little money, they go on an 800-mile road trip in their yellow Volkswagen Type 2.

Family tensions play out on the highway and at stops along the way, amidst the aging VW van's mechanical problems. When the van breaks down early on, the family learns that they must push the van until it is moving at about 20 miles per hour before it is put into gear, at which point they have to run up to the side door and jump in. Later on, the van's horn starts honking unceasingly by itself.

Throughout the road trip, the family suffers numerous personal setbacks and discovers their need for each other's support. Richard loses an important contract that would have jump-started his motivational business. Frank encounters the ex-boyfriend who, in leaving him for an academic rival, had prompted his suicide attempt. Edwin dies from a heroin overdose, resulting in the family smuggling the body out of a hospital and nearly having it discovered by the police. During the final leg of the trip, Dwayne discovers that he is color blind, which means he cannot become a pilot, a realization that prompts him to finally break his silence and shout his anger and disdain for his family. But he is then calmed down by Olive, and he immediately apologizes.

The climax takes place at the beauty pageant. After a frantic race against the clock, the family arrives at the hotel, and is curtly told by a pageant organizer that they are a few minutes past the deadline. A sympathetic hired hand instead offers to register Olive on his own time. As Olive prepares for the pageant, the family sees Olive's competition: slim, hypersexualized pre-teen girls with teased hair and capped teeth, performing highly elaborate dance numbers with great panache. It quickly becomes apparent that Olive is an amateur by comparison.

As Olive's turn to perform in the talent portion of the pageant draws near, Richard and Dwayne recognize that Olive is certain to be humiliated, and wanting to spare her feelings, run to the dressing room to talk her out of performing. Sheryl, however, insists that they "let Olive be Olive," and Olive goes on stage. Olive's hitherto-unrevealed dance that Edwin had choreographed for her is performed to Rick James's song *Super Freak*. Olive scandalizes and horrifies most of the audience and pageant judges with a burlesque performance that she joyfully performs while oblivious to their reactions. The pageant organizers are enraged and demand Sheryl and Richard remove Olive from the stage. Instead of removing her, one by one the members of the Hoover family join Olive on stage, dancing alongside her to show their support.

The family is next seen outside the hotel's security office where they are given their freedom in return for a promise never to enter a beauty pageant in the state of California again. Piling into the van with the horn still honking, they happily smash through the barrier of the hotel's toll booth and head back to their home in Albuquerque.

II. Introduction to the Video Clip

Little Miss Sunshine succeeds by making us all feel a little less weird and a little less alone. The film stands out from a moment of intense seriousness, such as the death of the grandfather, and from a comic scene where the family steals the body out of the hospital and puts it into the trunk of the car. A heartbreaking scene of despair will soon turn into a mission, which consists of stealing the body of Olive's heroine-addicted grandfather from the hospital where he died and eventually stick to the family's motto which is to never give up and keep moving forward no matter what happens. By hiding the body in the trunk of the car, the main characters once again defy the logic of common sense and bring together extreme emotions.

III. Script of the Video Clip

Olive: Mom? Dad?

Richard: What is it, hon?

Olive: Grandpa won't wake up.

Olive: Wanna take an eye test? Uncle Frank? An eye test?

Video Clip

Sheryl: Olive, come here. Put those away. We're gonna have a family meeting. Dwayne, family meeting. First of all, the doctors are doing everything they can to help Grandpa right now. He's had a long, eventful life, and l know he loves both of you very much. But if God wants to take him, we have to be ready to accept that, OK? Whatever happens, we're a family. And what's important is that we love each other. I love you guys so, so much.

Doctor: Are you the family of Edwin Hoover?

Richard: Yes.

Doctor: I'm sorry. We did everything we could. He was, uh... Well, it was too much. He probably just fell asleep and never woke up. I'll have someone come and talk to you about handling the remains.

Richard: Thank you.

Doctor: Linda!

Olive: Mom? Is Grandpa dead?

Sheryl: Yeah, honey. He passed away.

Linda: Hi. I'm your bereavement liaison, Linda. My consolations for your loss.

Richard: Thank you.

Linda: OK, these are the forms you need to fill out. A death certificate. A report of the death. An ME pink slip. Please try and be as detailed as possible. Um, this is a brochure for a grief recovery support group that meets on Tuesdays, and if you like, I can refer you to a funeral home so you can begin making arrangements.

Richard: Actually, prearrangements have already been made in Albuquerque.

Linda: Albuquerque?

Richard: We're actually on our way to California right now.

Linda: If the body is crossing state lines, you're gonna need a burial transit permit.

Richard: OK. But we're trying to get to Redondo Beach by three o'clock.

Linda: Three o'clock today? Hmm. Ain't gonna happen.

Richard: OK, um, can I just... I know that this, uh, might be a little unusual, but if maybe we could just go, and then we'll come back and take care of all the paperwork, and...

Linda: No. You can't just abandon the body.

Richard: No, no, no. Nobody's gonna abandon the body. We're just gonna go and...

Linda: Otherwise, the hospital becomes responsible.

Richard: We'll go, and come back.

Linda: Sir, there are ways we have of doing things.

Linda: You're not following me. Sir, you are not the only one that's had somebody die here today, okay?

Richard: Is there any way we might be able to view the remains?

Linda: We haven't had a chance to move him downstairs. So someone may come in a few minutes to take him to the basement. Tell them who you are, and they will wait.

Richard: Thank you.

Linda: And when you're done with the paperwork, I'll be at the nurses' station.

Richard: Great. Thank you, Linda.

Linda: Thank you.

Richard: God damn it, Dad. God damn it! Stupid...

Sheryl: We'll go to Little Miss Sunshine next year, okay, honey? Next year.

Richard: No. No. We've come 700 miles. I'll be damned if I'm not making that contest, Sheryl.

Sheryl: Well, Richard, we can't leave him here.

Richard: We're not gonna leave him.

Sheryl: Richard, what are you doing?

Richard: Fuck!

Richard: Dwayne, go around outside.

Sheryl: Richard, What are you thinking?

Richard: We're gonna take him with us.

Sheryl: No, no, that is not happening.

Richard: He's better off with us than these people. I want you to go round outside and underneath this window.

Sheryl: Dwayne, don't move. Honey, You stay here. We'll take Olive. Frank can drive.

Richard: No, Sheryl. We'll be there in two hours. Listen to me. I'll call a funeral home once we get there. One thing my father would have wanted is to see Olive perform in the Little Miss Sunshine Pageant. I believe we'd be doing a grave disservice to his memory if we were to just give up now. All right? There are two kinds of people in this world. There's winners, and there's losers. Okay? You know what the difference is? Winners don't give up. So what are we here? Are we winners, or are we losers? Huh?

Sheryl: OK. OK. Let's do it. You guys go. Olive, you watch the curtain.

Linda: I don't know. l have no reason to assume it's gonna be otherwise.

Richard: Watch. Get the back, get the back. Go, go, go.

Linda: Yeah, 1: 00. Now?

Richard: He's very heavy. Be gentle. One, two... Okay. Three. Wait, wait, wait! Not yet, not yet. Okay. Go, go, go, go.

Sheryl: Richard, I can't do it.

Richard: I got him. I got him.

Sheryl: Come on.

Olive: Come on! Hurry up!

Richard: Okay, he's slipping. Hold on.

Frank: I got him, I got him, I got him.

Olive: Be careful.

Sheryl: Hurry up! Keep watch, Olive. Watch the curb, watch the curb. Watch his head! Watch it!

Frank: Keys.

Sheryl: Swing him around this way. Olive, get in. Okay, let's go.

Richard: Sheryl. Let's go, Frank. Did I mention that I am the preeminent Proust scholar in the US?

Richard: Here we go! Here we go!

Sheryl: Are you Okay?

Olive: Dad?

Richard: Yeah, honey?

Olive: What's gonna happen to Grandpa? Uncle Frank?

Frank: Yeah?

Olive: Do you think there's a heaven?

Frank: It's hard to say, Olive. I... I don't think anyone knows for sure.

Olive: I know, but what do you think?

Frank: Um, well...

Olive: I think there is one.

Frank: Do you think I'll get in?

Olive: Yes.

Frank: You promise?

Olive: Yes.

Richard: Whoa! Hey! Son of a bitch!

Frank: What happened?

Richard: He cut me off.

Richard: It's stuck.

Sheryl: Okay, just leave it.

Richard: It's stuck or sth.

Sheryl: Maybe try pulling it from here.

Richard: No, no. Just leave it. I'll fix it when we get there.

Sheryl: Okay, fine.

Richard: Shit! Oh, Jesus! God! I'm being pulled over. Here we go. Okay. Everybody just
pretend to be normal, Okay? Like everything's normal here.

Policeman: How you folks doing?

Richard: Yeah, we're fine. Just...

Policeman: Little trouble with the horn?

Richard: What?

Policeman: Having a little trouble with your horn?

Richard: Yeah. A little trouble. Sorry. Uh. Sorry.

Policeman: Could you step outside the vehicle? Step this way, please.

Richard: No, no.

Policeman: What?

Richard: Don't.

Policeman: Don't what? Do you have sth in your trunk, sir?

Richard: It's nothing. I... Don't open it.

Policeman: Sir, you just gave me probable cause to search your trunk.

Richard: Just—I—I just...

Policeman: Sir, put your hands on the vehicle, now! Now! Don't move!

Richard: Okay. It's not illegal!

Policeman: I'd advise you to keep your mouth shut!

Sheryl: Oh, God. What is he doing?

Richard: It's not illegal. Goddamn!

Policeman: Sir, could you come back here? I love this stuff. I love it. God bless you, God bless you. Don't worry. I'm not gonna bust you.

Richard: Oh, thank you.

Policeman: How you doing? Cute. Cute family. That's nice.

Richard: Thank you.

Policeman: And this on the side. A little of this, a little of that. Sweet sweetness. That is sweet, yeah. Dirty. And this one is one of my favorites. Ah, good, yeah.

Richard: That's a little different choice. No?

Policeman: I'll leave that with you.

Richard: All right.

Policeman: You have a good day there.

Richard: Yeah.

Sheryl: What happened?

Richard: I'll tell you when I regain consciousness. Frank, Dwayne, get out and push.

Sheryl: Okay, there it is. Redondo Beach, 46.

Richard: It's 2:15. Might be a few minutes late.

Sheryl: They said three o'clock sharp. They were very explicit. We can't cross these people. Trust me.

Olive: Mom, Dwayne has 20/20 vision.

Sheryl: I bet he does.

Olive: Okay. Now I'm gonna check to see if you're color-blind.

Richard: Asshole!

Olive: What's the letter in the circle? No, no, no. Inside the circle. Right there. See? It's an "A". Can't you see it? Right there.

Frank: It's bright green. Oh, man. Dwayne, I think you might be color-blind. You can't fly jets if you're color-blind. We've got a little bit of... Okay, we've got an emergency back here.

Sheryl: What is it? What's the emergency?

Richard: Just pull over! It's all right, man. Dwayne, Dwayne. It's all right. Hold on.

Sheryl: Just pull over the car!

Richard: Okay. All right!

Sheryl: Get him to pull over, please?

Dwayne: Could you get him to pull over, please?

Sheryl: Richard, pull over! Pull over the car!

Richard: It's all right. We're pulling over. I'm pulling over. Please! No, no, no.

Frank: Dwayne! No. no. Dwayne! Sit down! God, this better be good!

Dwayne: Pull over.

Richard: I'm pulling over. All right!

Sheryl: Stop the car!

Richard: It's gonna be okay, Dwayne. All right. Do not open the door.

Sheryl: Dwyane? Oh, God.

Dwayne: Fuck!

Sheryl: What happened?

Frank: He's color-blind. He can't fly.

Sheryl: Oh, Jesus. Oh, no. Just give him a second. Dwayne? Dwayne, honey, I'm sorry. Dwayne, come on. We have to go.

Dwayne: I'm not going.

Sheryl: Dwayne...

Dwayne: I said I'm not. Okay? l don't care. I'm not getting on that bus again!

Sheryl: Dwayne, for better or worse, we're your family.

Dwayne: You're not my family! Okay? I don't wanna be your family! I hate you fucking people! I hate you! Divorce? Bankrupt? Suicide? You're fucking losers! You're losers! No. Please just leave me here, Mom. Okay? Please, please, please. Please just leave me here.

Sheryl: Shit. I don't know what to do.

Richard: Well, it's getting late. Maybe... Can somebody stay here with him?

Frank: I'll stay.

Sheryl: That is not happening.

Richard: All right. Well... Just worried about the time. Olive, you wanna try talking to him?

Sheryl: Richard, no! There is nothing to say. We just have to wait. Honey...

Dwayne: Okay. Let's go. I apologize for the things l said. I was upset, and l didn't really mean them.

Sheryl: It's okay. Come on. Let's go.

New Words

eventful 多事的

remains 遗体，遗骨

bereavement 丧亲之哀

liaison 联络

consolation 安慰，慰问

slip 纸片

brochure 手册，小册子

grief 悲痛

pageant 选美比赛

disservice 伤害

preeminent 卓越的，超群的

horn 喇叭

vehicle 车辆

trunk 汽车车尾的行李箱

asshole 令人讨厌的人

bankrupt 破产者

Phrases and Expressions

funeral home 殡仪馆

pull over 靠边停车

color-blind 色盲的

Notes

Proust scholar 马塞尔·普鲁斯特（1871—1922，
Marcel Proust），20世纪法国最伟大的小说家
之一，意识流文学的先驱与大师。

IV. Exercises for understanding

1. Decide whether the following statements are true or false according to the video clip you have just watched. Write "T" for true or "F" for false.

_____ (1) Sheryl decided to take the remains of Grandpa Edwin Hoover with them to the pageant in California.

_____ (2) In the United States, it is acceptable to take the remains of a dead person across state lines with no burial transit permit.

_____ (3) Linda, the bereavement liaison, said that the hospital would keep the remains of grandpa Edwin Hoover until the Richards came back from the California pageant.

_____ (4) Richard and Sheryl knew in the very beginning that Dwayne was color-blind.

_____ (5) Dwayne was in a rage when he knew that he was color-blind.

2. Put the following sentences in the right order according to the video clip you have just watched.

_____ (1) The family members worked together to take the remains of Grandpa Edwin Hoover outside the hospital into the car.

_____ (2) Doctor announced the death of Grandpa Edwin Hoover to the family.

_____ (3) The family car was pulled over by a police because the horn was honking unceasingly.

_____ (4) Olive speechlessly gave Dwayne a hug before Dwayne decided to continue with the journey to the beauty pageant.

_____ (5) Dwayne wrote simple notes for Olive to hug and comfort Sheryl Hoover.

3. Explore interculturally.

(1) How did Richard manage to strike a balance between handling his father's death affairs and sending Olive to the pageant in California?

(2) What did Olive do to persuade Dwayne into continuing his journey to the pageant together with the family members?

微课

Collaborative Efforts a Must!

"We didn't all come over on the same ship, but we're all in the same boat."

—Bernard Baruch, American financier

It's no secret that today's workplace is rapidly becoming vast, as the traveling environment expands to include various geographic locations and span numerous cultures. What can be difficult, however, is to understand how to communicate effectively with individuals who speak another language, or who rely on different means of reaching a common goal.

Tourism is the most superficial way of an intercultural encounter and one of the biggest industrial sectors in the world. From time to time, people may spend two weeks in Turkey, Dubai, or on Bali. When going abroad people need to be aware of different behavioral rules and patterns. Both tourists and employees need to face their upcoming intercultural communication challenges. People with different cultural backgrounds not only speak different languages, they think and act differently.

Intercultural Communication—The New Norm

The Internet and modern technology have opened up new places that allow us to promote our traveling businesses to new geographic locations and cultures. And given that it can now be as easy to work with people remotely as it is to work face-to-face, intercultural communication is increasingly the new norm.

For those of us who are native English speakers, it is fortunate that English seems to be the language that people use if they want to reach the widest possible audience. However, even for native English speakers, intercultural communication can be an issue: just witness the mutual incomprehension that can sometimes arises between people from different English-speaking countries.

In this new world, good intercultural communication is a must.

Understand Cultural Diversity

Given different cultural contexts, this brings new communication challenges to the workplace. Even when employees located in different locations or offices speak the same language (for instance, correspondences between English speakers in the US and English speakers in the UK), there are some cultural differences that should be considered in an effort to optimize communications between the two parties.

In such cases, an effective communication strategy begins with the understanding that the sender of the message and the receiver of the message are from different cultures and backgrounds. Of course, this introduces a certain amount of uncertainty, making communications even more complex.

Without getting into cultures and sub-cultures, it is perhaps most important for people to realize that a basic understanding of cultural diversity is the key to effective intercultural communication. Without necessarily studying individual cultures and languages in detail, we must all learn how to better communicate with individuals and groups whose first language, or language of choice, does not match our own.

Develop Awareness of Individual Cultures

However, some learning of the basics about culture and at least something about the language of communication in different countries is important. This is necessary even for the basic level of understanding required to engage in appropriate greetings and physical contact, which can be a tricky area interculturally. For instance, kissing a business associate is not considered an appropriate practice in the US, but in Paris, one peck on each cheek is an acceptable greeting. And, the firm handshake that is widely accepted in the US is not recognized in all other cultures.

While many companies now offer training in the different cultures where the company conducts business, it is important that employees communicating across cultures practice *Intercultural Encounters* patience and work to increase their knowledge and understanding of these cultures. This requires the ability to see that a person's own behaviors and reactions are oftentimes culturally driven and that while they may not match our own, they are culturally appropriate.

If a leader or manager of a team that is working across cultures or incorporates individuals who speak different languages, practice different religions, or are members of a society that requires a new understanding, he or she needs to work to convey this.

Consider any special needs the individuals on your team may have. For instance, they may observe different holidays, or even have different hours of operation. Be mindful of time zone differences and work to keep everyone involved aware and respectful of such differences.

Generally speaking, patience, courtesy and a bit of curiosity go a long way. And, if you are unsure of any differences that may exist, simply ask team members. Again, this may best be done in a one-on-one setting so that no one feels "put on the spot" or self-conscious, perhaps even embarrassed, about discussing their own needs or differences of needs.

Demand Tolerance

Cultivate and demand understanding and tolerance. In doing this, a little education will usually do the trick. Explain to team members that the part of the team that works out of the Australia office, for example, will be working in a different time zone, so electronic communications and/or return phone calls will experience a delay. And, members of the India offfce will also observe different holidays such as Mahatma Gandhi's Birthday, observed on October 2nd.

Most people will appreciate the information and will work hard to understand different needs and different means used to reach common goals. However, when this is not the case, make it clear that you expect to be followed down a path of open-mindedness, acceptance and tolerance. Tolerance is essential. However, you need to maintain standards of acceptable behavior. The following "rules of thumb" seem universal:

■ Team members should contribute to and not hinder the team's mission or harm the delivery to the team's customer.

■ Team members should not damage the cohesion of the team or prevent it from becoming more effective.

■ Team members should not unnecessarily harm the interests of other team members. Other factors (such as national law) are obviously important.

■ When dealing with people in a different culture, courtesy and goodwill can also go a long way in ensuring successful communication. Again, this should be insisted on.

Keep It Simple

When you communicate, keep in mind that even though English is considered the international language, it is a mistake to assume that every person speaks good English. In fact, only about half of the 800 million people who speak English learned it as a first language. And, those who speak it as a second language are often more limited than native speakers.

When you communicate interculturally, make particular efforts to keep your communication clear, simple and unambiguous.

And avoid humor until you know that the person you're communicating with "gets it" and isn't offended by it. Humor is notoriously culture-speciffc: many things that pass for humor in one culture can be seen as grossly offensive in another.

📝 Exercises for Understanding

1. Answer the following questions according to the passage you have just read.

(1) How do you understand that tourism is the most superficial way of an intercultural encounter?

(2) According to the passage, how to conduct effective intercultural communication?

(3) What are the ways out when different needs and common goals cannot be met?

(4) According to the passage, how many people in the world speak English as the first language? What should be kept in mind when speaking English in a foreign country?

(5) Why should people avoid humor in intercultural communication?

2. Choose the most appropriate answers to the following questions.

(1) Which of the following is NOT included in optimizing intercultural communication?

    A. Keep things simple and clear

    B. Transplant to a foreign country

    C. Develop consciousness of alien cultures

    D. Cultivate tolerance

(2) Which of the following is a common way of greeting in France?

    A. A firm handshake

    B. A wet handshake

    C. A peck on each cheek

    D. A namaskar

(3) In the passage, the meaning of "put on the spot" probably means _____.

    A. embarrassed

    B. threatened

    C. attacked

    D. confused

(4) In India, Mahatma Gandhi's Birthday is observed on _____.

    A. October 2nd

    B. January 1st

    C. December 15th

    D. July 14th

(5) According to the passage, the number of people who speak English as the first language is

_____.

    A. 400 million

B. 600 million

C. 800 million

D. 1,000 million

3. Decide whether the following statements are true or false according to the passage you have just read. Write "T" for true or "F" for false.

_____ (1) Tourism is the most superficial way of intercultural communication.

_____ (2) To develop awareness of cultural diversity is the first step for effective communication.

_____ (3) It is suggested that a meeting be held for team members to speak up their special needs in an international group.

_____ (4) For an international team to run properly, rules of thumb emphasize the team's cohesion instead of diversity.

_____ (5) Humor is culturally-specific as things that pass for humor in one culture can be offensive in another.

4. Case study.

Analyze the story of Zhang Yang, a foreign language tour guide from China Youth Travel Service, who is known as a "civilian diplomat" and leads nearly 10,000 foreign tourists to explore the land of China and showcase the charm of Chinese culture, as reported by *People's Daily* (Overseas Edition) in March of 2023. Discuss how to respond to the new challenges of tourism industry and better serve people's aspirations for better lives.

5. Small group task.

Read the following 3 pieces of travel tips in China, Myanmar and the Middle East and discuss their common and different points culturally.

China Travel Tips: Dos and Don'ts

Many travelers from abroad are confused and frightened by Chinese customs. This handy reference tool makes it easy for newcomers to China to fit right in.

So come along, my alien friend! Welcome to China!

The order of Chinese names is family name first, then given name. Among some 440 family names, the 100 most common ones account for 90% of the total population. Brides in China do not adopt their husband's surnames.

Among Chinese, a popular way to address each other, regardless of gender, is to add an age-related term of honor before the family name. These include: lao (honorable old one), xiao (honorable young one) or occasionally da (honorable middle-aged one).

Unlike the Japanese, Chinese do not commonly bow as a form of greeting. Instead, a brief handshake is usual. While meeting elders or senior officials, your handshake should be even gentler and accompanied by a slight nod. Sometimes, as an expression of warmth, a Chinese will cover the normal handshake with his left hand. As a sign of respect, Chinese usually lower their eyes slightly when they meet others.

Moreover, embracing or kissing when greeting or saying good-bye is highly unusual. Generally, Chinese do not show their emotions and feelings in public. Consequently, it is better not to behave in too carefree a manner in public. Also, it is advisable to be fairly cautious in political discussions.

Chinese do not usually accept a gift, invitation or favor when it is first presented.

Politely refusing two or three times is thought to reflect modesty and humility. Accepting sth in haste makes a person look aggressive and greedy, as does opening it in front of the giver. Traditionally the monetary value of a gift indicates the importance of a relationship, but due to increasing contact with foreigners in recent years, the symbolic nature of gifts has taken foot.

Present your gifts with both hands. And when wrapping, be aware that the Chinese ascribe much importance to color. Red is lucky, pink and yellow represent happiness and prosperity; white, grey and black are funeral colors.

The popular items including cigarette lighters, stamps (stamp collecting is a popular hobby), T-shits, and the exotic coins, make a good gift to the Chinese.

And the following gifts should be avoided:

(1) White or yellow flowers (especially chrysanthemums), which are used for funerals.

(2) Pears. The word for pear in Chinese sounds the same as "separation" and is considered bad luck.

(3) Clocks of any kind. The word clock in Chinese sounds like the expression—the end of life.

China is one of those wonderful countries where tipping is not practiced and almost no one asks for tips.

Traditionally speaking, there are many taboos at Chinese tables, but these days not many people pay attention to them. However, there are a few things to keep in mind, especially if you are a guest at a private home.

(1) Don't stick your chopsticks upright in the rice bowl. Instead, lay them on your dish. The reason for this is that when sb dies, the shrine to them contains a bowl of sand or rice with two sticks of incense stuck upright in it. So if you stick your chopsticks in the rice bowl, it looks like a shrine and is equivalent to wishing death upon the people at the table!

(2) Make sure the spout of the teapot is not facing anyone. It is impolite to set the teapot down where the spout is facing towards sb. The spout should always be directed to where nobody is sitting, usually just outward from the table.

(3) Don't tap on your bowl with your chopsticks. Beggars tap on their bowls, so this is not polite. If you are in someone's home, it is like insulting the cook.

Myanmar Travel Tips: Dos and Don'ts

Myanmar is a Buddhism country and it is famous as the Golden Land. Otherwise, it is also called the Land of Pagodas. So when coming to Myanmar, tourists should know the behaviors both in public and religious monuments.

Dos

Say "Mingalarbar" when meeting each other.

Add "U" (for male) in front of the names for adult persons.

Add "Daw" (for female) in front of the names for adult persons.

Wear decent clothes to the pagodas or monasteries.

Let the oldest be served first.

Show respect to monks, novices and nuns.

Offer articles with both hands.

Keep the feet on the ground.

Bend a bit when crossing close in front of the elders.

Dress and act decent.

Speak slowly and clearly.

Seek permission on retrieving an article above a person's head.

Behave in a proper manner.

Don'ts

Don't wear shoes and shorts at pagodas and monasteries.

Don't sit with back against Buddha Image.

Don't offer to shake hands with a monk.

A woman should not touch a monk.

Avoid being a nuisance when taking photographs.

Don't handle Buddha Images or sacred object with disrespect.

Don't keep Buddha Images or sacred objects in inappropriate places.

Don't step on a monk's shadow.

Don't touch anybody on the head.

Don't touch a woman on any part of the body.

Don't point a finger straight in the face.

Don't step over any part of the person.

Don't gamble.

Don't go where you are advised not to go.

Travel Tips in the Middle East: Dos and Don'ts

The trafficking of drugs and pornography are not the only crimes to carry the death sentence in extreme case. Homosexuality is highly illegal in most of the Middle East and, although Christianity is tolerated in most countries, attempts to covert Muslims can also carry very serious consequences.

But it is not all doom and gloom—travelers who employ common sense and a large helping of respect and consideration for Islamic culture will enjoy a trouble-free trip. Below are some basic tips.

Appropriate dress. It's a myth that Western women have to wear headscarves; tourists are recognized as tourists and as such are generally exempt from any such obligations. Women should, however, dress conservatively at all times, especially when traveling alone.

The sanctity of marriage. Unmarried women over the age of 25 tend to attract endless pity. If you prefer to avoid such attention, as well as excessive male attention, wear a wedding ring.

Leave the girls alone. Guys, it's not a good idea to even contemplate relieving a girl of her honor, even careless long glance can be very risky.

A bit of decorum. Try not to blaspheme, even in English—it tends to be dimly looked upon and considered disrespectful.

Wanna haggle? Always haggle—that's the way of the Arab world—and never pay more than one third of the original asking price.

Calling home. Get a prepaid international sim card rather than using the expensive local telephone networks.

 **Section C Case**

The Scenario

Scan and Listen

Apologizing to Your Customer—A Japanese Perspective

Outside, torrents of water streamed down Hong Kong's streets as the typhoon hit the city. Police recommended that vehicles stay off the streets. Safely inside the hotel, Japanese tourists were waiting impatiently in the lobby for the van which was to take them out to an elegant seafood dinner. Where was the guide?

Japanese tourists, used to prompt service at home, often expect departure time to be exact, down to the minute. He was now 20 minutes late. One older woman was particularly offended at his lateness, and kept grumbling to the others about his irresponsibility. Finally the guide came charging full speed up the escalator into the lobby, drenching wet, breathlessly apologizing over and over for the inconvenience he had caused. Not once did he mention that the typhoon had delayed him.

The woman beamed at him, and said, "You came running!" patting him on the shoulder. All evening, she kept saying approvingly to her companions, "He came running!"

☑ Exercise

Listen to the case above and answer the following questions.

(1) What was the weather like when the case happened one day?

(2) How did an old woman in the tour group show her dissatisfaction toward the lateness of the Japanese tour guide?

(3) What did the Japanese tour guide do when he arrived in the hotel lobby?

(4) From the Japanese tour guide's continuous apologies, what can we learn about Japanese service style?

(5) Why did the old woman keep saying "He came running!" again and again to her companions?

Unit 16 Intercultural Communication in Education Context

● **Knowledge Objective:**

Guide students to master different learning and teaching styles in different cultures as well as the relationship between language and culture in educational contexts.

● **知识目标：**

指导学生掌握不同文化中不同的学习风格和教学风格，理解教育语境中语言和文化的关系。

● **Ability Objective:**

Guide students to be aware of the national spirit and culture behind language learning and distinguish the pros and cons of different teaching and learning styles.

● **能力目标：**

指导学生在学习语言的同时了解其背后承载的民族精神和文化，并辨识不同教学风格的优点和弱点。

● **Educative Objective:**

Guide students to analyze the TED video *Learning Styles and the Importance of Critical Self-reflection* to understand that the significance of education lies in helping learners establish correct values and improve thinking and judging abilities. Guide students to think about the similarities and differences between the critical thinking mentioned in the video and Confucius' motto of "Learning without thought is labor lost, thought without learning is perilous". Guide students to understand that "People hope to promote inter-civilization exchanges, equality of educational opportunities and scientific literacy in order to dispel estrangement, prejudice and hatred, and spread the seeds for the idea of peace. This is precisely why UNESCO was established in the first place".

● **素质目标：**

通过分析 TED 视频《为什么学习风格并不存在》，引导学生理解教育的意义在于帮助学习者树立正确的价值观，提升思考和判断能力。引导学生思考视频中提到的批判性思维和孔子所提倡的"学而不思则罔 思而不学则殆"有什么异同。引导学生理解"人们希望通过文明交流、平等教育、普及科学，消除隔阂、偏见、仇视，播撒和平理念的种子。这就是教科文组织成立的初衷"。

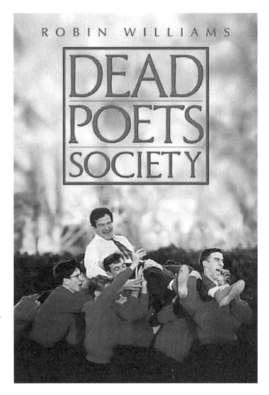

Section A　Video Clip Appreciation

I. Introduction to the Movie *Dead Poets Society*

Dead Poets Society is a 1989 American drama film written by Tom Schulman, directed by PeterWeir and starring Robin Williams. The film evoked an extensive reflection on education.

John Keating is the new charismatic English teacher at Welton Academy, a very traditional New England boarding school. Questioning authority and going against the conformist norm, he challenges his students to live life to the fullest, to "seize the day". He teaches them to act on their impulses and to be spontaneous, free thinkers. Some of the boys are inspired by his idealism and form a secret society based on their mutual appreciation of poetry. Here they learn to express their feelings and to find out who they are and what they really want.

But the school authorities refuse to tolerate this obvious rebellion against their traditional rules, and what follows is a conflict with tragic consequences.

II. Introduction to the Video Clip

Nolan investigates Neil's death at the request of the Perry family. Richard blames Neil's death on Keating to escape punishment for his own participation in the Dead Poets Society, and names the other members. Confronted by Charlie, Richard urges the rest of them to let Keating take the fall. Charlie punches Richard and is expelled. Each of the boys is called to Nolan's office to sign a letter attesting to the truth of Richard's allegations, even though they know they are false. When Todd's turn comes, he is reluctant to sign, but does so after seeing that the others have complied.

Keating is fired and Nolan takes over teaching the class. Keating interrupts the class to collect personal articles before he leaves. Todd shouts that all of them were forced to sign the letter that resulted in his dismissal and that Neil's death was not his fault. Todd stands on his desk and salutes Keating with the words "O Captain! My Captain!" Knox, Gerard, Steven, and over half of the class do the same, ignoring Nolan's order to sit down. Keating is deeply touched by their gesture. He thanks the boys and departs.

III. Script of the Video Clip

[*Chorus*]

All my life Shall surely Follow me

And in God's house

Forevermore

My dwelling place Shall be

Amen

Video Clip

Nolan: The death of Neil Perry is a tragedy. He was a fine student, one of Welton's best. And he will be missed. We've contacted each of your parents to explain the situation. Naturally, they're all quite concerned. At the request of Neil's family, I intend to conduct a thorough inquiry into this matter. Your complete cooperation is expected.

Charlie: You told him about this meeting?

Meek: Twice.

Charlie: That's it, guys. We're all fried.

Pitts: How do you mean?

Charlie: Cameron's a fink. He's in Nolan's office now, finking.

Meeks: About what?

Charlie: The club, Pittsie. Think about it. The board of directors, the trustees and Mr. Nolan. Do you think for one moment they're gonna let this thing just blow over? Schools go down because of things like this. They need a scapegoat.

Cameron: What's going on, guys?

Charlie: You finked, didn't you, Cameron?

Cameron: "Finked"? I don't know what the hell you're talking about.

Charlie: You told Nolan everything about the club is what I'm talking about.

Cameron: Look, in case you hadn't heard, Dalton, there's something... called an honor code at this school, all right? If a teacher asks you a question, you tell the truth or you're expelled.

Todd: You...

Boys: Charlie!

Charlie: He's a rat! He's in it up to his eyes, so he ratted to save himself!

Knox: Don't touch him, Charlie. You do and you're out.

Charlie: I'm out anyway!

Knox: You don't know that. Not yet!

Cameron: He's right there, Charlie. And if you guys are smart, you will do exactly what I did and cooperate. They're not after us. We're the victims. Us and Neil.

Charlie: What's that mean? Who are they after?

Cameron: Why, Mr. Keating, of course. The "Captain" himself! You guys didn't really think he could avoid responsibility, did you?

Charlie: Mr. Keating responsible for Neil? Is that what they're saying?

Cameron: Well, who else do you think, dumb ass? The administration? Mr. Perry? Mr. Keating put us up to all this crap, didn't he? If it wasn't for Mr. Keating, Neil would be... cozied up in his room right now, studying his chemistry... and dreaming of being called "Doctor"!

Todd: That is not true, Cameron! You know that! He didn't put us up to anything. Neil loved acting.

Cameron: Believe what you want, but I say let Keating fry. I mean, why ruin our lives?

[*Charlie punched Cameron*]

Cameron: You just signed your expulsion papers, Nuwanda. And if the rest of you are smart, you'll do exactly what I did! They know everything anyway. You can't save Keating, but you can save yourselves.

Nolan: Knox Overstreet.

Todd: Meeks.

Meeks: Go away. I have to study.

Todd: What happened to Nuwanda?

Meeks: Expelled.

Todd: What'd you tell'em?

Meeks: Nothing they didn't already know.

Voice Over: Todd Anderson.

Todd's Father: Hello, son.

Todd's Mother: Hello, darling.

Todd: Mom.

Nolan: Have a seat, Mr. Anderson. Mr. Anderson, I think we've pretty well put together what's happened here. You do admit to being a part of this Dead Poets Society?

Todd's Father: Answer him, Todd.

Todd: Yes, sir.

Nolan: I have here a detailed description of what occurred at your meetings. It describes how your teacher, Mr. Keating, encouraged you boys to organize this club... and to use it as a source of inspiration for reckless and self-indulgent behavior. It describes how Mr. Keating, both in and out of the classroom, encouraged Neil Perry to follow his obsession with acting... when he knew all along it was against the explicit orders of Neil's parents. It was Mr. Keating's blatant abuse of his position as teacher... that led directly to Neil Perry's death. Read that document carefully, Todd. Very carefully. If you've nothing to add or amend, sign it.

Todd: What's gonna happen to Mr. Keating?

Todd's Father: I've had enough. Sign the paper, Todd!

Teacher 1: Grass is gramen or herba. Lapis is stone. The entire building is aedificium.

****

Nolan: Sit. I'll be teaching this class through exams. We'll find a permanent English teacher during the break. Who will tell me where you are in the Pritchard textbook? Mr. Anderson?

Todd: Uh, in the, in the Prit...

Nolan: I can't hear you, Mr. Anderson.

Todd: In the, in the, in the Pritchard...

Nolan: Kindly inform me, Mr. Cameron.

Cameron: We skipped around a lot, sir. We covered the romantics and some of the chapters on post-Civil War literature.

Nolan: What about the realists?

Cameron: I believe we skipped most of that, sir.

Nolan: All right, then, we'll start over. What is poetry?

[*Knocking*]

Nolan: Come!

Mr. Keating: Excuse me. I came for my personals. Should I come back after class?

Nolan: Get them now, Mr. Keating. Gentlemen, turn to page 21 of the introduction. Mr. Cameron, read aloud the excellent essay by Dr. Pritchard... on "Understanding Poetry".

Cameron: That page has been ripped out, sir.

Nolan: Well, borrow somebody else's book.

Cameron: They're all ripped out, sir.

Nolan: What do you mean, "They're all ripped out"?

Cameron: Sir, we... Ac...

Nolan: Never mind. Read.

Cameron: "Understanding Poetry" by Dr. J. Evans Pritchard, Ph.D. "To fully understand poetry, we must first be fluent... with its metre, rhyme and figures of speech. Then ask two questions. One: How artfully has the objective of the poem been rendered? And, two: How important is that objective? Question one rates the poem's perfection. Question two rates its importance. And once these questions have been answered, determining a poem's greatness becomes a relatively simple matter. If the poem's score for perfection is plotted on the horizontal of a graph..."

Todd: Mr. Keating! They made everybody sign it.

Nolan: Quiet, Mr. Anderson!

Todd: You've got to believe me. It's true.

Mr. Keating: I do believe you, Todd.

Nolan: Leave, Mr. Keating.

Todd: But it wasn't his fault!

Nolan: Sit down, Mr. Anderson! One more outburst from you or anyone else, and you're out of this school! Leave, Mr. Keating. I said, "Leave, Mr. Keating."

Todd: O Captain, my Captain.

Nolan: Sit down, Mr. Anderson. Do you hear me? Sit down! Sit down! This is your final warning, Anderson. How dare you. Do you hear me?

Knox: O Captain, my Captain.

Nolan: Mr. Overstreet, I warn you! Sit down! Sit down! Sit down! All of you! I want you seated! Sit down! Leave, Mr. Keating. All of you, down! I want you seated! Do you hear me? Sit down!

Mr. Keating: Thank you, boys. Thank you.

New Words

fink 告密者

trustee 受托人

scapegoat 替罪羊

expel 开除

rat 背叛，告密

victim 受害者

administration 管理层，行政部门

crap 屎，废物

expulsion 开除

reckless 鲁莽的，不顾后果的

self-indulgent 自我放纵的

obsession 迷恋

explicit 明确表达的，公开显露的

blatant 公然的

abuse 滥用

amend 修正

metre （诗歌的）韵律，格律

rhyme （诗、歌曲）押韵

objective 目标

render 表达

horizontal 水平的，横的

graph 图表

Phrases and Expressions

blow over （麻烦、争论等）平息

dumb ass 笨蛋，傻子

cozy up 沉溺于

rip out 撕开，扯下

figure of speech 修辞手法

Notes

Nuwanda 化名，源自美国黑人给孩子的起名。电影中 Charlie 把自己的名字改为 Nuwanda，抛弃父母给的名字，表明他要开始新的人生。

IV. Exercises for understanding

1. Decide whether the following statements are true or false according to the video clip you have just watched. Write "T" for true or "F" for false.

_____ (1) Among the members of the Dead Poets Society, Charlie was a regarded as a fink.

_____ (2) Neil's parents wanted Neil to become a doctor while Neil himself dreamed of becoming an actor.

_____ (3) Both the principal Nolan and the students wanted to expel Mr. Keating.

_____ (4) Knox was the first guy to stand up against the principal Nolan.

_____ (5) Nolan became the temporary English teacher in place of Mr. Keating.

2. Put the following sentences in the right order according to the video clip you have just watched.

_____ (1) Students were required to go to Nolan to sign the description documents concerning Mr. Keating.

_____ (2) Students discussed about their future after Neil's death.

_____ (3) Mr. Keating came to pick up his personal belongings before he was expelled by the Welton Academy.

_____ (4) Students sang in memory of their classmate Neil who had committed suicide.

_____ (5) Some students showed their love and respect towards Mr. Keating by standing on desks and calling him "Captain".

3. Explore interculturally.

(1) According to Cameron, who is to blame for the death of Neil?

(2) Why did students address Mr. Keating as their "Captain"?

 **Section B Reading**

微课

Different Teaching Goals between China and America

The Chinese and American education systems have different purposes and goals. Many parents and educators view Chinese education as important for foundation, and American education as being helpful for the cultivation of students' creativity. As a matter of fact, Chinese education focuses on the knowledge of accumulation and more importantly on how students manage and use the knowledge they have learned in school. Americans are deeply interested in how students use their knowledge in everyday society.

Furthermore, the American system lets students criticize ideas, challenge as well as create concepts to a larger degree than the Chinese education system. Chinese education focuses on strictness and precision, which helps improve retention whereas American education focuses on assuredness, self-determination, and independence, which aids in improving students' comprehensive thinking. In comparing Chinese with American school approaches, one can easily understand why Chinese students get gold medals in Math Olympics Competitions, but Nobel Prize winners are often from Americans.

On top of that, the ways that American and Chinese students receive knowledge are also different. Memorization is viewed as the norm among Chinese students who generally spend hours trying to remember the content of their textbooks. American teachers would normally assess students' creativity, leadership, and cooperation skills and encourage American students to take part in extracurricular activities. American students strongly believe that every piece of information taught in their curriculum is part of life rather than part of school.

Different Roles of Teacher in Chinese and American Schools

Teachers in America regularly have a bit more freedom, especially when it comes down to building a unique curriculum to meet students' needs. In China, the most noticeable changes have surprisingly come down to advanced technology. Although test scores are still incredibly critical in China and schools continue to place high levels of pressure on students to compete and maintain high grades, students are starting to take part in more diversified activities to prepare for the competitive future that awaits them.

It is worth mentioning that Chinese teachers are responsible for larger student bodies in their classrooms. In fact, the majority of Chinese teachers work with more than 30 to 50 students per class whereas schools in America are more likely to have classes of 25 students or so.

In China's education world, the focus is based more on the collective group of students. Indeed, teachers would ask themselves "What can I do to improve learning as a whole?", while American teachers would rather focus on "What can I do to improve his or her (each student) learning?"

In the American education system, after each year or grade, students will usually move on to a different teacher as they continue their education journey. In the Chinese education system, however, one group of students may have the same teacher (the head teacher) throughout their education journey, especially in their primary school years.

Different Learning Goals between China and America

Examinations in China hold most substantial weight, and this pressure comes from both the home as well as the country. The expectation for high grades has become ingrained in the Chinese culture, and all citizens take grades and standardized test scores seriously. Grading not only determines the educational level of a student, but also is used to evaluate teachers' performance. As opposed to the latter, there can be slight consequences for teachers in America when it comes to students' outcomes and performances on both oral and written exams.

In America, arts and sports are highly encouraged from a young age. Now China has recognized the importance of these two subjects and has started to implement these as part of its education system.

In Chinese society, there is a high value on learning for future success. Beginning in preschool, Chinese parents communicate early that their children are expected to succeed in school, which has a very competitive environment. Students do not typically have time for extracurricular activities as the school day runs long. American parents tend to view education as just another part of their children's lives. A majority of American children play sports, learn an instrument and socialize with friends from a young age. School typically does not begin for American children until five years, which is usually the first formal school experience. And the American students do not have to strive in a competitive academic environment until late high school and into college as the American educational system is focused on any achievement, not just high grades.

To conclude, education is culture-specific, and different education systems show different social cultures. American education system is good, but it may not be exactly right for Chinese society, and vice versa. Both education systems have room for improvement. Neither system is better than the other. In the world of education, it is important to develop an international awareness and accept different learning approaches, cultures and knowledge.

🅔 Exercises for Understanding

1. Answer the following questions according to the passage you have just read.

(1) What are the different focuses of Chinese and American education systems?

(2) What are the differences of receiving knowledge between China and America?

(3) Speaking of middle school education, which is more stressful and competitive, China or America? Why?

(4) What different roles do teachers play in Chinese and American schools?

(5) What do Chinese and American societies differ in terms of learning goals?

2. Choose the most appropriate answers to the following questions.

(1) Which of the following is NOT the focus of American education system?

    A. Students' strictness and precision

    B. Students' assuredness and independence

    C. Students' leadership

    D. Students' creativity

(2) Which of the following statements is NOT true concerning the role of teachers in American schools?

    A. American teachers usually have 50 students per class.

    B. American teachers are more concerned about improving student's learning as an individual instead of as a whole.

    C. American teachers usually do not move on with students along their education journey.

    D. American teachers have more freedom to build a unique curriculum.

(3) Chinese students' pursuit of _____ in schools is ingrained in Chinese culture.

    A. high grades

    B. extracurricular activities

    C. leadership

    D. creativity and cooperation

(4) According to the passage, American students usually do not begin their first formal school experience until the age of _____.

    A. 3   B. 4   C. 5   D. 6

(5) Asserting that Chinese students take examinations more seriously than their American counterparts would be _____.

    A. accurate

    B. imprecise

    C. misleading

    D. baseless

3. Decide whether the following statements are true or false according to the passage you have just read. Write "T" for true or "F" for false.

_____ (1) Chinese education focuses on how students use knowledge in school while American education focuses on how students use knowledge in society.

_____ (2) Chinese education allows students to challenge and criticize to a larger degree than American education.

_____ (3) Primary school students in China usually have the same head teacher along their education journey.

_____ (4) When it comes to students' outcome and performance in oral and written exams, there would be slighter consequences for American teachers than Chinese teachers.

_____ (5) Learning is a way for future success in Chinese culture while learning is another part of life in American culture.

4. Case study.

Watch TED video *Learning Styles and the Importance of Critical Self-reflection* by Tesia Marshik and discuss about the similarities and differences between critical thinking in the video and Confucius's motto of "Learning without thought is labor lost, thought without learning is perilous" (学而不思则罔，思而不学则殆).

Section C Case

Scan and Listen

The Scenario

How Do Students Learn?

Karen Randolph had been teaching high school English in the United States before she accepted a teaching job at teacher's college in China. She found her new environment and her new teaching assignment exciting. Both her students and her colleagues seemed a bit shy of her, but Karen was sure that in time they would all come to be friends.

In the classroom, however, Karen was very frustrated. When she asked a question, the class was silent. Only if she called on a particular student would she get an answer, often a very good one. She could not understand why they wouldn't volunteer when they obviously knew the answers. They were very quiet when she was speaking in front of the class, and never asked questions, let alone interrupt with an opinion. But as soon as the class ended, they would cluster around her desk to ask their questions one by one. They would also offer their suggestions about the lesson at this time.

Karen often asked her students to work in small groups during class, especially when they were editing each other's writing. They were slow to move into groups and when they did, they often simply formed a group with the people sitting next to them. Finally she devised her own system of forming groups to get them interact with students sitting in another section of the classroom.

Most frustrating of all, after she taught her class how to edit essays, she found that the students were likely to write vague and not very helpful remarks on their classmates' papers. They would say nice things about the essays and correct small grammatical errors, but seemed unwilling to criticize them in a way that would help another student revise the essay. They usually accepted her criticism of their writing with good spirits and promised to improve. Karen felt that one hundred percent grammatical correctness was not as important as learning how to correct what they had written on their own and with the help of others.

Exercise

Listen to the case above and answer the following questions.

(1) What is Karen excited about when she arrives in China?

(2) When do Chinese students usually ask questions, in class or after class?

(3) According to this passage, do Chinese students like to study in groups? How do Chinese students find group members?

(4) When editing peer students' papers, what remarks would Chinese students give?

(5) What's Karen's opinion of good paper editing?